Silver Linings

Silver Linings: What Five Ninety-Something Women Taught Me About Positive Aging

Copyright © 2014 by Peggy Brown Bonsee

Published by Peggy Bonsee, Life Coach, LLC
PO Box 55
Middleburg, VA 20118-0055
www.peggybonsee.com

For ordering information, please visit the author's website: www.peggybonsee.com.

Biblical quotation in chapter 4 (Proverbs 31:25–27, 31) is from The Holy Bible, New International Version®, NIV®. Copyright © 1973, 1978, 1984, 2011 by Biblica, Inc.® Used by permission. All rights reserved worldwide.

Quotations from the works of Maggie Meredith in chapter 6 are used by permission of Chris Meredith, executor of Maggie Meredith's estate.

Any Internet addresses (websites, blogs, etc.) and telephone numbers in this book are offered as a resource. They are not intended in any way to be or imply an endorsement by the author, nor does the author vouch for the content of these sites and numbers for the life of this book.

Interior and cover design by Deb Tremper

Cover image licensed by Ingram Image

Publisher's Cataloging-in-Publication
(Provided by Quality Books, Inc.)

Bonsee, Peggy Brown.
  Silver linings : what five ninety-something women taught me about positive aging / Peggy Brown Bonsee.
  pages cm
  Includes bibliographical references.
  ISBN 978-0-9907668-0-3 (hardcover)
  ISBN 978-0-9907668-1-0 (trade paper)
  ISBN 978-0-9907668-2-7 (electronic book)

  1. Aging—Psychological aspects. 2. Older women—Massachusetts—Nantucket Island—Psychology—Case studies. 3. Retired women—Massachusetts—Nantucket Island—Psychology—Case studies.   I. Title.

BF724.55.A35B66 2014   155.67
                               QBI14-600147

Printed in the United States of America

14 15 16 17 18 19 / 10 9 8 7 6 5 4 3 2 1

Silver Linings

What Five Ninety-Something Women Taught Me About Positive Aging

Peggy Brown Bonsee

To my parents,

Edna and Bob Brown,

whose lessons and examples

continue to enrich my life

What we leave behind is not engraved in stone monuments,

but what is woven into the lives of others.

PERICLES

CONTENTS

WHY THIS BOOK?

EVERYONE KNOWS WE BENEFIT from good role models for growing up.

But what about role models for growing old?

As a baby boomer and as a life coach specializing in retirement transitions, I believe role models make a difference at any age. This book is about what I have learned from some of mine—a group of remarkable women who arrived in my own life at just the right time to provide me with wonderful travel insights for my own impending journey into aging.

I met them on the island of Nantucket, where my husband and I had purchased a tiny, cedar-shingled summer cottage. I was privileged to spend sizable chunks of time there in the summer—often working by phone or Internet, sometimes relaxing, always trying to take advantage of the rich cultural, spiritual, natural, and historical milieu that makes the island so special to me.

As I reached the landmark age of fifty, my dear mother—with whom I was very close—completed her life journey in graceful style. With her passing, of course, a significant void appeared in my life. But then, gradually, so did the wonderful Nantucket women whose stories are the heart of this book. They offered me inspiration and tools for the journey ahead and showed me diverse ways of traversing the briars and shoals of aging while still affirming life. They took up where my own mother had left off. And as I began to observe special qualities of positive aging in each of these unique women, I realized they had much to teach me and my contemporaries. I started to think of them as "my golden ladies of summer" and to treasure them as such.

About this same time, I was transitioning my life coaching practice to specialize in retirement and life renewal issues. The more time I spent with my golden ladies, the more I saw qualities in them that my clients—and I myself—could learn from. I began to see them as role models for positive aging.

Thus, what had begun for me as casual summer encounters with several older women on the island of Nantucket gradually developed into an unexpected book endeavor. I wanted to hear their life stories and learn whatever they had to teach me. So I spent more time in conversation with them when I was on-island, and I eventually began to make recordings of many of our visits in order to capture their stories in their own words. Correspondence and phone conversations during the off-seasons provided me with additional insights and allowed me to remain connected to my ladies from early fall to late spring, when things are less lively on Nantucket and I was at home in Virginia.

I found the process of hearing my ladies' life stories to be intensely interesting and felt honored to be traveling back in time with them. But the past wasn't the entire focus of our visits. We also talked about their present lives, including the challenges and joys of their respective journeys into and through old age. It was here that we mined some of the richest treasure, as my golden ladies taught me the art of finding silver linings in their sometimes reduced or restricted circumstances.

After I transcribed the recordings of our formal interviews and visits, I reviewed my notes from our telephone conversations and reexamined the letters each had written to me. As our relationships grew over time, the ladies continued to share additional anecdotes and memories with me that further revealed their talent for optimal living and positive aging. I have included many of these in this book.

At the end of the writing process, I checked back with my ladies to verify any information I was unsure about and to fill in any gaps I had discovered as I wrote. I also spent time perusing the professional literature and reflecting on the meaning of what I was discovering—for me personally as well as for those I hoped might benefit from reading this book.

All of the women whose lives I have reviewed in depth gave me permission to share both their stories and their names. Only one, the neighbor I have called Collette, asked to remain anonymous, though she was happy for me to share some of her story in the first chapter.

As I have listened to and interacted with these special women—and now as I introduce them to you—I do so through my own lenses and from my own perspective. I lean on my experience and training as a life coach, and I also come from the place of being a woman, a baby boomer, and a person of faith. I have related as accurately as I can what each woman told me about herself and shared her remembrances in her own words. My intention for this project is to respect and honor my golden ladies, and I have tried to be true to the character and spirit of each one.

I believe these women have provided me with treasure— treasure I want to share. Throughout the book I have tried to identify those traits, perspectives, and actions I see in their lives that characterize positive aging. I have also provided some resources to help you reflect on your own journey and identify your own positive role models.

My hope is that I have created a vehicle in which these women and their stories stimulate an awareness of the possibilities for positive aging. I hope you will be inspired, as I have been, by their positive attitudes, healthy perspectives, and resilient actions in facing the joys and challenges of older age. May the example of my golden ladies inspire you to seek the silver linings in your own particular circumstances, navigating the last third of your life with a sense of hope, wholeness, and well-being.

CHAPTER 1

First Ladies

"YOO-HOO, MEESUS BONSEE...."

I looked up from my novel to see Collette, my Nantucket neighbor,[1] out working in her garden as usual.

"Meesus Bonsee," she called over the fence that separated our yards, "gardening is very good for the figure."

That greeting, of course, made me feel a little self-conscious and prompted a quick comparison of how we were spending our time. There I was on our deck in my favorite rocking chair, enjoying an Anne Perry mystery, while my almost-ninety-year-old neighbor was cheerfully digging and cultivating. She had probably been out there since early morning.

On various occasions since we purchased our tiny summer cottage—our "little gray box"—on the island of Nantucket, Collette had made similar comments when she noticed I wasn't in motion. And though I admit to a bit of sensitivity,

---

1 Not her real name. Collette was the only one of my ladies who preferred not to be named.

I knew she wasn't trying to criticize me. She was just trying to rally me to get up and do something productive that she enjoyed—specifically, gardening.

The other familiar greeting, uttered in the beautiful French accent that had survived sixty years of living in the States, was "Meesus Bonsee, you are a real lady of leisure." Admittedly, that one teased out guilt feelings arising from the Protestant work ethic deep in my core—even though I knew very well that I'm not a lazy person. Although inspired by Collette's industry, I simply wanted to focus mine elsewhere.

Besides, how could I possibly live up to my amazing neighbor when it came to her enthusiasm for working in a garden?

Having Collette and her husband, Graham, as neighbors on our little lane in Nantucket afforded me a vivid example of what full engagement in life—despite age and health impairments—could look like. Like me, Collette was a seasonal resident; she and Graham had a home in western Massachusetts. But when she was on the island, she was fully present there, embracing her island life with an energy I found both inspiring and intimidating.

Summer after summer I witnessed Colette working tirelessly in her vegetable and flower gardens, nurturing both intentional and volunteer seedlings, transplanting, mulching, pruning, and energetically tackling all the other physical activities of an avid gardener. Her wash line with its laundered garden gloves gave evidence of her industry: a dozen hands pegged in a row from pole to pole.

Despite her arthritic hands and knees, Collette worked

with intensity—not for garden club recognition or ribbons at a fair, but for the sheer love of working and creating. She was also fully attuned to the balance of nature and exhibited the greatest respect for its care and nurture. She held strong views on the use of pesticides and often gave me an earful on what she saw as the evils of large chemical and agribusiness conglomerates. She was talking GMOs (genetically modified organisms) before most people even knew what they were.

I admired Collette's passion for her garden, but it wasn't for me. For one thing, I had serious concerns about the continuous need to dig in the soil and thrash about in the Nantucket brush where so many ticks reside. Many of Nantucket's ticks are quite nasty, bearing microorganisms that cause Lyme disease, babesiosis, and ehrlichiosis—most undesirable maladies. And, frankly, I did not want to spend all my precious island time on gardening pursuits. My deck containers and window boxes provided me with sufficient color and herbs. And their easy maintenance left me free to pursue the many other sources of rich nourishment—physical, intellectual, and spiritual—that the island offered.

But while I didn't want to follow Collette's specific example, I did find inspiration in her energy and enthusiasm. I loved seeing an older woman so actively and passionately engaged in vigorous and life-affirming activity—and she did a lot more than just garden. I'm not sure she ever sat down during daylight hours. She seemed to spend every moment doing something productive—gardening, fixing up things to donate, cooking, and apparently reading as well, because she always had significant knowledge of public affairs and the environment that hadn't come from any network news broadcasts.

Over the Garden Fence

Collette and I had many long and interesting conversations through the years, and it was over the garden fence that I came to hear her story. Collette had been born in Paris. But even after living in the US for so many years, she'd retained that strong accent—by choice, I believe—as evidence of her pride in her French heritage.

How did Collette end up in Nantucket? That story began with the romance of Paris and the joy of liberation from the Nazis by the Yanks at the end of World War II. A young American GI named Graham Carter wanted to see a film with his buddies but found himself confused by the French coins. He asked a couple of French girls for help in sorting them out—at least that's what he said. When the lovely Collette and her friends came to his rescue, he treated her to the movie.

Thus began an exciting courtship that resulted in Collette's postwar journey to the US as a young war bride. What started out as assistance with sorting French coins and interpreting movie dialogue turned into a strong partnership that lasted more than sixty years and produced three exceptional children.

I'm sure that Graham was struck by Collette's beauty and spirit, which must have been extraordinary then since so much of both had endured into her ninth decade. When I met her, she was still beautiful, her thick salt-and-pepper hair worn in a simple but chic style and her pretty face with its fine features, wide smile, and bright eyes showing remarkably few lines for someone her age. And that spirit—what an intriguing person!

Although usually occupied with some kind of task, Collette seemed to enjoy the diversion of our over-the-fence chats. In fact, I found I needed to allot ample time for these since some of them could be lengthy. The topics included health, the environment, and issues ranging from neighborhood to international. Collette provided supporting quotes from the *New York Times*, the *Economist*, and a variety of other notable sources, which she would often leave on my doorstep later for my further study. No one was as fluent on the issues of the environment or public affairs as my neighbor. And she had quite strong ideas about religion and politics as well. She was particularly attuned to hypocrisy.

A Generous Heart

Collette's gifts to us ranged from fresh-baked muffins or croissants to produce from her vegetable garden. But her generosity was not limited to the tangible; she also shared her time and energy. When we left the island—usually many weeks before she did—we gave her our potted annuals and herbs to enjoy beyond our stay, and she then emptied and cleaned out the pots to be ready for us the next season. During our absence she also weeded a bit in our yard and kept an ever-watchful eye out for untoward activities. She was even known to put down a bit of mulch and mow the yard if our service was delayed in coming. And I never knew what might meet me on my front porch after I had been off to the beach or town—a couple of small bushes ready to be planted, some French soaps, a collection of magazines or books, or even a sheaf of articles pertaining to my Scottish heritage that she had clipped from her reading.

Since I rarely, if ever, saw children visiting Collette and Graham, I was curious about the children's clothes I saw on Collette's wash line from time to time. In one of our over-the-fence conversations, she explained that she got them at the "Madaket Mall"—the take-it-or-leave-it section of our island landfill.

Nantucket, you see, is very committed to recycling. Along with various thrift stores and numerous yard sales, there is a fenced area and shed at the landfill where folks leave items they no longer want and others are welcome to take what they want or need. Feature articles have appeared in the *New York Times* and other publications about incredible finds people have made at the Mall. One family actually fitted out a house with items they found there. But when Collette went to the Mall, she was on a mission to find usable children's clothes, which she brought home, washed, and if necessary mended. She then boxed them up and sent them off to one of the several worthy causes she supported in the US and abroad—further evidence of her energetic generosity.

People of Leisure

Over the years my husband and I enjoyed a special security from knowing that Graham and Collette were looking out for our property when we weren't there. Sometimes she watched out for more than just our property. One summer evening when my husband was off-island, I passed her cottage on my walk into town and stopped to chat. I had changed out of my shorts, freshened up, and put on a casual sundress and some costume jewelry. Collette inspected my apparel as we talked.

"Such a sparkly necklace," she remarked with a mischievous gleam in her eye. "I will have to watch out for you for Meester Bonsee when he is gone!" (Even after all the years as neighbors, Collette never called us by our first names.)

Later, upon my arrival home, I found a bag with a tidy supply of books in it hanging on my doorknob—something to keep me busy and out of trouble. I honestly don't think I looked *that* alluring, but Collette was French, after all.

I wasn't the only one Collette kept an eye on. My husband, John, used to chide me about being too sensitive about those "lady of leisure" remarks, but it was a different story when his industry—or lack thereof—was the subject of scrutiny. John, like me, often brought his work to the island. One day, after being on the phone nonstop from about seven in the morning until one in the afternoon, he decided he needed a break. He was pulling out his bicycle from our shed, intending to pedal down to the beach for a swim, when he heard from over the fence, "Oh, Meester Bonsee, I see you are a man of leisure, relaxing and riding the bike."

When John returned to the cottage, he was sputtering a bit about how Collette had no idea how intensely he had been working. I could only laugh and say, "See what I was talking about? Now, don't *you* be so sensitive."

A Lesson from Earl

In early September of 2010, weather forecasters were tracking a category-4 hurricane named Earl that was predicted to be a direct hit on Nantucket. John was off-island, so I was on my own in the little gray box. Doing my best to remain as calm as possible, I did all I knew to do to prepare for Earl's arrival—gathering supplies like batteries, water, food, and plastic bags; securing the deck furniture and potted plants; and making sure the portable radio was working. I also called to check in with the police department regarding evacuation procedures, explaining that I had two ninety-year-old neighbors and wanted to know what I should do to help them if need be.

The first edges of the storm were predicted to arrive on the island by five thirty on Friday afternoon. By Friday morning I was as prepared as I could be, and I hadn't forgotten to say my prayers. I was also looking forward to seeing Graham and Collette, who were scheduled to come to my house for lunch that day. Earlier in the summer, I had shared some of my broccoli soup with the Carters, and Collette had raved about it. Because of her fine French dining sensibilities, the compliment on my cooking had boosted my confidence considerably. So broccoli soup was on the menu for lunch. I also wanted to make sure they knew they could call on me for help during the storm.

They arrived promptly at noon, but Graham announced he could only stay until two that afternoon because he needed to report to the high school. My mind scrambled into action, thoughts racing. The high school was the designated shelter for the island. Did the authorities have a list of all the ninety-year-olds and plans to pre-evacuate them to the shelter?

"That's fine," I said casually, not wanting to convey my concern about the impending storm.

"Yes," he explained, "they want me to report for duty with my ham radio, and I'll do my shift!"

"Oh," I squeaked, trying to switch my vision of my neighbors from evacuees to staff. "Great. We can have a nice lunch before you have to leave."

I don't think I will ever underestimate "the elderly" again.

What's Wrong with This Picture?

The summer of 2011 would be the last full season Collette and Graham spent together in their Nantucket cottage. I especially remember how active and engaged in life they were during that time—because my husband and I were not active at all. Upon our arrival in June, we had been overzealous in pruning our shrubs and not diligent enough in our daily tick inspections. We both wound up being bitten by nasty nymph ticks that were double loaded with both Lyme disease and babesiosis. We can attest that those tiny creatures can take you down several notches with fever, chills, and utter exhaustion.

While John and I spent our days napping or at least reclining, the Carters were hard at work next door—she on her knees in the garden from morning to evening (no exaggeration) and he up on a stool with his power saw cutting dead limbs. I said to my husband, "Look next door and then look at us. Isn't something wrong with this picture? We're not the ninety-year-olds!"

Collette and I were summer neighbors for more than twenty years. Over the fence and across the dinner table, I found a woman well versed in current affairs, world politics, and the environment. I saw a person with strong views, a sense of humor, and a hand she readily extended to help others. Someone fully engaged with life even in her tenth decade. Someone I was enriched to know.

Sadly, Graham passed away in January of 2013, and after that Collette spent little time on Nantucket. John and I kept in sporadic touch with her by mail, but our correspondence slowed as her vision faded and her arthritis made writing by hand difficult for her. Graham, with his electronic skills, had been the e-mail correspondent for the couple, and Collette didn't hear well on the phone.

Even so, in early spring of 2013, I received a package and a letter from Collette with the magazine *Scotland* enclosed. Graham had subscribed to it for me before his death (along with *France* for Collette), and Collette was sending it on. After that, just like my Nantucket doorstep, my Virginia mailbox would occasionally hold little gifts of organic granola or reading materials about the Berkshires or Scotland. Despite the geographical distance between us, my ninety-something friend was still giving.

Then one day, out of the blue, I received an e-mail from Collette saying, "So glad my son found your address on this machine of Graham's." She had learned that typing was easier for her fingers than writing. After that I regularly received delightful missives (via the "machine") that were peppered with French expressions and some interesting abbreviations that came through despite spell check. Since Collette was in her mid-nineties by then, I heard a bit about her health, but more about the frustrations of dealing with bureaucracy, phone menus, and real-estate property assessments. In 2014 she provided me with a colorful look at the punishing winter in western Massachusetts. And in a subsequent e-mail, Collette said she was hoping to return to the island soon.

I hoped so too, because John and I felt the loss of our island neighbors quite deeply. Nantucket just wasn't the same without having the both of them next door.

Yet even without Graham and Collette, our life on the island was something we treasured—a true gift.

A Summer Place

Every year for the last twenty-three, I have been blessed to spend at least part of the summer on Nantucket. I know this makes me fortunate in the extreme. Unlike some who are drawn to the posh or exclusive cachet the island has developed over the years, I am lured by the island's natural beauty, its palpable sense of history, the artistic and musical offerings, and the spiritual renewal I find there. Of great importance to me as well are the wonderful people I have come to know on the island over the years.

Perhaps the seed of my fascination with Nantucket was planted in my childhood. Growing up with plenty of pavement around me and a view of Manhattan out my window, I relished the brief summertime interludes I was able to spend at the shore with my family. Then the singer Patti Page expanded my perspective with her rendition of "Old Cape Cod." I loved hearing her sing about "sand dunes and salty air" and "quaint little villages here and there," her soothing voice painting a picture that appealed to me on several levels.

In addition to my love for the ocean and the beach, I had always enjoyed visiting historic places with family, school, or Girl Scouts. So those quaint little villages added a whole new layer of romance to my seaside vision at a time when I had only known the bungalow-and-boardwalk version of the shore. That vision was still with me in the spring of 1968, when John and I became engaged and I began researching a location for our honeymoon.

We knew that within weeks of the honeymoon, my new husband would be reporting for duty at Quantico, Virginia, as a newly commissioned second lieutenant in the United States Marine Corps. We also realized that within the next twelve months he would inevitably be shipped out to Vietnam. We wanted a very special place to start our marriage and build memories that could nurture us for the exciting and challenging life ahead. So instead of joining my East Coast contemporaries in exploring the typical resort options in the Bahamas or Bermuda, I sent off for literature about Cape Cod.

Among the packets I received was a brochure about an island just south of Cape Cod—Nantucket. The text and pictures revealed all the appealing Cape Cod charm Patti Page had sung about, with the bonus of island allure. I shared the brochure with John, and we immediately knew Nantucket would be our honeymoon choice.

So on August 18, 1968, John and I boarded a Steamship Authority ferry departing from Woods Hole, Massachusetts, to take the first of many trips across Nantucket Sound and begin our long relationship with the island. On our first visit we explored the beaches, from the calm waters of the family beach called Jetties near town to the powerful waves crashing at Madaket Beach at the western edge of the island.

We walked through the town on cobblestone streets, gazed at the magnificent whaling captains' homes built in the 1800s, and enjoyed the perfume from flowers that cascaded from window boxes, brightening the gray cedar shingles of the homes. At the harbor, John loved pointing out the different kinds of boats to me. Later we meandered across the island's undeveloped moors, breathing in the fragrance of *Rosa rugosa* and watching sailboats in the distance catch the wind.

Island Dreams

During that first trip, both John and I felt a special connection begin to develop with our newly discovered island. Even after we left Nantucket and began our new life together, I had periodic dreams that included the historic windmill, an island icon. Then, ten years later, with our two-month-old baby in tow, we returned to the island to celebrate our anniversary. It was all just as we remembered it, and our love affair with the island sprang to new life. We returned the following summer and the next, staying for a week at a time and wanting more.

Years passed. John's postmilitary career flourished. Our daughter reached her teen years. I engaged in a variety of vocational ventures. But we still kept returning to Nantucket in the summer. We even subscribed to the *Inky Mirror*—the *Inquirer and Mirror*, the island's oldest newspaper—and began to keep an eye on real-estate prices.

Finally, in February of 1991, my husband dispatched me to Nantucket on the mission of finding the least expensive property in the best location. He suggested I take along a friend of ours for company, a Marine wife whose husband was serving overseas in Operation Desert Storm. John thought the trip would be a good diversion for her during their separation.

We stayed at the historic Jared Coffin House, whose owners at that time, the Reads, were kind enough to accommodate our need for TV access to check for updates on the war. Our realtor drove us around the island to give us a feel for the various island locations and what property was available. ("For Sale" signs are not posted on properties on Nantucket.)

My mission was finally accomplished in those late days of February when I found a small, modestly priced cottage on a quiet lane located within walking distance of both town and Steps Beach. John would see it for the first time when we traveled together for the closing later that spring.

After that, I spent my Nantucket summers sampling the island's offerings and entertaining family and friends from back home who came to stay with us—adults in the bedrooms and kids in the loft. Feeling blessed to be in such a wonderful place, we enjoyed inviting those folks we knew who were going through some difficult patches and might enjoy being on the "faraway island."

I even toyed with calling the cottage Summer Haven, in keeping with the island custom of naming cottages. But I never followed through on that. Instead, because of the cottage's diminutive size and cedar-shingle siding, which aged to a lovely silver gray, it became the "little gray box."

As years passed, my time on the island evolved, depending on my job. At first, when I was working at a public library, I snatched short periods as my schedule would allow. Using my husband's frequent-flyer points, I would take a plane to Boston, board the Plymouth & Brockton bus to Hyannis, then catch the one-fifteen ferry to the island. When I became the librarian and independent-studies coordinator at a private college-prep school, my summers expanded to match the time when school was out—from late June to mid-August. Then in

1999, when I transitioned into having my own life-coaching practice, I was able to be on-island from mid-June through mid-September.

Except for my first years, my time in Nantucket wasn't exclusively what one might call a vacation. I was usually pursuing continuing education, doing professional reading for a publishing company, working with clients, or studying to pass certification exams. But I still tried to take full advantage of all the island offered—and, yes, read the occasional mystery novel. Best of all, I could walk to most places I needed to go instead of taking a car. So even when I was working, the exercise and change of venue provided a life-enhancing respite from life on the mainland.

Island Friends

In the early years, I didn't have a circle of Nantucket friends. There were our neighbors, Collette and Graham, of course. And I did participate in a few classes at NISDA (Nantucket Island School of Design and the Arts), attend lectures at the Nantucket Atheneum (the island's historic library), and visit different churches trying to find the right fit. John spent as much time as he could on the island, flying or ferrying in for long weekends, working out of the cottage on the phone and Internet when possible, and trying to get in a week or two of real vacation as well. But in between those visits, I was often on my own.

Gradually, though, I began to meet more people, and I didn't have to venture far for encounters that grew into special friendships. Many of these connections developed in three places that have offered me much, including—and especially—my golden ladies of summer.

First, the Nantucket Cottage Hospital Thrift Shop, which benefits Nantucket Cottage Hospital, was a virtual gold mine for me in many ways. The "Reuse! Recycle! Repurpose!" premise appealed to that part of me that respects the Yankee thrift and practicality that characterize so many Nantucket residents. A visit to the shop also offered me a diversion from work, allowing me to pop in or do some browsing when I needed a break from my work. And it was a great place to find a bargain on anything from a 14-karat-gold scallop-shell necklace to a set of dishes for my cottage to a lightweight wardrobe for my daughter's August trip to Egypt. (A friend often told me that she found nothing but "junk" when she went. But then she'd point to a cute jacket I was wearing and say, "Don't dare tell me—you got that at the thrift shop for three dollars.")

But the real gold at the hospital thrift shop had less to do with the merchandise and more to do with the collection of interesting folks who shopped and volunteered there. A visit there provided me the opportunity to connect with some inspiring souls, including two who would join the ranks of my golden ladies.

Another of my early opportunities for connection and shared community came when I joined a women's Bible study. My sister-in-law Edith saw the notice posted on the bulletin board at a book and gift shop and thought I might find the study interesting. And I did. The study brought together women of different ages, with different denominational affiliations, to provide learning, fellowship, and prayer support for one another. What appealed to me about the group was being involved with women who were eager to grow in faith and service and who were not gripped by the escalating materialism present in society in general and certainly not absent on the island. Even better, I met one of my future golden ladies in the group.

One more important venue for connecting with folks came through my associate membership in the First Congregational Church of Nantucket, which became my summertime spiritual home. The worship service was very similar to the church of my childhood. The hymns they sang were familiar favorites that brought me both comfort and inspiration. The sermons were thoughtful and pertinent. The congregation was welcoming. The excellent music filled the open expanse of the light-filled sanctuary, enhancing my sense of God's expansiveness. It was in this place of beautiful music and worship that I was touched by other golden ladies of summer.

My Premier Golden Lady

My mother, Edna Hansen Brown, also played an integral part in my early experiences in our Nantucket cottage. She had never owned a home of her own, so she took delight in helping me set up mine. She advised me on fabric for the curtains and pillow covers I made and enjoyed picking up small accessories to make the space cozier.

At the beginning of each summer, Mom would make the journey up north with me in our fully packed Ford Explorer, which she had stocked with homemade sandwiches and other treats to sustain us on the journey. She would help me open the cottage, stock the shelves, and fill the flower boxes. Then, once we completed our early-season tasks, we'd reward ourselves with visits to the island's unique shops, making several stops at the hospital thrift shop so as not to miss any possible treasures it might have to offer.

Mom and I continued this special seasonal ritual until her death in 1996. Our relationship had always been close, and I missed her presence in my life intensely. On Nantucket, when the summer days were longer and the pace of life slower, the void she had left felt even deeper.

I had always admired my mother. She, like my golden ladies to come, was the kind of woman George Eliot describes in her novel *Middlemarch*:

> Her full nature . . . spent itself in channels which had no great name on Earth. But, the effect of her being on those around her was incalculably diffusive: for the growing good of this world is partly dependent on unhistoric acts.[1]

Widowed at age forty-eight, my mother lost her only brother, with whom she was very close, just six months after

---

1 George Eliot (Mary Ann Evans), *Middlemarch* (New York: Oxford University Press, 1996), 785.

my father died.[2] At that point she hadn't worked outside of the home for twenty-five years. But without complaining or exhibiting any self-pity, she said her prayers and read her devotions each morning, polished up her typing and shorthand skills, and four months later commuted into New York City to take a job that would reintroduce her to the world of business as it existed in 1964.

By this time my brother Joe was grown and married, with children of his own, but my maternal grandfather still lived with us. The Chief, as we called him, had come to live with our family when I was three years old, two years after my grandmother died. Although he was still working when he came, he had retired and was well into his eighties by the time my dad died. Being a positive-spirited person, he was not demanding in any way. Nevertheless, he was very much dependent on my mother for meals, health and medical care, and all other homemaking needs.

This responsibility, coupled with the demands of her new job and the double loss of her husband and brother, must have made her feel depleted much of the time. She had to have shed private tears, and I knew she sorely missed these vital figures in her life. But to me, her seventeen-year-old daughter preparing to graduate from high school, she remained the strong and gentle mother I had always known. My memory

---

2 Technically Joe Mullaney was my mother's cousin. But when his mother died in childbirth, my grandparents raised him as their own. He called them Mom and Pop, and my mother considered him her brother. They were as close as any brother and sister I have known.

of this situation is no doubt influenced by a typical adolescent self-focus as well as by my mother's fortitude and grace.

My going away to college would leave an additional empty seat at the dinner table and deprive my mother of a source of companionship and support. Yet she never tried to sway me from my college dreams or make me feel guilty about leaving. Instead she threw her energy into studying to take the civil service test. Passing it would allow her to apply for a job as a school secretary in our town, eliminating her commute across the Hudson River and allowing her to have summers off when I would be back home from college and looking for my own summer job. She passed the test easily—she had always been a strong student—and became the beloved Mrs. Brown, secretary at Roosevelt School. The community was small and the school wasn't far from home, so she could check on her dad as needed.

The school position ushered in a new phase of my mother's life. She worked in a lively and demanding environment that allowed her not only to use her typing skills, but also to employ her strong suit, that of empathy and compassion for students, parents, and teachers alike. They became a bit like another family for her.

Gradually, too, she began to get out and participate in social activities beyond home and work—a deliberate act on her part, since my father's death had severely limited her social life. I remember her commenting that once you were widowed, you were no longer invited to the "couple" events you were accustomed to attending. So she set out to refashion a social life for herself as a widow. She made several new friends while still maintaining a close friendship with Mildred, her best friend from childhood. She and Mildred had served as maid/matron of honor in each other's weddings and over the years had shared many confidences, cares, and joys.

As part of her more expansive life, Mom joined what she would always call her "painting group," although it would evolve into more of a ladies group that occasionally worked on artistic or craft projects but more often traveled together and socialized. She also signed up for an adult-education group in our town that offered reduced-rate tickets for Broadway shows, concerts, and the ballet. After my granddad's death and her own retirement, she traveled to Hawaii, Europe, and throughout the US with a retired educators' group that afforded greater learning opportunities than average tours did. Always an avid reader, she kept a list of book titles and authors she had read. And she enjoyed some favorite television shows—*The Guiding Light* during the day, *Murder, She Wrote* and *Matlock* in the evenings—but was never governed by the television.

Two Golden Qualities

Even as a young girl, I was aware of two important qualities my mother possessed—loyalty and moderation. If you happened to be her husband, her friend, her child or grandchild, she was totally devoted to you. She accepted your shortcomings and stood firmly in your corner no matter what happened. And her personal lifestyle gave her modest preaching on "moderation in all things" a powerful legitimacy.

For example, she enjoyed "a little something sweet," as she called it, after a meal—cookies, cake, custard. But she was always satisfied with a "taste," a small serving or just a few bites. Her response to offers for more was "No, thank you. I have had an elegant sufficiency." She found contentment in moderation and spared herself the continuous unrest associated with a quest for more and more. My mother "got" the concept of balance, something so many seek.

Mom also knew herself. She knew she needed to be engaged in life. And she understood the importance of having a purpose, something to live for and work toward. I saw this sense of purpose evolving in different ways as she grew older and no longer needed to care for my grandfather. An incident from late in her life illustrates this vividly.

My mother was in the hospital at the time. She'd had a very close call, and we'd thought we'd lost her. My brother was traveling in Europe and couldn't be there, but his daughters Robbin and Daria, my nieces, kept vigil with me at the hospital. When she regained consciousness and realized how sick she had been, she commented, "Well, I have lived a long and good life and would be content to die now—but I really want to know whether Robbin is going to have a boy or a girl."

You see, Mom loved her grandchildren, and she *really* loved babies. She had often told me that had it not been for the war, she would have had more children. And as her great-grandchildren arrived, she had made a point of knitting or crocheting a gift for each of them. And ever since learning that Robbin was pregnant, Mom had been badgering her about the gender of the baby so she could get started on her knitting project.

Robbin, who already had two boys, explained that she preferred to be surprised. But weak as my mother was, she persisted. "If you have that doctor call me and tell me," she bargained from the hospital bed, "I won't tell you, but I can begin knitting in the right color."

We laugh now when we remember that moment because it so clearly illustrates my mother's resolute sense of purpose. She never stopped thinking forward. And she held on to life, even though Robbin did not give in about the gender. Although Mom never completed that last project, she did have a purchased gift ready for the new arrival—a Peter Rabbit jacket, a special remembrance to this day. More important, she was able to hold baby Jared in her arms and give him her blessing. Six weeks after that, she passed away.

Seeking the Light

The day of my mother's funeral, November 8, 1996, was cold and rainy. We shivered as we stood at the graveside, but the sun finally broke through as they lowered the casket. Mom's friend Mildred turned to me, then looked at the sky and said, "Your mother didn't like dark days, so now the sun is shining. She'll be happy."

Mildred was right; my mother wasn't fond of the dark days. But to counter their heavy effects, she created projects to distract herself from the gloominess and keep herself moving. Often when I called she'd describe a project she was working on, maybe starting a baby blanket, organizing her clothes or dishes, or cataloging her letters or photos. Her projects helped her hang on to that sense of purpose, especially if they were done on behalf of someone she loved.

Looking back, I can see so many other ways my mother pushed toward the light and stepped away from darkness. She knew the importance of getting her exercise, for instance, and took regular walks either with friends or alone. And she made daily phone calls to an elderly friend of the family, Mary McNaughton, who was at home by herself while her daughter Lillian was at work. Those daily check-ins gave Mary something to look forward to and added to my mother's sense of purpose.

My mother reached out lovingly to so many people, but quietly. Drawing attention to herself was not her style. After my mother's funeral, for instance, I received a letter from a neighbor my mother had befriended. Sarah[3] suffered from depression and insecurities and often felt lonely and overwhelmed. My mother had spent hours with her, encouraging her, affirming her, and just being there through difficult times. She had even stayed in touch with letters and occasional visits when Sarah was hospitalized for what used to be called

3 Not her real name.

a nervous breakdown. Sarah told me it was my mother, not her family, who had been there for her when she came home, with a chicken dinner and a warm welcome.

Mom also regularly visited an older cousin who was virtually an orphan, totally deaf, and living in a nursing home a distance away. By then my mother was no longer driving, so the logistics of her regular pilgrimages were daunting. On many occasions she would ask for favors from friends—one being Lillian, the woman whose mother Mom had called daily—and make those visits happen. She then could communicate love through her touch and her presence.

Although I wouldn't describe my mother as a funny person—she wasn't one to crack jokes or entertain people with funny stories—she looked at life with a light spirit and a sense of humor. Her ability to laugh at herself and not take herself too seriously was a distinct blessing for everyone.

Sometimes, for instance, we got into conversations about situations or people who were frustrating us. If we reached the point of viewing the person quite critically, she would interrupt, doing what I call pulling us up to humility. "Oh, isn't it too bad," she would say in a mock-serious tone, "that everyone can't be as perfect as we are?"

Nailed! And then we'd start laughing.

My Mother's Legacy

Unlike her dear friend Mildred,[4] who was extremely vivacious and outgoing, my mother was a quiet and rather shy person. She still made quite an impact, however, mostly through her actions and gentle words. And she was no pushover. "I won't shout," she once told me, "but in my own quiet way, I will make my voice heard." And she did. She would politely persist, stating the facts as she saw them, and she wouldn't give up until her voice was acknowledged. She didn't need to get her way all the time, but she always demanded a respectful hearing. I consider her model of communication to be a valuable legacy.

During my mother's final days in the hospital, my daughter, Kristin, and I traveled from Virginia to New Jersey to be near her, staying at Mom's house and shuttling back and forth to the ICU to visit during the hospital's designated hours. While at her house, with her familiar belongings surrounding us, we felt a strong nostalgia and that comfortable "going home to Mom/Grandma" feeling, both heightened by the imminent possibility of losing her.

As we fixed ourselves something to eat one day, Kristin recalled "those soft oatmeal cookies" her grandma used to stock. During our next ICU visit, she mentioned them, and

---

4 Mildred herself was the face of positive aging. I loved her dearly and called her Aunt Mildred when I was young, as did my daughter when she came along. Mildred remained a part of our lives until her death. She adored entertaining and had just thrown a Father's Day party for her three sons with all her large family attending. After the party, Mildred went up to bed and went to sleep—her final sleep. I have often thought of her exit from life and hoped I would be so blessed to go the same way.

my mother's response still makes my daughter laugh: "Help yourself to whatever you want, but stay away from my custard. I just made that fresh." Even on her deathbed—and I believe she knew her time was coming very soon—she refused to be morose, and she kept looking forward.

But perhaps the most memorable remark my mother made during this time came when Kristin inquired about a simple drawing she had done years earlier. "Grandma, I noticed you framed my swirl drawing and put it on the shelf at your house. I don't remember giving that to you." From her hospital bed, connected to IV lines and hooked up to monitors, my mother flushed red and sheepishly responded, "I lifted it!" We laughed at her words and impish demeanor.

"I couldn't believe Grandma said that!" Kristin told me later. "'I lifted it.' She was in such a playful mood that day. We had such a good time together. And she died that night." My mother's unlikely and endearing comment on their last day together reflected her special connection with my daughter and gave Kristin a warm and affirming memory to treasure for the rest of her life.

As she was dying, my mother gave us all our instructions. "Take care of each other," she said. And with respect to her worldly goods, she used a familiar expression to indicate her idea of total fairness: "Share everything even-steven." That was another gift—the legacy of peace with those I love.

But one of the most precious gifts my mother gave me in those last days at her bedside concerned someone who had been less than kind and supportive to her. She knew I was troubled about the situation. So she took my hand and said, "We must forgive and let go of it. *You* must do that."

I could clearly see that she had already forgiven those who had hurt her. How could I do otherwise? Even on her death-bed, she gave me a lesson in forgiveness—in letting go and moving on.

Bridging the Void

Needless to say, my mother's passing left a huge hole in my life. It wasn't just that I was sad, although of course I was. But I also missed having her to talk to. I missed her wisdom and her example. I missed her ongoing lessons in the art of growing older with grace. I felt I had lost my primary mentor as well as my mother. And so I consider it a true gift that during the slower pace of my Nantucket summers, with my first golden lady no longer a part of my everyday life, I met and then grew to know the other women who would teach me so much. I was ripe for the various opportunities to engage in conversations with these women whenever those opportunities presented themselves—across the fence, in a study group, shopping at the hospital thrift shop, or attending church and concerts.

Collette, our whirlwind of a neighbor, was first, of course. But then came Claire . . . and Jane, Lilma, Estelle, and Maggie. As we spent time together, I became aware that these women—my golden ladies of summer—were helping bridge a void that my mother's passing had left. I found myself wanting to get to know them better and hear their stories.

I was especially impressed by how these women, like my mother, carried their age with strength, spirit, flexibility, and a vital engagement with life. As we spent more time together, a seed of curiosity began to grow. What was it that set these special women apart from others their age? And what could I learn from them that would help me on my own life journey?

Concurrently, within the venue of my professional work as a life coach, I happened to be studying positive psychology[5] and optimal functioning. I also grew fascinated with the concept of resiliency and began to study it more closely. I read the findings of various research studies on these topics and found this material especially applicable to baby boomers like myself. As my retirement coaching practice developed, all these interests naturally led to a focus on positive aging, which I included in the presentations and workshops I gave on retirement transition and well-being in the later years of life.

Then, at one point, something clicked in my head. I realized that the qualities, attitudes, and habits I was reading about on an academic and professional level and sharing with clients were being modeled for me by these very women to whom I had been drawn in my personal life. They seemed to be real-life examples of what the research claimed. I became

---

5 Positive psychology is a relatively new academic and clinical approach to psychology. Unlike the older psychological paradigm, which focused on pathology and mental illness, positive psychology focuses on positive emotions and uses a model of mental health and wellness that helps people develop and flourish. One of the founders of this approach is Martin Seligman of the University of Pennsylvania, whose work is cited in this book.

excited about learning more on both the academic and personal fronts.

More important, I grew to treasure my deepening relationship with each one of these women. I very much appreciated their willingness to share their stories with me . . . and now with you.

As you'll see, my golden ladies shared a generation, having grown up during the Great Depression and lived through World War II. That meant all were in their eighties or early nineties when I met them, and all lived well into their nineties. (Estelle made it to one hundred before she passed away.) All except Colette lived full-time on Nantucket, although they arrived there by very different routes. And all were what Nantucketers call "washashores"—meaning they had not grown up on the island. In fact, they hailed from different parts of the country.

Shaped by their respective natures and circumstances, the women's stories play out across the realms of education, career, romance, and family, punctuated by various celebrations and losses. Their voices reflect their personal faith and philosophy of life. And although each woman was unique, the common thread uniting their stories is their endurance and spirit in facing challenges, including those in their later years.

As such, I believe my golden ladies can serve as models for any of us, offering wisdom and hope for finding contentment and a positive perspective in our golden years. My intention in sharing these stories is to allow you, the reader, to journey with each woman through her life, to get a sense of who she was and who she became, and to be encouraged to live your golden years with grace, contentment, and even joy.

I am fond of sending this Madeline L'Engle quote to my baby-boomer-and-beyond friends on their birthday: "The great thing about growing older is that you don't lose all the other ages that you have been." My ladies lived out that reality, bringing the good from every decade of their lives into their later years. May you and I learn from them and do the same.

MY FIRST LADY

My favorite photo of my
mom at the wedding of
my niece, Daria (1985).

My mom on the ferry
to Nantucket.

My mom on the deck of
our "little gray box."

A visit from Mom when
we lived in Illinois.

CHAPTER 2

❧

Claire Dwyer

"You can't just exist. You have to live."

I met Claire during one of my browsing days at the Nantucket Cottage Hospital Thrift Shop. With no small children or grandchildren of my own, I'm still not sure why I wandered into the children's department of the shop. It must have been providential—or perhaps Claire's magnetic personality and sense of humor simply drew me into her sphere. She howled with laughter when I shared that possible explanation with her, but neither of us could come up with a better suggestion as to how we came to cross paths with each other.

Claire was a short, roundish, white-haired woman with a gentle countenance, a distinct Massachusetts accent, and an irrepressible sense of humor. Chatting with her always left me with a lightened spirit, no matter what the topic. Whether she was puttering around at home or attending to her shop duties, pricing children's clothes or tidying her stock, she devised a humorous approach to everything.

As I got to know her better, I continued to be amazed at how she could express a complaint in a way that dissolved any bitterness into a flood of laughter. I envied her knack for repartee, her quick wit, and her impeccable comic timing. I would need ten days and twelve rewrites to come up with the kind of hilarious responses she reeled off without a thought. She was a genuinely funny person. But that's not to say that Claire lacked depth or was a philosophical lightweight. We had many serious conversations over the years that spawned new insights as well as welcome affirmations.

Throughout her years at the thrift shop, Claire had achieved amazing results with the sorting, marking, and display of merchandise in her department. The fact that she was still working at the shop at age ninety was a source of inspiration in itself. But the most valuable service she provided was her special insight into the needs and realities of motherhood. She had raised ten children and was still encouraging others on their journeys of motherhood. No wonder her customers adored her.

No matter the situation, Claire had a positive and enviable way of meeting the world and its challenges. She was always demolishing stereotypes that one might be tempted to use given her age and situation—such as the lonely old woman who lived alone, the worn-out mother of a large family, or the ninety-year-old hobbled by aches and pain.

Claire did live alone. She had indeed raised ten children in a busy household. And she had faced her share of ailments. But she didn't seem the least bit lonely, worn out, or sick. Living life with compassion, gratitude, self-knowledge, and intentional focus, Claire was engaging and open-minded, an exceptional source of wisdom as well as fun. I felt blessed to call her a friend and tap into her positive energy. With Claire it was never the same old, same old. There was always something new.

I knew Claire was widowed and not a Nantucket native—she and her husband, A. J., had raised their ten children in Plymouth, Massachusetts—but I was surprised to learn she had arrived on the island so recently. I was curious about how a woman who had lived her entire life on the mainland made such a big change late in life, when she was in her eighties. She told me she'd had a friend from Plymouth who came over to Nantucket regularly and invited her to visit. After hosting Claire on the island, this friend had put Claire's name on the list for an apartment at Academy Hill, a large converted schoolhouse right in the center of town.

At the time Claire was living with family on the mainland—"lovely folks," as she described them to me. However, when her name came to the top of the waiting list, Claire didn't hesitate. "The door opened and I jumped at the chance," she told me. She explained that two of her grown sons and a daughter had since come to live on the island as well. The rest of her living children were scattered across the country and even across the Atlantic. I had to use a cheat sheet to keep them all straight: two sons and two daughters in Plymouth, Massachusetts, two daughters in Denmark, two sons and one daughter on Nantucket, and one son—Michael—in heaven.

What was it about Nantucket that appealed to Claire? "I liked the idea of a village setting," she told me. "Being able to walk to everything, the beauty. . . . I used to be out and about walking every day." She threw me that familiar mischievous look. "I always say, 'Oh, to be eighty again.'"

Visiting Claire

Out of the abundance of offerings available during my summers on Nantucket, none was richer than a one-on-one visit with Claire in her Academy Hill apartment. The place was lovely, with large windows—think old school-building windows—and lots of light. I loved to go there. However, orchestrating such an opportunity during the busy summer season was often a challenge because Claire's calendar was always full. I marveled at how she managed all her activities—working at the hospital thrift shop Thursday through Saturday, going back in on Sundays to catch up when the shop was closed, playing hostess for visiting family and friends, and being clever enough to pace herself so she could enjoy it all.

I was sometimes able to sneak a quick visit with Claire while she was on duty at the thrift shop, but that could be a rather distracted and disjointed experience at best because she took her responsibility seriously and kept her mind on her work. So I was always delighted when Claire invited me for lunch. When I inquired about bringing something, she invariably responded, "Nothing, my dear. Only yourself." Then she would greet me at her doorstep with outstretched arms and a big smile.

On one of my first visits to Claire's apartment, she took me on a tour, pointing out the wonderful paintings, artifacts, and family photos she had displayed on her walls, bookcases, and tables. The picture of A. J. in his World War II aviator's uniform was spectacular—great smile, loving eyes, and a face as handsome as any movie star of the day. Behind her bedroom door was a portrait of Claire painted by her granddaughter. I struggled at first to see the resemblance (greenish face, pink feather in a black beaded headband, black braids), but I could definitely see my friend in the generous smile and laughing eyes. Claire treasured that picture, and I could understand why.

Among the other items of interest Claire showed me were two mirrors that had belonged to A. J.'s great-grandmother, a statue from a trip to Denmark, a beer stein from Copenhagen, an abandoned bird's nest, and a colorful stuffed bear, each of which had a story of its own. A large, carved wooden tree (that Claire says she paid sixty dollars for) spanned the wall between her windows. The tree bore tiny lights and whatever ornaments Claire fancied at the time, a kind of revolving exhibit. The eclectic array was artfully displayed, suggesting that the curator had an eye for nature and had selected her collection with love and care.

Claire told me the stories of some items and explained why they were meaningful to her—each relating in some way to

A. J., the family, or friends. A perfect example was the stuffed monkey Claire babysat for a granddaughter who was away at school, being sure to dress it appropriately for the changing seasons. She also mentioned a few cherished items that she had decided to give away to particular family members. "It's not to get rid of them," she explained, "but for them to have and enjoy." Shifting gears and scrunching her face into a comic mask, she added, "I hope they take good care of them, though, or the next one I give will be only a box of napkins!"

"Claire, it's only stuff," a friend had once said about her collection of things. But Claire insisted that wasn't true: "It's a lifetime of memories." Then she clarified that the items themselves didn't hold intrinsic value to her, but the memories they represented were priceless. They were part of what made the apartment home for her.

Life with A. J.

On another visit, not wanting to miss a minute of our time together, I joined Claire in her compact kitchen while she prepared lunch. As she bustled about, she kept interrupting our conversation by talking to herself—audibly guiding herself through the various culinary steps. Then she looked up and shook her head. "To think, I cooked for twelve people." We both laughed as she went on: "We all sat down at the table for breakfast, the children came home for lunch, and all twelve of us sat down for dinner with my husband." Starting to giggle, she told me, "When I was first married, my biggest claim to fame"—now she was sputtering in an attempt to speak through her giggles—"I served a tomato stuffed with tuna fish and a side of frozen French fries. I was a genius!" Finishing her revelation, she twirled her arm in the air in artistic punctuation. Then, deadpan: "As a result, A. J. became an excellent cook. I learned along the way."

Talking about her husband triggered more reflections: "Sometimes I wonder if our lives are mapped out—because I met A. J. on a blind date, went out for five years. . . . It's so good to have someone to go hand in hand with, sharing life. . . . He was the funniest man I had ever met. He had a heart the size of this room."

I guess he was a good sport as well because Claire told me, "I fell off a horse two days before my wedding on the twenty-seventh of December. We jumped the wall, and the horse hit a patch of ice. I was black and blue all over, and I limped down the aisle."

Still looking back, she revealed the great irony of her past: "I was going to have only one child." She laughed, "But then, as I always say, 'I never had a headache.'" She told me how beautiful her children were as little ones and how good their manners were. But most important to her, she explained, was that they were good people with warm hearts. Her voice softened. "How beautiful that all was. . . . Not easy—no way. But it was beautiful."

Claire lost her beloved A. J. to a swift and deadly heart attack when he was only fifty-four. "I am just so grateful that it was quick and that A. J. didn't suffer." She told me that eight of her children were still at home when that happened.

I could hardly fathom what that must have been like for her. But when she spoke of it, she focused more on the children's pain at losing their father and didn't dwell on her own agony. She did speak briefly about her son Michael's immediate response to his father's death: "Michael tried to resuscitate him. And when it failed, he said, 'I'm going to church.' 'But it's two o'clock in the morning,' I told him. And he responded, 'I'm going to church.'" In his shock and sadness, perhaps he hoped to find solace in that place of prayer.

Michael would die young as well, and Claire always held his spirit gently. She spoke of him as easily and as often as she spoke of her living children.

During one of our visits, Claire talked about the first house she and A. J. had owned—how badly she'd wanted it, but how little sense she had about the logistics of buying it. "I was positive we could do anything," she says of her partnership with A. J. And they had in fact managed the purchase despite the unlikelihood of it all coming together.

Claire still retained a strong degree of that can-do attitude when she talked about her present needs. She had learned to find contentment and sufficiency in the midst of a culture that was always seeking more and more. "Everything I need I was born with," she told me on several occasions.

Dancing Through

I was always struck by Claire's capacity to find little treasures in places where others found only darkness. When I asked her about this remarkable quality, she reminded me of a story she had already told me about a traumatic early-life experience she credited as a source of important coping tools.

Claire's father had been a casualty of World War I, and her mother, struggling to support Claire and her little sister, Lorraine, had been forced to put them in a convent boarding school. "I was five years old and my sister three-and-a-half when [our mother put us] in a car—my Aunt Molly's. She was my father's sister from Springfield. I had never been in a car," she explained in a soft voice that told me she was seeing back to that place in the past. "I remember we drove up to the big doors, and there was this little short person by the stairs. It was a nun, but we didn't know what that was. Imagine trying to get all that into my head. Then my mother said good-bye to us and we were left."

The two girls had then been taken upstairs, where they saw a sizable group of children sitting on the floor with nuns all around them. "Lorraine started to weep, and I'm biting the inside of my mouth trying not to cry so she won't, and I'm holding her hand," Claire remembered. "And then they took her away," she said, revisiting both the amazement and the grief of that experience. "And I didn't see her, I'll say, for four days. I don't remember exactly."

Claire saw this event as a turning point for her, the point at which she began to protect herself from painful circumstances by reframing them in her mind to focus on the good. Unable to face her difficult reality, she used her imagination to create something better in her mind—a "beautiful visual," as she called it—that allowed her to keep her spirits up. Such a habit could, of course, become unhealthy, a way of with-drawing from life by denying reality. But from what I know of Claire, that didn't happen. She simply learned to use the "beautiful visual" as a tool when needed to protect her heart. It was a way of coping with her difficulties and, more import-ant, pushing past them.

This imaginative focus was a tool she would use again and again during those days at the convent school, which were often very difficult. When she was able to go home in the summer, it was in what she termed "a malnourished state" because the convent food was so bad. Some summers she and her sister weren't able to go home at all.

"My mother was bringing us up alone," she explained to me in sympathetic tones as she related some of the stories from the farm they sometimes had to go to in the summers instead of going home. She remembered a farm boy who treated a kitten cruelly and also recalled his complete disre-gard for some beautiful geraniums—both things of nature and beauty that Claire treasured. She explained that she'd had to "build my inner fence around myself" to navigate such experiences.

Claire also reached back during that time to find connec-tion with the father she had never really known. She'd been told he was a great storyteller and mimic, a wonderful, fun guy. "I think I inherited that from him." So as she grew older, especially when painful aspects of the convent experience intruded into her life, she started to draw on her dad's legacy. She developed her talent for fun and imagination as a survival technique. "In retrospect," she told me, learning to do that "was a great stone in my foundation."

The reality was still there, of course. But looking back, Claire could see how those survival techniques—focusing on beauty, leaning on humor, bringing joy to others—had helped her not only survive, but thrive. "I danced!" she told me, acknowledging her own strength. "I danced through it. I really did."

The habit of reframing experience and focusing on the good protected Claire from bitterness as she looked back. "There were some nuns who were so kind to me," she told me in reverent tones. "I whisper their names" in remembrance and honor.

And as for her mother's role in her difficult childhood, Claire drew on her own experience as a mother and spoke from her heart without rancor or blame as she explained: "Mum was doing her best, you see. It wouldn't have been easy, In fact, it was worse on her as I look back on it."

"Great Respect in the House"

Being the mother of an only child, I was fascinated by Claire's accounts of what it was like to raise ten children. She revealed an issue that had never even occurred to me— the then-prevalent stereotype of large families. "Once you have five children," she told me, "you have to be careful because you get put in a special column." So she had become extremely sensitive about being judged by people who assumed her household would be shabby, chaotic, or even dirty. "Really, it was an obsession with me—keeping house," she told me.

She then related an awkward yet amusing incident that had occurred when she had only five children, half of her eventual ten. Her second oldest had come home from school and reported that there was an epidemic of head lice at school and that the school district nurse would be coming for a visit. The nurse obviously arrived with a set of preconceived notions about what a home with five children would look like. Upon entering the house, she looked around and cooed, "Oh, this is lovely. This must be the Bradshaws' home." Because Claire's home was neat and organized (and lice-free), the nurse had assumed she was visiting the Bradshaw family, who had only one child.

That wasn't the only uncomfortable situation Claire faced in those days. Having ten children continually elicited curious reactions and comments from folks. Addressing such remarks, Claire used her trusty humor to neutralize these awkward conversations. To the aghast faces and the inevitable questions, she just pulled out her "I never had a headache" line, which usually silenced the questioners quickly.

To my unasked practical question of how she managed it all, Claire volunteered, "The only way to live with twelve people in the house? You have to have rules and can never bend one half an inch. Once you give half an inch, you've lost the whole battle." That surprised me, because I had never viewed Claire as the strict disciplinarian that statement seemed to imply. But she tempered her stance by pointing to one of her essential values: "We had great respect. When we sat at the table, there was no horsing around. I used to say, 'Soft feet and soft voices in the house.' Outside, of course, it was different. Great respect in the house," Claire repeated. I heard it as the defining mantra she had offered her family.

Satisfied Customers

Claire was always delighted to talk about her work at the hospital thrift shop, where she was considered a fixture by her many friends and admirers. She took pride in her efforts there and achieved near professional results with clever merchandise displays and a welcoming atmosphere. Despite a long list of physical limitations, she actively sorted and tagged the never-ending flow of incoming merchandise, keeping the displays orderly and eye-catching, and warmly greeting the moms and children as they crossed the threshold. The little ones would often dash over to hug her or share their latest milestone or newest treasure.

When the shop was closed over the weekend, she sometimes enlisted her nearby son, Wizza (a family nickname), and her daughter-in-law to help with especially large piles of donations that needed attention. The trio often surprised the manager with the amount of work they dispatched during those off hours to get Claire's department in top shape for a brisk Monday-morning business.

But as I've mentioned, Claire's most valuable service at the shop wasn't her skill at handling tangible merchandise, but the intangible warmth and encouragement she shared with mothers and children who needed a soft, supportive touch. On my visits I often saw her reach out to overwhelmed mothers and their children. She would notice a mom with one child perched on her hip, trying to manage two others who were reaching for the colorful displays. Claire would begin to chat gently with the children, they would calm down, and the mom's relief would be obvious. Understanding, not judgment, means the world to a stressed mother, and Claire understood that.

"Hi, Adam,"[1] Claire called to one particular tousle-headed little guy, who rushed over to give her a bear hug. "I knew him from the time he was in his mommy's womb," she explained to me. "At first he was shy when he came in and only stood at the door. Then he would stand there and yoo-hoo. And you see him now."

Little Adam was only one of Claire's many satisfied customers. Over the holidays she received cards and notes from the many customers and assistants who over the years had benefited from her help, insight, humor, and encouragement. I certainly counted myself among her fans. Whenever I was feeling a bit frustrated or low, Claire was just the person to slide things into perspective and buoy my spirits.

I'll never forget one such occasion. My grown daughter, Kristin, had been kind enough to accompany me on the long drive up to Nantucket from Virginia. We had spent a few days working together to get me settled in for the

1 Not his real name.

season—unpacking, grocery shopping, choosing plants for the deck and window boxes, setting up the computer and Internet, and hitting a few of Kristin's favorite food spots. As the days passed, a few of our minor style differences began to surface, but nothing that interfered with our camaraderie.

In fact, everything went well until I took her to the airport for her flight home. We said good-bye, and I proceeded to my luncheon appointment. Then I got a call from Kristin. Her flight had been canceled and, due to complications typical of flying out of Nantucket, it would be two more days before a seat opened up. Kristin was understandably stressed and upset, as was I.

I picked her up and we returned to the cottage, which soon began to feel very small. Kristin was fretting about how to take care of her responsibilities at home during her unexpectedly longer absence, and I felt frustrated and helpless—able to empathize with her predicament but unable to make those planes fly. I began to feel a little of that push-pull dynamic I remembered from the years of parenting a teen, and I knew we each needed some space. So I walked into town to get a little exercise, complete some errands, and experience some solo time.

After submitting my "Resume Delivery" request card at the post office, I thought I'd visit the thrift shop, and of course I hoped Claire would be on duty. She was. "Dear Peggy, how good to see you," she called to me as I crossed the shop's threshold. "Did you just get here?" Then her mother's sixth sense kicked in. "Oh dear, you look like something's troubling you. What's wrong?"

"The flight was canceled, and things are pretty stressful at the cottage."

"Well, dear, you have to understand that once men reach a certain age, all they really want is a mother and a nurse."

I chuckled, realizing she had assumed it was my husband whose flight had been canceled. I set her straight as to the source of my distress. "Oh well," she said, "Then I have a good story for you." Then she proceeded to tell it.

"We had a friendly lady who volunteered here, a nice woman with a grown family, but a salty and rather outspoken gal. At one point for about two weeks, when she arrived at the shop, she was somber, without her usual spirit. We didn't know what was happening and were reluctant to ask. Then, suddenly, she was back to her smiling, chatty self. Curious, I asked what had happened to make her look so happy. Her jarring response took me aback. 'I put the bastard on the boat!' she said. What we didn't know was that her grown son had been visiting for several weeks, and apparently they had begun to get on each other's nerves."

With these unlikely words coming from my dear, white-haired friend, I exploded into therapeutic laughter, and she joined me. With one brief story, Claire had given me the gifts of humor and perspective. She'd taken me out of myself and helped me release my tension.

She then beckoned me to lean over as she offered her benediction: "Now, dear, if it gets rough, I'd just focus on that new departure date." And we laughed some more.

As I walked back home, I was refreshed and even eager

to see how my daughter and I might make the most of our unplanned bonus time together. How could I not want to learn more from Claire's rich repertoire of positive ways to deal with stressful situations?

A Model for Giving

Claire knew I found her inspiring—a model for reaching out and giving to others in old age. She sometimes joked about this role I had identified for her, and she was quick to tell me, "I get more than I give." Claire saw her work at the thrift shop as an opportunity for "giving back, for reaching out, and for communing with the community." "The thrift is so important to me," she added. But perhaps her most enlightening revelation was "I'm ageless there."

Among the wide array of conversational topics we explored together, food often topped the list. Our conversations touched on the various eating establishments on the island, with Claire providing humorous commentary. She mentioned a particular long-time restaurant in town that was quite good—but expensive. "I hear if you get there at a certain time, the potato won't be sixteen dollars." She shook her head in amazement. "Vegetables are a la carte. Somehow, I just can't get the mind-set of the prices."

I countered her complaint about high prices by suggesting a small spot that I had discovered with delicious food, moderate prices, and generous portions—a winning combination. She admitted she had been there. But then, with that naughty-girl expression on her face, she confided her objection to the place: "Oh, but, dear, you can't tell anyone across the table from you that you are having an affair because the tables are so close." That took me aback, but just for a moment. Then I burst out laughing, as I often did when I was with Claire.

Joy in the Storm

One of the things I learned about Claire as we got to know each other was that she loved storms. She reveled in the rumble of thunder, the flash of lightning, and the sound of pounding rain. When clouds grew dark or a front swept in, she would sit by an open window and enjoy the show. She was doing just that one day when her phone rang. It was one of her sons.

"I know exactly what you are doing," he said.

Caught at her game, she challenged him. "What do you mean?"

He responded, "Oh, I know you—and I'm doing the same."

Claire's enjoyment of storms—which she'd clearly passed along to her children—began when she was little, and it was something her mother introduced quite deliberately. Claire's Aunt Nell, who had adopted a rather fearful and sheltered approach to living, dealt with imminent electrical storms by "shutting herself in the closet and saying the rosary." But Claire's mother took a very different approach with her children.

"My mother [would] put us in our carriages" in an area proximate to an approaching storm. She did this "even when we were little, because she didn't want us to be afraid." She wanted her children to be strong. And her strategy worked, because Claire grew up to employ this approach when facing the literal and figurative storms of her life. Yes, she reframed her circumstances and focused on beauty. Yes, she used humor and imagination as coping tools. Yet she didn't give up or hide from her troubles.

This lifelong strategy for facing storms informed Claire's approach to aging as well. In one wistful conversation, we remarked about how fast the summers were going, and we each knew the broader implications of time's swift passage. As a baby boomer, I was becoming more sensitive to it, and I knew it had to be a looming reality for a ninety-year-old.

But not one to dwell on what she couldn't control, Claire pivoted the conversation with her levity: "I ask everyone, 'Did I sleep through June and July?'" She continued, "I have a watch that I wear pinned on my shirt because I can't wear it on my wrist. When I look at it, it's always an hour later than what I think." And in another conversation she shared a new, liberating insight: "Did I tell you my new approach to time? I don't do time. I just say whenever."

Claire wasn't just marking time, though. "You can't just exist," she told me one summer, all joking aside. "You have to *live*." I knew that over the previous winter she had had significant problems with her knees as well as other health issues. "Last winter I was just existing, and I'm very ashamed of myself," she confided. "I told myself I just have to be thankful for all that I have. I want to keep on learning. It all [the health problems] had me down for a while, but I just see it as a phase of the moon."

A Broader View

Although Claire lived in a relatively small apartment on a small island, she had a broad worldview, thinking about and caring about those outside her immediate world. Her heart broke when she saw pictures of unfortunate children in war-torn countries or of people living in poverty around the globe. Although unable to offer direct assistance, she did what she could: "I visualize one poor child I saw, and I pray for her." Drawing on her convent exposure to the traditions of intercessory prayer and offerings of personal sacrifice and action, she told me, "I honor them in everything I do and offer my day to them." Prayer and meditation, in fact, were a regular part of Claire's life.

During a 2011 conversation, Claire acknowledged the passage of time and assessed her situation. "I'm happy where I am. It's comfortable. I think that I am very well. But when you think of what my body [has] been through—oof, it's extremely tired and not really in the mood for too much anymore." She winked. "Sometimes, even when I push the favorite ice cream—no way. She's not going to play.

"Wizza won't let me walk [outside] by myself, so I depend on him, which becomes another problem. But I said to myself this morning, 'If you go through life telling yourself you can't, you can't, you can't—you can't!' So I'm going to take my cane, leave a note on my door—'You know where to find me'—take my key, and we'll see." Apparently all went well, since I talked to Claire many times after that. I knew she had participated in many activities in the interim, including her ninetieth birthday celebration off-island. Then she'd capped the milestone event with a trip to visit her two daughters in Denmark and continued the party there.

At that point—in 2012—Claire had also done some serious preseason thrift shop sorting and even posed in a group shot for the Nantucket phone-book cover. I couldn't wait to get my hands on a copy of that phone book with the thrift-shop volunteers on its cover. I had been instructed by Claire to look for the one with the purple boa, which she had donned to distinguish herself from the other silver-haired ladies in the group. I scanned the pictured of all the volunteers posed in front of the shop. Sure enough! There on the porch was my friend Claire flamboyantly draped in purple feathers. When I asked when she would be doing the centerfold, she told me she had already done one for *Yankee Magazine*.

"My Own Priority"

When I asked Claire how she liked her current living arrangement, something that is often of concern to many folks in Claire's age group, she told me, "I live alone, and I love it. I think I might be too powerful to be living with others." Although she had enjoyed living with a son before coming to Nantucket, she'd been concerned she might be tempted to take sides in family disputes and upset the harmony of the home. Being on her own allowed her to "find my peace, rhythm, and balance. I've become my own priority."

Many would have to agree that after raising ten children, Claire was entitled to be her own priority. "You know, I had five children under five—in five years. It was a beautiful time. My whole *me* was *them*. I got to be a girl again, enjoying it all since I hadn't had a real childhood." But she was also quick to extol the benefits of not having to answer to anyone else. "I do not really mind being alone. It's the first time in my life I've been alone. It's a luxury," she added with a laugh. "If you want to get up and make a tuna-fish sandwich at two in the morning, who's going to say anything?"

During one of our long-distance phone conversations, Claire told me about a fire drill in her apartment building that morphed into a three-day evacuation of the premises. The basement flooded due to a broken pipe, and that knocked out utilities in the building. Claire provided colorful commentary on the process: "Of course we're all there sleeping in the nude"—I suspect that was a joke, but I don't know for sure—"and it takes time to get our clothes back on. With the alarm still going, they say, 'All clear,' so I return to my apartment and start reading my prayer book, eliciting all the calmness in the world—with that old alarm still clanging away. Then at three fifteen in the morning, we get the word to leave our apartments. I pull on my sweatshirt and sweatpants, grab my address book and my money, and exit. Downstairs they told us we would have to evacuate, and my first thought is *I have to go back and get my underwear and my pills*. Imagine, at ninety, those are my priorities."

During the three-day evacuation, the crews worked to drain the flooded basement and restore the heat, water, and electricity. Fortunately, a Red Cross volunteer took Claire to her daughter's house, where she was able to relax. An evacuation such as this could be disturbing for anyone and particularly stressful for someone Claire's age, but she took the event in stride. Writing me later with the story of her evacuation, she ended her letter with "So, girlfriend, I'm well. Home again . . . a bump in the road and, in truth, life is beautiful."

Despite living alone, Claire often told me that she really wasn't lonely. She developed many strategies for staying connected with others. "I still write letters," she reminded me, and I can attest that her letters were great reflections of her personality. Another connection tool was the telephone. One morning, she told me, she received seven telephone calls from friends and family before ten o'clock. And why wouldn't they call? Talking with Claire on the phone was always an entertaining experience.

My own phone conversations with Claire ranged from news updates and playful humor to deep spiritual or philosophical explorations. Whatever the content, the conversation was seasoned with laughter. If I was feeling low, a call with Claire never failed to lift my spirits. The message she modeled was "Don't take yourself too seriously, or you'll make yourself miserable, not to mention those around you."

Even Claire's voicemail greetings reflected her positive outlook. I particularly loved the one that stated, "Hello! Red, green, blue, yellow—please leave a colorful message," followed by a full, infectious laugh that let callers know they had indeed reached the right party. Claire's laugh was unmistakable. She told me once that she and her youngest son would sometimes agree to "be serious about this or that during a call, but to no avail. Before you know it, we're laughing."

Common Sense

But as I have mentioned, there was a lot more to Claire than laughter. She was an astute observer of her world and of the world at large. I learned that I needed to do my homework before talking to Claire about current events or politics. I was moderately impressed at her knowledge of Massachusetts politics, though I figured she had lived in the state her whole life, so why not? But I was floored to realize how well-equipped she was to speak about Virginia politics. She was as knowledgeable—if not more so—than many Virginians half her age.

I often thought we should send Claire to Washington, and she herself suggested that in one of our conversations about government. "I'm going to dress up in my business suit and go throughout the halls shouting, 'Common sense! Common sense!'"

When I heard that, I told her I might follow her shouting, "Ditto! Ditto!"

We were both laughing at that when she suddenly grew quiet and announced somberly that she had something to tell me. Her abrupt change in tone made me catch my breath, thinking of her age and fearing a heart-heavy revelation of some sort.

Tension crackled through the phone line as she announced in an almost funereal tone, "My dear, I have to say . . ."

I waited, preparing myself for bad news.

"You are getting to be like me now."

I practically collapsed with relief. "Claire," I said, "that's *good* news to me."

Though Claire stayed interested in the world around her and sought to understand and learn, she also seemed to comprehend the concept of "enough"—a rare thing in our media-saturated and often narcissistic culture. Instead of dwelling on the constant stream of media negativity, she would listen to what was said, use her common sense to evaluate it, then change the channel if necessary to maintain her sense of balance.

Claire employed the same strategy when it came to reading material. An avid reader even in her nineties, she had learned to be selective. "I can't read anything that's too much reality," she specified, adding that "I have to flow with [the material], and my thoughts can't be shaken." Claire usually chose "cozy" mysteries and biographies and explained that the subject matter had to be what she termed "pure"—nothing too graphic or disturbing. For instance, she ruled out reading anything involving harm to animals or children. She knew such things existed, but she chose not to fill her mind with them, especially as entertainment.

That's wisdom for healthy living, no matter what the age. And Claire came by it honestly over the years—through experience. Describing herself as a young woman, Claire claimed,

"I thought I knew everything. The older I get, I know that I know nothing." She told me that in her youthful cockiness, she used to think that everyone died at seventy. The irony didn't escape her when she told me her apartment building was 75 percent eighty-year-olds. We shared stories and jokes about memory challenges. "I always tell folks that the only room that I go into and remember why I'm there is the bathroom," she confessed.

"The Greatest Cathedral"

Claire honored her religious roots and maintained an abiding faith, but her spirituality reached far beyond any church walls. She saw God everywhere—in nature and in people. She especially appreciated communing with her Maker while "kneeling outdoors in the greatest cathedral." And she wasn't afraid to fight to protect the nature she loved.

When she learned about plans to take down the large tree in the back of her building, she was very upset and gave the folks in charge a good tongue lashing. What possible reason could there be, she asked, to cut down that tree during the hottest summer on record? "It looks fine, provides shade, and helps keep the air clean," she informed them. When told the tree was sick at the top, she retorted that she "hadn't seen any monkey climb up there to check its health!" She even suggested that a neighbor "Scotch-tape me to the tree"—Claire loved tape!—"and boost me up into the crotch of it. I'll stay there defying the tree killers!"

Once Claire analyzed the situation further, she realized

that some of the branches of that tree must have been dropping leaves or seeds on a newly renovated high-end house on the street behind her. "You know how it works," she told me, "when there's a loud voice and a lot of money." But the last time I looked, the tree was still standing, so maybe strong, wise voices trumped money that time!

In the yard beneath the tree in question and its leafy neighbor, Claire had planted a garden of violets, lilies of the valley, and hostas, from which she derived enormous pleasure. The flowers reminded her of her mother, whom Claire had come to understand better and better over time. "She was a crook, you know," Claire told me once, then looked to gauge my reaction. "On a visit to Monticello, she stole some violets— that was her crime. At home she planted those violets, and they reproduced even faster than I ever did."

And, not far from Claire's apartment was another wonderful friend—"the tree over on Quince Street." The minute she mentioned it to me, I visualized that stately old chestnut tree. "She has so many bumps and breasts off of her. When I go by her, I touch her and say, 'Thank you so much.'" Suddenly pensive, she said, "We take so much for granted, and we don't stop and think about anything. We rape everything."

Another time, when I mentioned how much I liked the Nantucket summer skies, Claire's eyes danced as she jumped on my bandwagon. "Sunsets! Oh, I tell my son, 'I don't care where you are. Jump up on the roof and look west, look west, look west. It's never the same twice.'" When I commented on how the sky was like life in its swift changes, she concurred.

"Sometimes it takes your breath away, and sometimes it's a gray day."

No matter what the day was like, Claire wanted nature to be the dominant scene for her. "I could never live in New York [City]," she confided to me. But she was content living in Nantucket with her wonderful trees, open skies, and signs of nature nearby.

She never took the natural beauty of her surroundings for granted, and she loved sharing her love of nature with others. Whenever I left Claire's apartment, she would press some parting gift into my hand—a unique shell, a colorful feather. They seemed to come from thin air, little remembrances of Claire and her love of nature, each accompanied by a benediction: "Bless you, my child."

Mao's Mother

Sometimes, during our visits, we would tread into philosophical territory—discussions on death, afterlife, forgiveness, understanding, and other such weighty topics. One day, when on a philosophical bent, Claire commented on the fact that she had experienced a "lot of living," and her eyes appeared to be watching a faraway film. We talked about death, and Claire told me she had explained to her children that she wouldn't really be gone—she would be living on through them. I know she believed this since she had often commented on how, through her sons, she still has A. J. alive with her.

I particularly remember a lovely conversation I had with Claire near the end of one summer season as we sat in our usual spots at her table for two. "Life is so wonderful," she affirmed. Then, standing up, she walked in place as she said, "First we walk through life, and then"—she reached out her hand—"we go to walk hand in hand with God . . . beautiful." Claire didn't fret about the future or about what death was like. Instead, she trusted in an almighty God.

On another occasion, when we were talking about forgiveness, I shared the powerful lesson about forgiving and letting go that my mother had taught me when she was dying. Claire reached back to retrieve her own mother's words as well: "Don't say any words about someone who is doing something wrong to you. Time takes care of everything." She had come to agree it was best to let slights and injustices sort themselves out, and she emphasized that doing so was "not easy, but right."

She then told me about an opportunity she'd had to share some forgiveness wisdom with a son she described as having "an enormous heart." He was having difficulty understanding an associate of his. "You don't need to understand everybody," Claire had counseled. "What you need to remember is that God lives within all of us. Maybe you can't stand [the other person] or his ways are so ungodly. But mentally fold your hands and tip your head and say, 'Good morning, God.' And then all of a sudden the negatives of this guy will pass away, and you're honoring the power of creation. We're all different," she added, "and we can't expect to understand everybody." More important, "You cannot expect life to be perfect."

Then she bent toward me and sheepishly whispered, "That's where, when I'm thinking, *how in the world can they do that [to me]?* I have to say to myself, 'Claire, practice what you preach.'" She concluded with a hearty laugh. Humility was what I heard in her laughter . . . and a touch of my own mother.

Claire and I occasionally discussed the state of the country and the world, and I felt myself privileged to hear the perspective of someone who had experienced ninety years of living. She cringed at the polarization in our country's domestic politics and found herself troubled by the world situation as well. "What's the matter with us? Wars and wars. We have to have a better understanding of [our supposed enemies] and their history. Oh, and what about such people in these countries with genocide?" She shook her head, understanding that her ideal of seeing God living within all of us was not the dominant theme around the globe.

Claire also remarked on our society's collective impatience: "We want it yesterday." She lamented our unwillingness to meet one another's needs and alluded to our selfishness. "If the world is hungry and you have just a half a sandwich [a foldover, she often called it], you would be the richest person in the world. You don't need a banquet" in order to share, she insisted. "We just have to get down to doing something."

Never one to leave a topic on a depressing note, Claire had a way of shifting and neutralizing an unsettling conversation with an amusing, often self-deprecating anecdote. "When I was in seventh grade, the Catholic school I was in had a big drive for orphans in China. That was the early thirties, I think." As part of this effort, the students were charged with collecting and balling up silver paper from gum, candy, and such, which could be recycled for cash. "I was like a street picker, looking for all I could find. And then, years later, I said to myself, 'I wonder if I'm Mao Tse-Tung's mother!'"

When I looked confused, Claire's words became infused with her giggles: "What if I saved *him* from starvation!"

My Funniest Friend

As I did with the other of my surviving golden ladies, I conducted a read-through of this manuscript with Claire to be sure I had the facts correct and hadn't made any other errors. "Well, you got one thing wrong," she said when I finished. I shifted into alert mode, eager to know where I had erred. "Well, dear, you described me as short and roundish. Don't you see how tall and slim I am?" I was instructed that when I photographed her, it would need to be in her "tall, thin pose," which we laughingly executed. (See the photos in Claire's gallery at the end of this chapter.)

I often thought that Claire was one of my funniest friends—if not *the* funniest. She could, without exception, be counted on for a laugh and a spirit-lifting anecdote. Her stories reflected a playful and mischievous nature that, though somewhat suppressed during her difficult childhood, had surfaced in adulthood and was now in full voice.

On one visit to Claire's apartment, I noticed a pair of sequined, pointy-toed, spike-heeled purple shoes on a chair in her living room. Knowing Claire's need for sensible shoes,

I questioned their ownership. "Oh, they're mine," she said. "Overflow from Designers Day at the thrift. I plan to put them and a pair of men's slippers next to my bathtub to see what the children say when they visit Mama to see what's she's been up to. What do you think?"

In another story she told me, she was coming out of the grocery store, and one of her sons was waiting for her in the parking lot. Claire, busy arranging her bundles, got into the vehicle, closed the door, and turned to the driver, who by this time was calmly amused—and was most definitely not her son. "Oh, I think I'm in the wrong car," she told him. "He was very handsome and nice," she told me, "and said, 'I'd be happy to drive you anywhere you need to go.'" At this point she leaned in close. "If you see me driving about with some handsome man, I'll ask him if he has a brother for you."

Another vehicle incident occurred after grocery shopping. Petite Claire climbed up on the running board of her son's Jeep and exclaimed, "See how tall Mama would be if she was normal height—oh, look at that tree over there." She pointed to a gnarled and twisted tree in the center of the parking lot. "That's how Mama looks naked." Well, her son didn't find these antics quite as amusing as I did when she described them to me later. "Now get in the car!" he said, shaking his head and rolling his eyes.

Hug the Man You Sleep With

One gray winter's day when I was at home in Virginia, I decided to tackle a long-overdue household task—cleaning out two closets. As an incentive, I promised myself a phone call to Claire when I was through. The expectation of a dose of laughter with my friend motivated me to get the job finished quickly. Then I picked up the phone. When Claire answered, I explained to her that our phone visit was my reward for completing the closet work.

We chatted for a long time. Claire filled me in on the status of her son's health, the aftermath of "the evacuation," and the thrift shop's end-of-season accounting and celebration lunch for the shop's volunteers. That year had been the "best ever," she told me. "That little shop probably did better than all the big-name shops in town." I could hear the sense of ownership and fulfillment in her voice.

"At the lunch I sat with the managers," she said. "They told me how well we had done to raise such a record amount of money. But they said to me, 'Now, Claire, no more twenty-five-cent items.' I'm pretty territorial about my department," she confessed, but said she'd promised to "think about it."

At the end of the conversation, Claire bestowed her usual lighthearted benediction—with a little zinger at the end: "Good, warm hugs to you, my dear, and it wouldn't be me if I didn't say, 'Hug the man you sleep with.'"

When I told her that my husband had been out of town on business the previous night, she replied, "Oh well, then.

That's the answer for why you're doing all that cleaning. Remember then, in the future, so you have plenty of energy for your chores: don't sleep with him the night before you need to clean."

"We're Not All the Same"

Regular social involvement has long been recognized as an important component to maintaining well-being in later years. Claire found ways to fulfill her need to interact with other people. "I can't say enough about how important the thrift has been to me, because I'm not social here," she said, pointing to her apartment. Claire wasn't what you might call a social butterfly, but she connected in ways that were significant to her. "I know a lot of people. I love a lot of people. I keep in touch with a lot of people. But I've never had what you might call a regular girlfriend," she told me, referring to a best friend or single confidante.

Many of Claire's friendship needs were filled by her relationships with her children and grandchildren—a ready-made community unto itself, with Claire as matriarch. Claire's children remained close to her whether they were on-island or across the Atlantic. "The youngest calls every single morning. She and I laugh over I forget what, but we're hysterical. Then the oldest calls, and we discuss all kinds of things and laugh about a couple of things too. I want to honor him; he's such a beautiful person. And I had an hour-plus call from one of my daughters in Denmark, which I love because she's great, telling me all kinds of wonderful things. She takes me on a great ride—you know, visual." (Claire appreciated this daughter's ability to paint word pictures and accepted these beautiful "visuals" as gifts that brightened her day.) Work demands kept another daughter from being in touch as frequently as they both would have liked. But Claire was understanding about that daughter's hectic schedule. "She calls when she can give me quality time."

I was curious as to how Claire managed her relationship with each individual in her large family as well as the dynamics of the larger group. Given human nature, I would expect it to be a complicated enterprise. But I didn't sense significant conflict or dissension when Claire talked about her family. Though she was quite frank and honest in discussing her children, she rarely seemed angry or frustrated. Instead, she demonstrated a kind of peace not all older parents are able to manage. If discord arose, she chose not to dwell on it.

Claire seemed to maintain an exquisite balance between staying involved with her children and allowing them freedom to live their own lives. There was balance, too, in the way Claire encouraged each of them—enough to lift their spirits, but not so much as to impose a burdensome amount of expectation. She modeled strong values for them, joined in full celebration when warranted, and offered comfort when needed, but she also honored her children's ability to make their own decisions. She gave them a safe place to be themselves.

I was particularly impressed by the way Claire navigated the challenges of relating to her children as individuals.

Her view of each child and her relationship with him or her was special unto itself. She took a clear-eyed view of both strengths and weaknesses and appreciated the beauty and gifts of each child. She enjoyed one-on-one connections that fit the circumstances and the nature of each child while also understanding her grown children's relationships with others.

In all the years I knew Claire, I never heard her play the prideful parent or brag about her children's status or achievements. Instead, she defined her children by who they were as individual people—by their souls, as she expressed it. I found the way she talked about each of them quite refreshing. She always focused on the sweet aspects of their hearts or their special ways of being in the world.

How did she do this? I think one answer lies in a belief Claire both embraced and proclaimed: "We're not all the same." This open attitude saved her from the frustration of trying to put one child into another child's mold—or her own mold. She acknowledged each of her children as a distinct individual. For instance, Claire often mentioned the things Wizza did for her and how attentive he was to her. But then she would demonstrate her fine-tuned sense of fairness by saying, "I don't want you to think he's the only child I've got who helps—he's not. But he's here [on the island]."

Claire chose not to cover her children with blankets of guilt. She believed that once you know who a person is and accept them as who they are, you can relax and look at things differently. So I didn't hear a lot of shoulds when it came to her relationships with her children. She spared herself—and them—the burden of judgment.

She told me of one daughter who had arrived at Claire's home fully engaged to help after maybe four weeks of no contact at all. "She shows up to help yesterday. There you are! You know that yesterday was a gift, instead of 'Where the heck have you been for four weeks?' and all that crazy stuff."

Claire was also able to keep in mind the specific circumstances, personality, and responsibilities of each of her children. One son, for instance, lived close by but had serious health problems to deal with. Claire explained to me in her poetic way, "He is very dear to me. And everything he does for me is a gift because he has to get through all the bushes to come to me." Leaning back and looking up, she thought out loud, "There's so much to take into a relationship, so much to think about, isn't there?"

Cremating the Past

Change can be a struggle for many of us, and the aging process demands that we face it often. In discussing the subject with me, Claire confirmed that we "need to be able to move with the change—like the loss of my oldest son and the move from Plymouth, my home, to Nantucket. It's a great gift I have, being able to deal with change. I see it like turning the page in my book of life. Oh, there are lots of bad things to get through, but the good is so beautiful."

Claire illustrated her ability to navigate change—a very difficult change—when I saw her in the summer of 2013. For a variety of reasons outside of her control, I learned, Claire would not be working at the thrift shop for the 2013 season. Given the important role the shop had played in her life, I was concerned about her, wondering how deeply this change might affect her.

Clearly she wasn't happy with what was happening. When I saw her early in the summer and she told me the news, she employed her special way of expressing dislike—a kind of closed-mouthed, churning mumble that resembles the way a human food grinder might look and sound. I wasn't happy either. I mourned the fact that my friend wouldn't be doing something she loved and that I wouldn't have those chance encounters with her during my lazy strolls through the thrift shop.

But when I saw Claire later at our church fair and broached the subject, she was back to her big-picture perspective. With a graceful smile, she simply referenced "turning those pages in my life book."

Despite her age, Claire saw herself as growing, not stagnant. She faced change not only with perspective, but enthusiasm. "I don't know what I want to be when I grow up," she once declared to me with a cherubic grin. Then she turned more serious. "I'm rich," she said. "Rich and extremely happy." I knew she was not talking about finances.

"Now, I do have a torn ligament in both knees," she conceded, "osteoarthritis in my spine, and a touch of diabetes. I've lost the sight in one eye, and I have arthritis here and there. But I don't concentrate on these. I'm too busy." Sensing my reaction, she allowed, "I know I can't do some things. But I do what I can, and [then I] sit down."

With regard to regrets, Claire advised, "Cremate the past, but take a lesson. No matter what you do, be noble enough to learn a lesson." Her contented and joyful spirit told me she has taken care of many cremations and has learned many lessons.

A Mother's Heart

As any mother knows, watching our children face adversity can be an intense, frightening, and ultimately a depressing experience. Claire related such an instance to me one day over the phone. One of her sons had undergone a series of procedures, including some small surgical interventions at the ER. He'd been sent home with medication, only to return to the hospital and be subsequently airlifted off-island by helicopter to Boston. After five days of hospitalization, doctors still didn't know what had caused his life-threatening symptoms. And during that same period, another son had been forced to go to the ER for a kidney stone.

For many, Claire's weighty list of family health problems could have precipitated a significant case of "woe is me" or even paralysis. Claire just sighed and said to me, "But today is a new day, and life is good." She didn't dwell in the valley of the shadows, but instead reached for the light of a fresh morning.

Claire also chose to focus compassionately on the needs of others instead of her own troubles: "It's not easy being a mother, is it?" she once asked me. Then she expressed her empathy for the struggles of other mothers she had been thinking about: "Especially when you are the mother of a soldier leaving—or not coming home. Especially when you have to go through those kinds of things."

This line of conversation transported Claire to pictures she had recently seen of an orphanage in Russia. "Everyone was making a big deal about this little boy the couple was adopting, but I saw the little girl in the background on crutches who was left, not chosen." That picture had stayed in Claire's mind. "So when I meditate lately, I picture that little girl and send her a message of hope. There are so many things you've got to keep doing."

On occasion Claire tended toward wistful. "I find at this age, I live in the land of memory a lot, turning the pages of the book." This reference to her memory book triggered reminiscences of her late son, Michael, who had died when only a young man. She celebrated his gentle spirit and generous ways, comparing him to the "giving tree" in Shel Silverstein's famous children's book.[2]

Like Silverstein's tree, Michael was the kind of person who was always giving of himself to others. When he lived in California, for instance, he went out of his way to show kindness to older women, helping them with things they were no longer able to do. One time Claire saw him wearing a knitted beret. "It was *quite* a color, but he wore it. He explained that

2 Shel Silverstein, *The Giving Tree,* 30th anniversary ed. (New York: HarperCollins, 1999).

it was from one of the ladies he helped." She emphasized that her son never accepted money from them in return for his services. "That lady liked to knit and made it for him. She learned she could trust him, and she loved him."

When Michael died, "his funeral was standing room only as every little old person filled the place with their stories about how beautiful what he did was." Afterward, Claire and her family visited the places where Michael hung out, and they heard story after story of things Michael had built or created. "That was the gift," Claire told me, her face glowing with peace.

"Some people don't want to get old, or they fear it," Claire once explained to me. "But I say it's wonderful! I can do anything I want to do. If I want to have another piece of pumpkin bread, I can." She was able to appreciate the liberating possibilities and unique perspectives of a long life. She filtered through the negatives and grasped the shining positives—the pearls—even when they were hard for others to see.

Gifts from Claire

One February day when I was back home in Virginia, I found an unexpected package at my doorstep. I noticed it was swathed in packing tape—a signature Claire practice—but was puzzled by its prodigious size. Wizza must have assisted her in this operation.

What fun it was to unwrap this trove of surprises. The box was filled with an array of separately wrapped (and taped) packages—Nora Ephron's book, *I Remember Nothing,* a tin of Earl Grey tea, a colorful yarn figure from a local craft fair, an address book, some candy, and other fun things.

As I unpacked all these treasures, a beautiful card fell out. Enclosed within it was a note written on a lined piece of paper. (Claire hadn't wanted to spoil the card by writing on it.) She explained that upon learning of my birthday in January and my advanced age of sixty-five, "I was thrown for a loop. I thought we were both in our midforties—I really did—I became depressed—reality set in. But now it's February—I'm halfway back to my midforties and hope you are too." I assumed that everything in the box had a story, so I had to call Claire to hear all the tales.

I loved that gift from Claire—both the items and the stories—but it was just one in a wonderful series of gifts she gave me over the years. More than the hilarious quips, delicious lunches, and unique mementos, I treasure the time she spent with me, the wisdom and insights she shared, and her example of how to live into old age with grace.

She offered me the privilege of observing her version of positive aging as she modeled her unique strategies for viewing and living life in her later years. Her openness and sensitivity showed me the possibilities in this last chapter of life. Claire came to be my friend, and her generous friendship enhanced my own journey into aging. I am intensely grateful for these gifts.

One of the important qualities to possess in life is a healthy degree of self-awareness, and Claire certainly had that. She wasn't stagnant in her thinking or narrow in her interests, but she also knew what she needed to do to care for herself. She kept abreast of current affairs, but stepped back from sensational or repetitive coverage that could drag her down. And though she read widely, she chose to stay away from material she knew would upset her unnecessarily.

But self-care for Claire involved more than what she didn't do. It also involved what she *did* do. Like several of my ladies, she tapped into her memories for warmth and comfort. In this way she could enjoy her relationships with loved ones who were no longer with her and mentally visit places that fed her soul and created a sense of calm and gratitude. She recognized that doing so was important for her. "I've become my own priority" was not a selfish proclamation, but a simple acknowledgment that she was responsible for addressing her own needs.

Claire frequently said things like "I have all that I need" or "Isn't life wonderful?" Filled with gratitude, she acknowledged her obvious blessings, but she also chose to seek and identify blessings she might otherwise have overlooked. To do so, she had to remain open and aware, seeking the good in the everyday as well as in unlikely places.

She was particularly astute at finding the gifts in other people and honoring them. I think that quality enhanced and reinforced her connections with others. She also recognized that we are all different—unique creations of God whose uniqueness is to be embraced. She didn't spend time and energy trying to make everyone the same or judging those who were different. Instead, she accepted and celebrated each one-of-a-kind person.

Claire had also mastered the concept of perspective and harnessed it to her advantage. Defining her challenging situations as being "just a page in my book of life," "just a bump in the road," or "just a phase of the moon" helped her to define and limit them. By choosing not to identify her situation as permanent, personal, or pervasive, Claire typified the optimistic approach and outlook identified in the writings of the well-respected psychologist Martin E. Seligman.[3] According to Seligman, those who adopt this frame of mind have a greater chance of sustained happiness or contentment. I have learned in my further studies about aging that such a perspective also supports resilience, wellness, and overall positive aging.

An optimistic outlook like Claire's does not mean being a Pollyanna or being totally unrealistic. It means being able to acknowledge the negative, put it into perspective, and then set a course to move forward. As far as I could see, Claire practiced that art with considerable proficiency. She modeled for me what I have come to call balanced optimism. She would talk about how "rich and extremely happy" she was. Then she might tick off a laundry list of her various physical ailments, some of which were quite serious. Then she would switch again: "I don't focus on these. I'm too busy." Claire got into action, looking at problems realistically but then stepping around—or dancing over—the obstacles.

Claire also modeled the power of a lighthearted approach to life. Humor was a constant in all of our encounters—a

3 For more on Seligman, including a list of his relevant books, see chapter 7 and appendix B.

respectful, laugh-at-yourself kind of humor. She was adept at finding the funny side of any situation and, by doing so, lightening the burdens of others and helping them shift perspectives. She also had a great capacity for creating fun—her words, observations, funny gifts, or mimicry added joy to the lives of those around her. And occasionally the gentle, respectful Claire would hit me with a zinger I would never have expected from someone of her generation. She could lift a mood—her own and other people's—better than any pharmaceutical, a strategy she had discovered long ago and had been using ever since.

I had occasion to tap into Claire's "humor wisdom" during the summer of 2013, when I was struck by Bell's palsy, a paralysis of the major nerve on one side of the face due to viral infection, trauma, or Lyme disease. In my case the disease manifested as an inability to close my right eye and the contortion of the other side of my face into a grimace—not a pretty picture.

As I confronted this new reality, I felt Claire's inspiration and modeling kick in. I was able to look realistically at the situation, do all I could through medications, exercises, patches, and so forth, and then actually joke about my appearance. I dubbed myself Pirate Peggy (because of my eye patch) and kept a small sign handy that said, "This is my smile, not a sneer." I also invited everyone who helped me along the way to a "Wink, Blink, and Smile" party to be held once I had regained all the fine motor skills necessary to execute those facial expressions.

Everyone on my medical team commented on my positive spirit and upbeat approach to a condition that often, they said, left people frustrated and depressed. For that I must thank Claire as well as my other golden ladies. I certainly don't think I would have fared so well without Claire's humor training.

Claire was also a prime example of the value of positive self-talk, a technique often used in life coaching to help clients stay on track by affirming, directing, and encouraging themselves. Claire well understood the power of what she told herself, declaring that "If you go through life telling yourself you can't, you can't, you can't—then you can't!" She employed self-talk to remind herself of salient perspectives, and she scolded herself when she thought or said something out of sync with her sense of integrity. She also told herself when it was time to let go of things—a news story, a medical regimen, or even her thrift shop work, which meant so much to her. Claire benefited from her strong, intentional self-talk "conversations," and we can choose to do so as well.

Claire continued to maintain a strong sense of purpose throughout her life. For years she reached out and served in the community. When that was no longer possible, she mourned the loss of that opportunity and then found other ways to reach out to others—through phone calls, notes, and prayers, plus the occasional tape-wrapped package. Motherhood, too, took on a new face once her children were off on their own, but it continued to be an important part of Claire's life purpose. Once a mother, always a mother, as they say.

The capacity to adapt to new circumstances is crucial to navigating the older years, when change and loss can be all-too-familiar experiences. Claire had faced both many times, and she considered herself fortunate that she'd always had the ability to adapt.

I have seen this skill of Claire's in action, watching her accept her physical limitations and then find ways around them. I've seen her reaction to being forced to evacuate her home and later being unable to work in a place where she felt she received more than she gave, a place where she had felt herself "ageless." She faced each new situation and adapted. Her confidence in her capacity to handle change was built on former successes. She tapped into that confident energy for present challenges.

In life coaching we help clients build on their strengths and past successes to meet their current obstacles. That's exactly what I saw my friend Claire doing. As she once reminded me, she kept "evolving." What a great approach for someone in her nineties to be able to imagine new adventures and new ways to contribute. Such thinking serves as a reminder to me and my generation not to become stalled or hung up when things don't go quite as planned or when life isn't "the same as it used to be."

My friend Claire modeled for me what a person can do in "old age" with humor, compassion, and strength! Yes, it's possible. Claire is proof. For me as an aging baby boomer, knowing that is a gift indeed. If only I can follow her example, I'll consider myself truly blessed.

CLAIRE'S GALLERY

The young Claire about the time of her engagement to A. J. (1940s).

Claire in the "tall, slim" photo I took (2013).

Claire and I on one of my visits to her place (mid-2000s).

CHAPTER 3

❧

Jane Manning

"The nurses call me Sunshine."

I FIRST MET JANE while attending a women's Bible study. A petite, soft-spoken woman, she usually wore khaki slacks and pastel blouses, and she sat in the same spot each week. I'd been told she was a full-time island resident who lived with her son in Madaket, on the western end of the island. Beyond that, I knew little else about Jane until another full-time resident, Jackie, took me on a hike.

As a child, Jackie had spent her entire summers on Nantucket with her family in their tiny cottage on the easternmost part of the island, Siasconset—or 'Sconset, as it was usually called. When Jackie discovered that neither Jane nor I had experienced the 'Sconset bluff walk, she invited the two of us to join her.

We followed the lovely right-of-way that runs along the edge of the sand bluff before it drops to the beach below. Because it crosses private property, we were mindful of keeping our voices low and treading lightly so as not to beat a path in areas where we had to traverse someone's lawn. Winding our way along the edge of the bluff, with its spectacular views of the sea, we enjoyed the bright yellow blossoms of Scotch broom and inhaled the sweet perfume of *Rosa rugosa* that gentle breezes mixed with the scent of the sea.

On the landward side, we marveled at the large old cedar-shingle homes collared by hydrangea bushes and trimmed with rose-covered trellises. The green lawns stretched down to the "walk," and the occasional chair, ball, or toy hinted at the leisure activities of each household. Jackie guided us on a special tour, recounting her childhood experiences and telling us "how things used to be in the old days."

On the day of our walk—in the late 1990s—we were able to walk all the way to the Sankaty Head lighthouse located at the end of the bluff path. (Since then, the sea has reclaimed large sections of the 'Sconset bluffs and the lighthouse has had to be relocated further inland, so the current ocean-view walk is much shorter.) On our way back, walking along Baxter Road, I began to learn more about the quiet and intriguing Jane.

I learned she was a widow and had retired after a career in meteorology. Never having met a meteorologist in person, and a female at that, I was fascinated. Since Jane was in her seventies when I met her, I suspected there must be an interesting story behind a woman of her generation becoming a professional in that field.

I learned that seventy-something Jane had only recently taken up the violin and especially liked learning to play her favorite hymns. Jackie also mentioned Jane's locally admired dollhouse, something that caught my attention as well. I had played for hours with my own dollhouse as a child, and I loved the fact that Jane had created one as an adult.

As we were heading to our respective cars at the end of our walk, I asked Jane how she had come to Nantucket in the first place. "Was it because your husband was here?"

"No," she replied, "I met him here." She said she had arrived on-island alone to work at the Nantucket weather station.

Hearing all this, I knew I had to learn more about this woman who forecasted weather, created dollhouses, was game to take up the violin in her eighth decade, and had come to this "faraway island" all by herself after World War II. I wanted to hear more of Jane's story than a mere walk along the bluffs could provide.

Jane thus became one of my special Nantucket discoveries, one that could have easily gone undetected if I hadn't shared that time and conversation with her on our 'Sconset walk with Jackie. Prior to that little adventure, I had only seen Jane's quiet nature and modest demeanor at the Bible study. She never pressed her own agenda or expressed herself in dramatic ways. But I would come to learn much more about the depth of this quiet soul.

Starting Out

Jane was a child of the Depression. Born in Ohio, she moved with her family to Florida and then to North Carolina, going wherever her father could find work. But in North Carolina, upon her graduation from high school in 1939, she discovered that no local jobs were available. She would have loved to go to college, but her family "couldn't swing that."

Without specialized skills, Jane returned to her high school to take a business course—which, she told me with a chuckle, "I promptly failed." She took a few little jobs that she didn't like much while she kept careful watch on the newspaper want ads. Finally, an ad recruiting workers for the United States Weather Bureau caught her interest. She was excited to learn that, due to escalating prewar efforts, positions were beginning to open up to women. "Before that," she told me, "it was an all-man job."

When Jane applied for the weather position, another stumbling block presented itself. She was disappointed to learn they were only taking women candidates who had completed college. But throughout the roller coaster of raised and lowered hopes, Jane kept an even spirit.

Some of this equanimity may have emanated from her faith. Around this time, a pivotal event in Jane's spiritual journey occurred. In her words, "I came to the Lord at about age eighteen."

Her childhood days had included Sunday school, but the "disconnected stories" she heard there hadn't really seemed to apply to her life. It wasn't until she became a teen that her understanding started to shift. She had always loved school, playing teacher from the early grades and placing her brother, dolls, and teddies in chairs as her students. During her teens, though, she had been disappointed to realize her "teachers weren't all I thought they were. They weren't perfect. And my parents weren't perfect. And finally," she said, laughing, "it came down to me, and I wasn't perfect. I needed the Lord, and I had doubted he even existed."

When I met Jane more than fifty years later, it was clear that her Christian faith had remained with her all that time, providing her with a constant source of strength and peace. Back then, no doubt, it helped keep her steady at a very uncertain time for Jane, her family, and her country.

Making WAVES

When the war broke out, Jane wanted to do her part. But when she suggested going north to work in a factory, her parents said no. They also nixed the idea of her joining the Women's Army Corps because the WACs would likely be sent overseas, and Jane's dad, who had served in Europe during World War I, was strongly opposed to that.

The next flicker of hope arrived when the United States Navy established the WAVES (Women Accepted for Volunteer Emergency Service). But again, at that point, they were accepting only college graduates, preparing them for the officer corps. The recruiter did offer her some hope, though, suggesting she try again when they "took enlisted," as he put it.

Unlike officers, enlisted personnel would not be required to have college degrees.

So when the call finally went out for enlisted candidates, Jane joined the Navy. She was twenty-one and leaving home for the first time. She experienced a bit of second-guessing when she peered out the train window and saw her mother standing there on the platform. "I was on the train that was leaving for who knows where. I shed a few tears then and asked myself, 'What have I done?'" as she set off on her multi-legged odyssey to boot camp—in Iowa, of all places.

Why would the Navy situate one of its bases in such an unlikely location? Jane explained that an Iowa teachers' college had been turned over to the Navy as a boot camp site for their new women's corps. Her eyes twinkled as she recounted some of her adventures on the way to that landlocked camp.

For reasons unbeknownst to her, for instance, she had been handed two tickets for her next train connection—hers and another woman's. She had no idea who or where that person was. The mystery was solved when the two women looked around and simultaneously realized they were the only two on the platform with the required "short hair and black Oxford shoes"—hardly the fashion of the day. They soon found they had something else in common. Both were named Jane Ellen—a comforting, if confusing, beginning.

Having executed a successful train connection in South Carolina, the two Janes were able to settle in a bit for the ride. They knew they wouldn't starve because, in addition to the extra ticket for her new friend, Jane had also been given the meal tickets for all the women recruits on the train. As for distributing the meal tickets, she told her new companion, "I'm not going to worry about it. I'll just sit here, and they'll find me, I'm sure."

Thinking back to her initial enlistment experience, Jane remembered, "They had promised me I would get first-class accommodations." And she did secure a sleeper compartment with a lower bunk for the first night. But after her connection in Chicago, her accommodations were "hardly first class." She boarded an "ancient, old-fashioned, iron-seated car" packed with young women who had to either squeeze into any of the uncomfortable seats that might be available or stand. Some sat on their suitcases. "With everyone so excited," Jane recalled, "there was no sleep for anyone."

After two sleepless nights, Jane arrived in Iowa to begin her training. She was in for several surprises. She waited in long lines for bedding and room assignments and then hoped to get some rest. But she had no sooner stretched out on her bunk when she was disturbed by shouting in the hallway. The cry "Muster! Muster!" was interrupting her nap, and she didn't even know what *muster* meant.

She and her fellow recruits quickly learned how to line up in exact platoon positions. They were taught the basics of marching and made their way to the mess hall. "That was the next surprise," she told me. "I was handed a metal tray with compartments, and someone then slopped the food onto it, giving me twice what I would normally eat and only fifteen minutes to eat it!"

After that initial mess hall experience—when, as she told me, "I didn't get much eaten"—Jane thought she would finally be able to return to her bunk. Instead, the women toured all the places where they would be having classes. They even visited the gymnasium. Then came a required ("boring") lecture. Jane did not have a chance to sleep until ten o'clock that first night. Welcome to the Navy.

Shock Waves

The first full day of Jane's boot camp was "filled with shots," Jane remembers, "in both arms." The Navy was just beginning to adapt to having women in its ranks, as Jane learned to her shock when she saw her medical chart. "I was a little startled when my health record had a man's figure on it," she told me with a giggle. "I guess they finally got around to changing it."

As the women completed their health checks, they each needed to get a chest X-ray, tuberculosis being a prevalent concern in those days. And at that point Jane, who had been raised in a home that valued modesty, got another shock. "They had us all stripped to the waist and lined up in a hallway when this maintenance man came walking down the hall." She continued, "He was a perfect gentleman—he didn't look left or right. But he had a grin a mile wide on his face, and of course all the girls were screaming."

I asked Jane if she had done her weather-service training at the Iowa location. "No," she answered with a revealing note of triumph. "This was boot camp—and *I survived.*"

At the end of boot camp, Jane took a variety of tests to determine where she would go next for specialized training. She fared well enough to have some choice in the matter. Due to her soft voice, the role of trainer was ruled out. She chose weather, but for that she needed to take a special test. She felt uncomfortable and less competent when she learned that she and another girl were the only ones taking the test who were not college graduates.

To boost her courage, she reminded herself that she had been the only girl in her physics class in high school and that she did love math. But she couldn't help but be intimidated by those other girls, who talked about "their colleges and *calculus.*" "Calculus," she said to me with a laugh. "I had never even *heard* of calculus."

"I'll never make it," she said to herself at first. But then she summoned her innate positivity and told herself, "The Navy took me. It's their problem what to do with me." She calmed herself down, and the test turned out not to be a problem at all. It just measured general intelligence—"Quite easy, actually."

Drama on the Slow Train

Jane was excited about having successfully completed boot camp—and being able to go home on a short leave before reporting to her next assignment. When she received her orders, she discovered that she would depart for home the next morning and then, right after her leave, proceed to weather school in Lakewood, New Jersey. The abrupt departure schedule added the pressure of urgency to her excitement. She hastily packed her belongings—"Not much," she told me—and scrambled to retrieve her dirty laundry from the hamper.

At the train station she was assisted by a porter. ("We had porters in those days," she reminded me.) She boarded the appropriate train, but as it pulled away from the station, she realized her bag was not on the train with her. She felt the grip of panic but quickly sought a solution to her problem by seeking out the conductor.

"The conductor said there was no way for him to get my bag, which he assumed had been put on the local—the slow train. 'But,' he told me, 'we do pass that train at a station, and you can get off this train and get onto the other.'" That's exactly what Jane had to do—take the slow train when everything in life seemed to have such a sense of urgency and swiftness about it.

The remainder of Jane's journey home would provide her with a bit more drama. "That's when I found out I had run off with a hundred dollars of the Navy's money." When the train was ambling through Harrisburg, Jane had become bored and, for something to do, decided to look through her new purse.

"I opened my billfold and asked, 'What's this one-hundred-dollar bill doing here?' Then it dawned on me. Realizing what had happened, I said, 'Oh no! They're going to court-martial me, and I haven't even started.'"

Then, of course, she had to explain to *me* what had happened.

Just prior to their departure, each of the WAVES had been given two hundred-dollar bills. "I think it was to save paperwork," she said. "We were to get our uniforms in two different stores, and we were to give one hundred dollars to one store and the other hundred dollars to the other store. But in all my excitement to be going home, I forgot the second store. I worried the whole time until I got home."

As soon as she arrived, she barely said hello to her folks, who didn't own a phone at the time, and rushed over to the neighbors, who did. "Would you mind if I made a long-distance call?" she implored.

Jane called the camp and asked to speak to the commanding officer. "It happened to be a WAVES officer," she told me. "I gave her the whole Navy spiel—name, rank, and serial number—and told her what had happened."

As Jane told me the story, I could almost hear the childlike supplicant voice she must have used that day. "I didn't mean to do it," she said again and again. And as she explained it to me, "The officer couldn't get a word in edgewise. She laughed her head off."

At the time, Jane wondered what the woman found so funny. With all the Navy regulations that had been drilled into her, she was convinced this was a court-martial-worthy offense. But the officer calmed her down, told her where to send the money and the explanation, and finished by saying,

"I'm sure it will be all right." Jane followed directions and heard no more about it.

Weather Trainee

Despite the intensity of her weather training in Lakewood, Jane had several amusing experiences during her time there—including her very first experience on a two-hour fire watch.

The Navy had acquired a facility that had previously been a Catholic boys' school—an unlikely venue for technical military training. The beautiful campus included a lake surrounded by a sea of daffodils and a lovely grove of trees. The gymnasium had been left intact, but one of the large storage buildings had been converted into a fully functional weather station.

The large main building, which resembled a big old manor house with wings on each end, made for an imposing presence. The trainees had quarters on the top floor of one of the wings, with offices, classrooms, and a library below. The other wing was home to the chapel, with officers' quarters above. Joining the two wings was a large classroom with a high ceiling and a skylight.

I tried to envision tiny Jane, newly arrived and unfamiliar with the place, moving through that big old building in the middle of the night while "standing fire watch." ("Now that didn't mean you got an extra two hours sleep during the day," Jane informed me.) For this duty, she had been issued a flashlight with a battery that was "just about gone. Its little orange light didn't shine very much. And they handed me a billy club," she added, laughing.

"So I came down to do my watch and first flashed my light all around the library. Remember that [radio] program *Inner Sanctum,* with the squeaky door making that eeeeking sound?" she asked me. "Well, it was like that when I came to the room with the skylight. It was eerie because the light that did come in was through the skylight, and it was a dark night, so there was very little. I just got through the squeaky door into the dark when this bright light flashed right in my face—one of those huge lights—and I couldn't see what was behind it."

Jane's orders had been to challenge anyone she met. "So I dutifully said—I'm sure in a timid voice—'Halt! Who goes there?'"

The answer came in a booming male voice: "It's only me. I'm checking the heat."

Jane explained, "I didn't see who 'me' was because he had too bright a light." So she continued on her rounds through the chapel and elsewhere, shining her weak little light.

We laughed about the incident, and she clarified that the purpose of her watch really was to check for fires. "There were other guards outside." When I asked if she had been frightened, she said, "Not really, but it was kind of a creepy and scary spot. I guess I had seen too many movies."

Fire watches aside, Jane's concerns about the weather training class proved unfounded. She finished in the top third of her three-month intensive training classes—and that was without college or the mysterious calculus under her belt.

Jane's next duty station in the Anacostia section of Washington, DC, would prove frustrating for her because "I didn't get to do any observations. All I did was tear off teletypes and file them and hand out flight gear to pilots. I wasn't really doing what I was trained to do." Despite being soft-spoken, Jane made her voice heard when her superior officer asked her how things were going. "I asked to be transferred," she explained to me, "before I forgot everything I had learned. I told them, 'You're not getting use of my education.'" As it turned out, the station was disbanded a month later, and Jane and half the other women received orders to St. Louis.

Jane loved working at Lambert Field, located "way out in the country" outside of St. Louis. At the airport weather station, she was able to get plenty of practice making observations and giving reports, the things she liked to do. "But I didn't like the city," she told me. "It was so smelly from the beer and the leather. The smells were awful." Even so, she did venture into St. Louis on occasion to visit what she affectionately remembers as "the beautiful zoo" and to enjoy outdoor theater performances.

As it turned out, Jane was at the theater on a fateful day and missed observing a "horrible accident" at Lambert Field. "They were test launching a new glider made in the area that was meant to take the troops behind enemy lines," she explained. "The local dignitaries—including the mayor of St. Louis—were on board for the flight. Their families were there." She hesitated. "The wing fell off and the whole thing came plummeting straight down a thousand feet, with all the families watching." She shook her head. "I'm so glad I wasn't there."

On Duty

Once her training was complete at Lambert Field, Jane was sent back to Washington, DC, for a weather-related assignment. There she had some experiences working in classified military areas ruled by "need to know." The idea that it was her duty to keep information secret to protect those on the front lines was so deeply instilled in her that even many decades later she was reluctant to say much about it. She was appalled at the various leaks that had appeared online and in the press more recently, when the front lines were less clearly defined.

When a friend of Jane's, who worked in a high-security area, named her as a good candidate to substitute for her while she was on leave, Jane was "unhappy with the idea." My initial reaction to that was surprise, since Jane always seemed eager to do her duty. But the situation became clear when my con-scientious friend explained, "I was very concerned because, in a week, I had to learn the maps of the Pacific, China, New Zealand, the islands of the Pacific . . ." She ticked off all she needed to know, and I could see her shoulders fall as she recalled the weight of that responsibility and her desire to "get it right."

To add to the pressure of the task at hand, Jane had to walk to the building in the middle of the night and then work her shift locked in a very small room with only one key. Her orders were clear. She was not to let anybody into that room, even if "they were an officer—no one." She was on her own.

The room "had a teletype, which was encoded," she recalled, plus "a map table, a great big map on the wall, and a stool to sit on. If I went to the bathroom, I had to lock the door. . . . I had to stay in [that map room] for eight hours— talk about solitary confinement." She laughed. "And I have claustrophobia too."

Jane explained her night's work there: "The only communication I had was the teletype machine, and it had only one line. There were not any telephone numbers. So when I turned it on and typed, it went directly to—somewhere." Jane never knew where that somewhere was.

"I could ask a question if I got into difficulty," she told me, and the response would come in via the teletype. During the night, as weather information came in, Jane put it onto the map according to code. The next morning an officer would come, and by prearrangement, Jane let him in to make a forecast. "But before I could leave my watch, I would have to gather all my paperwork and teletypes from the night, take them to a fireplace in another room, and burn them. There was no such thing as a shredder back then.

"I didn't like that duty," she told me. "I was so glad when [my friend] came back. I was able to do it, though, amazingly. Eight hours was sufficient to finish [put all the weather data on] the map."

Scrambled Eggs

One of my favorite stories from Jane's time in the WAVES occurred while she was walking down a street in Washington, DC. At the time she held one of the lowest ranks among the enlisted members of the Navy—aerographer's mate third class. Her enlisted rank required that she come to attention and salute any uniformed officer she encountered.

How would she know an officer's rank? The uniforms were marked with either an emblem or a pin, and some officers might have a bit of gold braid on the brims of their caps—the higher the rank, the more braid. The highest ranking officers, admirals, wore caps that were covered with a significant amount of gold braid, typically called "scrambled eggs."

On that particular day Jane and a WAVES friend decided to go for a walk. Jane admits to having a bad habit of walking with her head down, watching her feet, quite the opposite of the chin-up, straight-and-tall carriage required by the Navy. As they proceeded, she noticed her friend stiffen. Jane looked up just in time to see her deliver a snappy salute to what Jane told me "was all this gold braid. I'd never seen so much in my life. And of course he was returning her salute."

Between chuckles as she pictured the scene of so many years ago, Jane told me, "I didn't know what to do. So I, of course, did what I'd do at home. I said hi."

I admit I gasped at that, then burst out laughing. As a former military wife, I knew that you *never* just said hi to a higher-ranking officer when in uniform. And Jane knew that too, of course. But, she explained, "I was in awe with all those scrambled eggs he had."

I asked her, "Did he do anything when you failed to salute?"

"No," she responded. "He didn't even put me on report. He just grinned."

"Good thing he had a sense of humor," I said, to which Jane countered, "Well, if I'd been an ensign, I'd have been put right on report." She guessed she had been given some leeway because of her low rank and possibly her gender.

Her companion was horrified at the whole scene, however. "That was an admiral," she sputtered. "And you said hi!"

Ending the War

Jane remained on duty in Washington, DC, from the fall of 1943 until spring of 1945, when one of her longtime dreams came true. "I got sent to Hawaii—one of the two places I'd always wanted to go," Jane told me. "The other was Switzerland, and I've never been there."

Jane's journey to Hawaii began with a cross-country railroad trip. Initially, she had difficulty finding a place on the train, and it was suggested that she double up in a bunk for the ride. Jane took that opportunity to speak up for herself and said, "No way." At the last minute, space became available on another train heading for San Francisco. From there she would depart on a passenger ship refitted to accommodate troops.

"We weren't allowed to tell anyone our schedule," Jane told me. "We couldn't telephone anyone. It was very hush-hush.

We sailed out at night. We didn't go in convoy, but we had air cover, with planes flying over us from time to time, and antiaircraft guns were onboard."

The five-day trip went smoothly. The WAVES were separated from the other troops and were "bunked over the ammunition," Jane told me. We both agreed the location of their quarters was a great deterrent to smoking below decks, though Jane herself was not a smoker. And no one was smoking on deck either, because no lights were allowed. "Even though it was close to the end of the war, there were still submarines out there."

When the ship reached Hawaii, the WAVES were dropped off on the island of Oahu. Jane was assigned the same duties she had performed in Washington, DC. The weather unit where she served turned out to be smaller than she had expected because the Pacific Command headquarters had been relocated from Hawaii to Guam, but she still stayed busy conducting regular weather breakouts. "We had cracked the weather code awhile before," she explained, "but [the enemy] didn't know it, and they didn't find out. So we were breaking out [checking their coded weather forecasts and status] regularly"—a significant advantage to our aviators and troops.

From her workplace, Jane could see where the war had begun. "I looked down on Pearl City and all of Pearl Harbor," she told me. When I asked Jane about a particular detail of the war, she responded, "For being part of history, I don't know much about it." Perhaps she didn't recall the chronologies of various battles, but what she did remember was what it was like when the end of the war came to Hawaii. "The celebrating was, was—something," she recalled with a faraway look in her eyes, unable to capture the experience in words.

Jane's family, like many others during the war, had more than one member serving in the military. Her brother served on the European front in France with the Eighth Army, participating, she thought, in the Battle of the Bulge. But she didn't know for certain because "he never talked about it," she told me. "My mother said he had nightmares for a long time after."

Explaining that her brother had been a high school dropout, she said that after the war he told his family he had learned a lot. "Next war," he told them, "I'm going to fight from Washington." And he did. After going back to complete high school and then college, he pursued his doctorate, only to be interrupted by the realities of raising a family and running out of GI benefits. So he took a job with the National Security Administration, working first with codes and then with computers. "But it was so much easier when the computers came along," Jane declared. His work, like her wartime service, was secret.

Back to School

After Jane arrived back home in November, she began to explore going to college on the GI Bill. Her pastor was able to facilitate a midyear entry into a small Christian school, Lenoir-Rhyne College in Hickory, North Carolina. She began in January and then attended all summer to make up for the semester she had missed.

A friend of Jane's, who wanted to become a doctor, felt that they were not being challenged enough where they were and suggested they apply to Women's College of the University of North Carolina at Greensboro. Jane was accepted and continued her studies in math. "I almost had enough physics credits for a major in that. Physics was my love. But in order to do physics, you almost had to have a degree in math too—it's so connected," she explained. "I really had meteorology in mind, but so few schools offered it, and the ones that did were so far away. I wanted to be closer [to home]."

After graduating from college, next on Jane's agenda was applying for a job with the Weather Bureau, but there were few openings in the geographical areas she preferred. North Carolina had only one opening—at Cape Hatteras—and "they hesitated to send a woman there [because] it's so isolated." So they suggested she change her division option to the northeast.

That was agreeable to Jane. "New England was what I had in mind," she told me. But no jobs were available in that division either. So Jane took her brother's suggestion and requested another year of school through the Veterans Administration. They approved her request. Jane was accepted at North Texas State University, which agreed to take any number of veterans as long as they had a place to live, housing being scarce at that time. So Jane traveled to Denton, Texas, and moved in with her brother and his wife, who let her sleep on the sofa of their one-bedroom apartment.

While at North Texas, Jane studied graduate math and physics, but she didn't abandon her Weather Bureau ambitions. When the opportunity arose, she traveled to Fort Worth for an interview. She also devised a backup plan to take education classes in case a job in meteorology didn't materialize. However, she didn't need that plan because she was called for her first Weather Bureau assignment and had to leave Texas before completing her master's degree.

A Tiny Dot in the Ocean

"They sent me to Nantucket," Jane told me. "I had to look it up in the library. I'd never heard of Nantucket." When she took out the world map and located the island, her heart took a bit of a dive. "It was a tiny dot out there in the ocean," she exclaimed. "I thought, *Oh boy*. But I was desperate to get on at the Weather Bureau and thrilled with the hire, thinking I could always put in for a transfer."

Her brother asked her, "Do you really want to go?" and she replied, "Oh yes." He then offered her a helpful perspective on the adventure. "Well, why don't you go and look at it as a vacation? If you don't like it, you can turn around and come back again."

In those days, traveling from Texas to Nantucket was a significant journey. Jane took the train to New York and then had to transfer to a bus that would take her to the seaport of New Bedford, Massachusetts. From there she traveled on to Woods Hole, where she sat up all night waiting for the ferry. She spent five hours on the steamship ferry, which stopped first in Martha's Vineyard and then continued on to Nantucket. Finally, on March 20, 1950, Jane arrived on-island.

She took a taxi to a guest house the driver recommended and booked a room there for a week. Hungry but too exhausted to seek out a place for dinner, she just sank down into a chair and looked around her. At the end of that bleak March day, she asked herself, "What have I done?"

"I felt pangs of homesickness and despair," she remembered, "greater than any I had experienced before on my trips away from home." But then she remembered her brother's suggestion to think of the trip as a vacation. And in faith, as was her custom, she offered a prayer for strength and guidance before collapsing into bed for some much-needed sleep.

Despite the inauspicious beginning to Jane's Nantucket venture, the next day would be what she had come to call "the most marvelous day of my life. In one day," she declared, "I got a job, a car, a place to live, a church, and even met the man who would eventually be my husband."

Early that morning, Jane went to the airport and reported for duty at the weather station, a two-story wooden building with a potbellied stove in the middle of the main room. There she met the chief of the weather station, who would be her boss. With no food service available on the premises, the chief brought Jane home to his house for lunch. She met his wife and their three boys, and they invited her to live in their spare bedroom. She would pay fifteen dollars a week for room and board and help out some with babysitting. The chief's wife also invited Jane to join their family for worship at First Baptist Church (later Summer Street Church), which soon became Jane's church home.

The next issue was transportation. With no bus service on the island, Jane said, "I guess I will have to get a car." So off they went to the local car dealership, owned by a friendly man named Burt Manning. Burt sold Jane a Chevy, and a colleague at the weather station offered to give her driving lessons.

The future no longer looked uncertain for Jane. She now had her job, home, car, and church. And she didn't know it yet, but she had just met the man she was going to marry.

Mr. Manning

Jane's face lit up as she told me about how her relationship began with Burt Manning, a man she would grow to love and respect deeply. "Well, he was Mr. Manning to me when I first came to the island. I never really got to calling him Burt until after he was gone." She laughed. "First it was Mr. Manning, then Honey, then Dad, then Grandpa."

Some of her great respect for Mr. Manning was based on his devotion to his first wife, who had multiple sclerosis. She explained that Burt worked during the day at the dealership— which was also a garage and gas station—then cared for his wife and young son at night. When his wife's MS progressed to the point that she needed more care than he could give her, he arranged for her transfer to a hospital on the mainland. But he still traveled every other weekend to see her—at a time when travel to and from the island involved both time and intention.

Mrs. Manning passed away just about the time that Burt's son graduated from high school and joined the Coast Guard—around 1956. Burt spent some time off-island visiting relatives after that, then returned to run his business. One day Jane stopped at the garage for gas, and she and Burt got to talking. He invited her to ride out to see the progress he was making on getting his Madaket cottage ready for visiting relatives. "Okay, maybe I will," Jane told him, and she did eventually go out to see the cottage.

One evening not long afterward, Jane came home to the house on Milk Street that she shared with its widowed owner. Her landlady, who was preparing to go out for the island's Fourth of July celebration, said she had left two chicken pies in the freezer, so Jane could invite someone for dinner. "I thought, *who in the world will I invite?* The only people I knew well were married. But then, all of a sudden, I thought of Mr. Manning. I thought he'd be lonesome all by himself with his son gone to the Coast Guard. And he had invited me to see the cottage, so why not invite him over to eat?"

Jane drove over to Madaket to extend the invitation. Mr. Manning accepted. And no sooner had Jane arrived back home to begin the dinner preparations than a neighbor came running over. ("News travels fast on Nantucket," Jane reminded me.)

"I hear you're having company," the neighbor said. "I'll bring over some rolls for you, and if he asks you to marry him, do!"

Aghast, Jane responded, "I just asked him for dinner. I had nothing like that in mind. But later [that same neighbor] asked us both to dinner at her house. She was a regular little Cupid."

It wasn't long before Jane and Mr. Manning "started going together." Jane recalled how "he would get off work and we'd go to the beach. At the time he owned Island Chevrolet."

With a shy laugh she admitted that Burt wasn't the most effusive of fellows. One time Jane was taking a new Weather Bureau employee on a tour of the island. At Altar Rock, the highest point of the island, they ran across a woman with car trouble. The woman insisted she needed a garage and asked if they knew Burt Manning. Jane and her colleague, who knew that Jane and Burt were seeing each other, had a giggle over that.

As it happened, the person who came out for the repair service was, in fact, Burt. The woman asked him, "Why did the girls laugh when I said your name? Are they related [to you]?"

Burt replied, "Not yet." And Jane responded to that answer with a nervous laugh because, as she explained to me, "He hadn't even asked me!" But his response warmed her heart and suggested the possibilities of things to come. Burt and Jane would look back on this story with fondness and laughter in the years to come.

Burt and Jane's courtship consisted mostly of dinners and TV at his home. Then he would drive Jane home, stopping to talk a bit in front of her place. "One night he said, 'Someday

I'd like to take you home and keep you. Would you come?' I said yes, and he was so startled. You know, I had made up in my mind a long time ago, but I didn't think he would ever ask. When I said yes, he reared back in the seat and said, 'That's that,' like he had just sold a car." I thought, *Boy, how romantic can you get?*

Jane was thirty-five and Burt was fifty-three when they married on January 1, 1957. A year later they had a baby son, whom they called Tim. By the time I met Jane, her son was grown and living with her in Madaket. Burt had died two days before his ninety-third birthday.

Several times Jane and I discussed the experience of motherhood. She said, "My mother used to say, 'God gave the hardest job to the least experienced.' It *is* a tough job," she added. "And all children are different. There's no secret formula." I concurred. Jane and I also agreed that motherhood was the most challenging yet rewarding experience a woman could have. We both felt blessed to have the privilege of being mothers.

Lasting Acts of Kindness

In telling me her life story, Jane didn't dwell on the difficult times of her life. Instead, she stressed the blessings she had received from others over the years—her parents and brother, her fellow WAVES and commanding officers, her family and friends on Nantucket, and even random strangers. I couldn't help but wonder how this focus on counting blessings had contributed to Jane's positive approach to life in her eighties and nineties. When we discussed this, Jane shared her belief that kindness can have both an immediate and a lasting impact.

She recalled a time when she was traveling by train with her husband and young son, who became sick to his stomach right there in New York's Penn Station, with all the people hustling by. Burt tried to locate a restroom while Jane stood alone with poor little Tim. "Of all the people there, only one person stopped," she recalled, "and the least likely. A businessman all dressed in his nice suit and [carrying his] briefcase came over to see if he could help." The memory of his kindness, she told me, had always stayed with her, warming her soul.

On another, earlier occasion during her Navy days in Washington, DC, Jane left a skating party that her shift had arranged at the only time the rink was available—from midnight to two in the morning. Having just learned to ice skate, she'd been eager to attend, but she hadn't considered that her return home in the wee hours of the morning might prove problematic. When she learned that the crosstown bus, her usual way home, didn't run at that hour, she found herself alone on the dark streets, trying to figure out which combination of streetcars she could use to get home.

The drivers were helpful to an extent, but she still found herself standing in the dark on a traffic island, waiting for an unfamiliar streetcar. A man approached her to say, "This car doesn't run now. You'll have to walk over to the next street."

"Before I could even say no," Jane told me, "a black woman who had been quietly standing much farther down the island was at my side. 'Don't you believe him,' she said. 'That street-car's due to come over that hill in just a minute.'"

Jane reminded me that Washington was segregated at the time and that this African American woman was putting herself at risk by speaking up like that to two white people. It would have been far safer for her to simply mind her business. But she didn't.

Fortunately, the man backed down and stepped aside. As he did so, Jane told me, "Sure enough, here came that streetcar."

As Jane boarded and told the driver where she needed to go, the other woman made her way to the back of the streetcar. Jane was so shaken up by the incident that she sat right up by the driver. But more than fifty years later, she still regretted not taking the opportunity to thank that woman.

"That was indeed a self-sacrificing act on her part. She really did a wonderful thing. Well, she will have a reward in heaven."

At Home at the Homestead

In 2007 Jane moved from the Madaket house to the Homestead, a cozy Nantucket independent-living residence that provided three meals a day in an inviting dining room. In order to remain eligible to live there, a resident had to be able to navigate to the dining room to eat. Because of some spinal issues, Jane received some help with bathing and dressing but was otherwise on her own.

I asked how she liked living at the Homestead and how she came to move there from Madaket. Her answer to the first question was that she unequivocally loved living at the Homestead. She found the balance of support and independence at the facility to be just right. "The people here are wonderful—residents and staff both."

As for the second question, Jane said she reached the point where she realized she needed more help. She didn't want to burden her son. So she called her friend Jackie—the same Jackie who had taken us on the bluff walk. Together they checked the availability of suitable options and discovered that a vacancy had just come open at the Homestead. Jane had to make a snap decision to take the apartment or she would lose it. She decided to take it and thinks she made the best decision for both herself and her son, who still lives in the Madaket house.

Hearing that story, I had to admire Jane's strength and decisiveness in making such a significant transition so quickly. Clearly, this very mild lady was made of tough stuff.

Jane quickly got into the rhythm of life at the Homestead, playing backgammon with other residents and attending the weekly teatime gatherings on Monday afternoons. But she found that the level of conversation needed a boost, and she set out to remedy that. She explained to me that many of the residents didn't have much life outside the residence, so there was potential for becoming insular. "Of course, they all like to reminisce, but starting other conversations can be difficult."

Jane facilitated those teatime conversations by using her subscription to the magazine *Cappers* as a source of good jokes, human-interest stories, quotations, and thoughts to remember. She read some of these to me when I visited—"Smiles never go up in price or down in value" and another that could certainly tease out some comments: "You can learn more about a person by what he says about others than by what others say about him."

One thing Jane liked about the Homestead was its convenient location on Main Street, which facilitated Tim's regular visits. Jane enjoyed seeing him and appreciated his help with various chores. He even brought his cat along at times, providing a source of entertainment and joy for them both. (Animals are widely recognized as contributing significantly to the well-being of older folks . . . and younger ones as well.)

Once she settled in at the Homestead, Jane found plenty to occupy her time. One day, for instance, a staff member who needed be gone in the afternoon asked her to take charge of the exercise time that day at the residence. "Most all of us are in wheelchairs or on walkers, but we do get together for our exercises each day. It's fun. Actually we do have a lot of fun," she told me. "People wonder what a bunch of old ladies over seventy-five do all day. But I have to say," Jane added with conviction, "we have a lot of laughs here. . . . Who would have thought it?"

I didn't doubt Jane's word for a minute. And her words infused me with a sense of hope for myself and my fellow baby boomers.

Staying Sharp

Observing Jane's impressive mental acuity at age ninety, I asked her if she did something special to keep herself so sharp. "Yes," she replied, "I work puzzles. Right now I do Sudokus"—referring to the popular number puzzles where players must fill out a grid according to a set of placement rules. "Of course I have a system worked out, so it's just a matter of concentration and accuracy, because they sort of work themselves." (I must confess that that has not been my experience with Sudoku!)

But Sudoku wasn't Jane's only puzzle outlet. "I like cryptograms," she informed me. "And I like acrostics—it's one of my favorites." When I looked puzzled (no pun intended), she explained that acrostics were a combination of a crossword and code work, which can be worked back and forth. "I used to like logic problems," she told me, "but they're a little too much for me these days."

She went on to say something I have heard from other of my golden ladies as well: "Anything that isn't fun, I don't like to do. I like to do things that keep my interest up but aren't too hard." Then she described another game I had heard of but had no experience with. "Backgammon is a nice game for just recreation," she told me. "It's a two-person game with some chance and some thinking. The rules are simple, and it's a fast game. That's why I like it."

Over the years Jane had enjoyed a variety of activities that fell into two categories: learning and exploring. Despite some eye problems, she read widely in various formats—books, magazines, newspapers. She had taken Elderhostel trips, which combine adventure, learning, and new horizons. I also knew that Jane was interested in birds and had made some drawings and paintings of them, but I had no idea of the extent of that interest until one recent summer day.

Many Ways to Be Smart

The more I learned about Jane, the more impressed I was with her intelligence and accomplishments. But finding out about these took some digging, because Jane was not one to toot her own horn.

On one of our afternoon visits, I had the chance to see her celebrated dollhouse again and admire the changes she had made in its décor since moving into the Homestead. As we chatted, Burt's two grown granddaughters arrived for a visit. Priscilla lived in Nantucket, but Jessica had come all the way from Utah. Jane explained to me that they had never met their natural grandmother, Burt's first wife, so she was the only grandmother they knew.

In the course of the visit, they asked to look through Jane's memento and jewelry box. I remembered doing the same thing with my grandmother's treasures.

As they took out various items, Jane related little stories or gave a context for each one. Tucked away from most of the other artifacts was a little covered box. One granddaughter opened it and held up a small metal object. "Grandma, what's this?"

Jane waved her hand dismissively. "Ach, put that away. It's just my Phi Beta Kappa key."

Our eyes all opened wide, and we whispered a collective "Wow." Neither I nor they had any idea their grandmother had received such a prestigious honor for her academic achievement.

Gently and with sincere humility, Jane explained that there were many ways to be smart and that not everyone had the opportunity for the kind of education she'd had. "Burt was the best mechanic on this island. There wasn't an engine on the island he couldn't fix—that's smart."

During another visit, Jessica unveiled another facet of Jane's talents that I hadn't known about. When Jane asked her to retrieve some hard-to-reach materials from her closet, Jessica came across a portfolio of drawings. She and I were both curious, so Jane allowed us to look through it. Jane's affection for birds shone in her excellent portrayals of these small creatures. The colored-pencil drawings had a photographic quality, the birds' features as well as blossoms, berries, branches, and leaves rendered in exquisite detail.

We learned that Jane had actually sold some of her work. One piece, she told us, was bought by an admirer right off the easel before it was even complete. On another occasion, she had been commissioned to paint some hummingbirds from a photo the commissioners had taken during a trip to Arizona. A five-hundred-dollar commission is not bad at all for an amateur artist. But if Jessica hadn't happened to find those drawings, we would never have known about it.

Nanotechnology

When I visited Jane the summer after her ninetieth birthday, she commented on how much she missed school, saying that she had always loved learning. "So, I sent to the Teaching Company—something I had done in the past."

The Teaching Company produces and distributes a variety of college-level audio and video courses for home study. Jane had selected a course on writing—"never my best subject." Why had she chosen to tackle this least-favored pursuit? "I have some stories I'd like to write down, and I thought it might help." Later, when I checked on how the course went, she shook her head. "Well, it just reminded me of why I was never an English major and why I loved math and physics."

Despite that experience, Jane wasn't discouraged. I visited her the next summer after her ninety-first birthday. With a broad smile, she told me she had signed up for a new course, nanotechnology. When I commented to my modest friend about how such a course would intimidate me, she didn't seem at all worried. "I am confident I will understand and learn it. But I won't remember as much as I like because my memory isn't what it used to be."

Once again, Jane inspired me with her spirit and initiative. For the sheer love of learning, she was willing to dive into complex material that she might have only a remote chance of ever applying.

During the winters, when I was home in Virginia, Jane often sent cheerful letters updating me on what she was doing and what was happening at the Homestead. In one she thanked me for a puzzle book I had sent her: "My record of solving isn't very good. So far, I have attempted twenty-nine and succeeded in solving eleven! I'm not going to give up, though. It's good mental exercise."

Not surprisingly, each of Jane's notes included a weather report from Nantucket and a comment on my Virginia weather, which she explained she learned about on the Weather Channel. What else would I expect from a meteorologist with an active, inquiring mind?

Well, not quite a meteorologist. Ever-modest Jane wanted to make sure I set that record straight. Although she did work in the field of meteorology in the Navy and in civilian life, Jane did not have a degree specifically in meteorology, so she didn't feel it was accurate to call her a meteorologist. She did agree, however, to be called a meteorological professional. A small distinction, but yet another example of Jane's humility.

"You Can Learn to Adapt"

On one of my visits, I wanted to talk with Jane about the topic of loss, a common experience in the later years of life. Arriving in her suite at the Homestead, I found her upbeat and contented as she waved me over to where she sat in her specially angled chair, designed to accommodate her degenerative spinal disc issues. Her walker stood on one side, and tables holding variety of items surrounded her.

Seeing her situated like that, I asked how she viewed the obvious limitations this stage of life had brought her. "Well, I don't really have a problem with that," she replied. "I just kind of go with the flow." She was quick to state that she had always been a realist: "I recognize that I can't be twenty again and do this or that. You can't change your limitations, but you can learn to adapt."

With excitement in her eyes and a wide smile, she pointed at various items around her. "You'd be surprised at how many things you can do with your hands—and look at the tools I have." Picking up an unusual-looking gadget that looked like a boot or ankle brace, she explained, step by step, how to use it. "This allows me to put on my socks without bending forward, which I'm not supposed to do because of the problem with the discs in my back." I confess to not really understanding the mechanics of how the gadget worked, but since she had her socks on, I figured it worked just fine.

Sweeping her hand in a semicircle around her, she said, "So you use the tools to adapt. And it's a wonderful thing to learn all these things from the physical therapists and nurses. I'm pretty independent," she declared.

On another one of my summer visits, Jane showed me both her adaptability and independence. We had been discussing a local landmark called Greater Light, a summer home and art studio built by two Quaker sisters in the 1930s, known for being one of the more intriguing properties owned by the Nantucket Historical Society. Unlike the many sites that reflected the island's early history, Greater Light served as a reminder of the art colony that thrived on Nantucket during the period between the world wars. I had heard about the place and wanted to visit, but I didn't know exactly where it was.

"The Greater Light is just around the corner from here," Jane told me, detailing the location. For some reason I wasn't able to visualize the directions she gave me—my problem, not hers. "Well, we could walk over there now if you want, and I can show you—as long as I get back in time for my exercise class at one thirty." Agreed.

Jane then demonstrated a special trick for getting her shoes on without that forbidden bending—arranging them with their backs down so she could slide her feet into them with ease. Then she grabbed her walker by the handles, opened her apartment door, and led the way down the back hall to take advantage of the ramp located at the side of the building.

We made our way to the rear garden of the Homestead, which was more beautiful than it had been when I had seen it several years before. Jane pointed out her bird feeder and commented that it needed filling. She enjoyed taking care of that from time to time because it connected her with the delicate creatures that held a special place in her heart.

Looking around, we both enjoyed the array of colorful flowers, especially the clear pink mallow, a favorite of mine. Leading the way across the yard, Jane then took us to another gate. It opened onto a lane whose surface switched from pavement to pea gravel as it meandered behind us. Cedar-shingled Nantucket homes lined the lanes, their window boxes spilling over in a shower of lavish pink, purple, and yellow flowers. Jane pointed out her favorite house as we walked—the one with its own charming sunken garden.

Along the way, Jane explained the benefits of her particular walker and showed me that it was fitted with sturdy wheels that could handle ruts, bumps, and other uneven terrain. We chatted along the way, with Jane filling in the name of a mutual friend when I was grasping for it in my memory bank.

Of the many beautiful and interesting tours available to me during my summers on Nantucket, I believe I enjoyed this one the most. My ninety-one-year-old friend not only showed the way to a historical site I had never seen, but also introduced me to a lovely corner of Nantucket I hadn't known existed.

A Gift for Each Other

Before leaving the island that summer, I stopped by Jane's to pick up a photo taken of her during her Navy days. When I arrived, Jessica was there again visiting. The three of us enjoyed viewing some photos as well as the art that decorated Jane's apartment. We also had a lively conversation about Jane's busy schedule, which she kept track of in a small pocket calendar that was always at her side. I learned that Jessica had already stopped by the Homestead to visit twice that day, only to find Jane not at home.

When the time came for Jane to go to the dining room for dinner, followed by a Homestead sing-along, Jessica and I left together. Her love and respect for her grandmother was clear, as well as her enthusiasm over Jane's active approach to life. "She is an inspiration for me, Peggy. At an older age, she's done all these new things—the trips to different places, the violin, the hammered dulcimer, and who knows what classes."

This particular granddaughter is an artist like Jane. Her paintings and pencil drawings hung on a wall in Jane's apartment next to Jane's own pastel portrait of her mother. Grandmother and granddaughter were a special gift to each other. They possessed a common bond in their art as well as their spirit.

Trust and Don't Worry

For someone who has lived beyond ninety years—especially someone in a retirement residence—the prospect of death looms large. Jane faced that reality of death with the same calm practicality and faith that she used to engage life. She outlined her approach in a letter to me. She listed a variety of Scripture references and quoted several assurances from Jesus, including the promise of "everlasting life." Then she concluded, "So I do the best I can each day and leave the future to the Lord."

She echoed that quiet confidence in a later conversation, in response to my question about how she managed to keep her spirits up as she got older. "I have no trouble with that," she said. "I trust in the Lord." Then she went on to tick off some of her strategies for keeping herself positive.

"I remember the good things—I think that's a blessing. I had some bad ones, everyone does, but the Bible says to forget about what's gone behind us." She spoke about her attempts to help a friend who had had a difficult past and was having difficulty shaking it. "This is a beautiful day," Jane had told her friend. "Let's enjoy it."

Jane seemed able to live in the present, look for the good in it, make the most of it, and let go of the past. She believed that refusing to let go is a failure of faith. And she held tight to the belief that "God's grace is good, and as [the apostle] Paul says, 'His grace is sufficient.'" Jane went on to say that "you can think and plan and do what you know is right," but in the long run, "trust and don't worry" was the best approach. Recognizing this was difficult for some, she prayed daily for loved ones she knew to be "worriers."

Ever realistic, Jane understood that we don't have control over everything. As she put it, "Some things are unresolvable." And at times, she admitted, staying positive required a bit of work. Yet she did her best to keep a positive perspective, believing that "to be a good witness to the Lord, you have to reflect his good news."

Jane admitted she was fortunate to have been born with an upbeat temperament, part of her father's legacy to her. However, she told me that her "faith kept it alive." Besides, she added, "There's so much beauty and love. I believe in people. One of the best ways to fight discouragement is to count your blessings.

"I'm blessed in that I think I'm naturally cheerful," she added. "Some of the nurses call me Sunshine."

From what I know of Jane, I have no choice but to agree.

Lessons from Jane

Jane was a wonderful example to me of how being gentle and serene does not preclude being strong, intelligent, and determined. Without drama or calling attention to herself, Jane moved through life with intention. She repeatedly ventured beyond her comfort zone, relying on her native intelligence, her education and training, and her persistent Christian faith, which provided her with motivation and direction as well as comfort. As she put it, "I wouldn't be a very good witness of my faith if I was down and not hopeful or believing that the Lord would provide."

Jane built on the experiences and lessons of her earlier life and consistently wove them into the fabric of her later years. A good student in her youth (a piece of information I had to dig to find out), Jane had continued to enjoy learning all her life. She wasn't intimidated by tackling something new, even something like nanotechnology, despite her realistic concerns about her memory. And she wasn't afraid to risk failure by working in an area of relative weakness—writing. Both of these endeavors were inspirational for me because they contradicted the popular myth that old people cannot learn new things.

Jane was proactive and intentional in managing the typical challenges of old age, remaining involved and taking responsibility for her own well-being. She read as much as she could. She worked puzzles that challenged her mind and played games that provided the additional benefit of socialization and companionship. She found companionship as well as exercise by participating in—and occasionally even leading—exercise classes. And through it all, Jane kept a healthy sense of self-protection and balance: "If it isn't fun, I don't do it."

Jane's response to her physical limitations—spinal problems, eye issues, and the like—was especially inspirational to me: "You can't change your limitations, but you can learn to adapt." The willingness to learn and adapt is a crucial element in positive aging. Jane showed me how this can work in a very practical sense as she employed the various tools or workarounds that allowed her to stay active. Rather than giving in to frustration, she was grateful for having those tools and being taught new ways to do what she needed to do. As always, gratitude fueled Jane's positive outlook.

When she was in her seventies, Jane stepped into new territory again when she took violin lessons, an undertaking that combined the challenge of the new instrument with the goal of playing her favorite hymns, something important to her spiritual life. Wisely, she chose an accessible goal for which she was internally motivated. And, as I learned from her granddaughter, she had also taken up the hammered dulcimer. Jane never let herself go stagnant.

Art provided another creative outlet for Jane. She remained involved with nature, especially the birds that she loved, while at the same time embracing the challenge of capturing on paper what she saw. Doing so provided a generative component in her life, which research tells us is an important ingredient in positive aging. (The term *generative* refers to creating something new.) Jane derived great pleasure from the process of creating drawings and paintings and enjoyed a healthy sense of accomplishment when they were finished.

Jane's beautiful dollhouse provided her with yet another creative outlet. With the changes in décor she made to reflect the seasons, it was an ongoing project. The dollhouse also afforded Jane a social outlet, connecting her with people who were eager to see how it looked and thus keeping her involved with friends in the community.

Though a quiet woman, Jane was far from withdrawn. She involved herself in the community as best she could, using the bus available to seniors to get around town. And she kept her focus off herself. She reached out to others and humbly offered wisdom to a friend who had difficulties. She acted as a conversation leader in her Homestead community, and she served as a regular substitute exercise leader. She kept in close touch with her family and continually prayed for those she loved.

Jane's disposition, as the nurses noted, was sunny. She believed she had been born with that quality and considered it a blessing. But Jane was also intentional about maintaining her positive perspective. She consciously fed it with the warmth of gratitude, looking at what she had rather than focusing on what she didn't have. She immersed herself in good memories and appreciated the good qualities of people she had known, tapping into their positive energy. She did her best to put away negative thoughts and feelings, reminding herself not to "dwell on the bad things."

Most of all, Jane held tight to a sense of purpose guided by an indestructible faith. "My daily morning prayer," she told me once, "is that the Lord, through the Holy Spirit, will work in me to be a good witness for the Lord."

A model of gentle strength, Jane is someone I want to emulate as I journey through these decades. Thinking of her provides me with a good measure of sunshine for the path ahead of me.

JANE'S GALLERY

Jane as a WAVE in the 1940s.

Jane graduating from college after the war.

One of Jane's bird sketches.

Jane at Bible study (2013).

CHAPTER 4

❦

Lilma Cook

"You have to look for the good."

MY INTRODUCTION TO LILMA came at the First
Congregational Church, my summer church home, where
every Sunday she sang in the choir high up in the loft over-
looking the congregation.

The First Congregational steeple offers a compelling landmark to those approaching the island by sea. It stands high
and proud, marking the historic community of faith that was
first established in Nantucket in 1725. Back then the congregation worshipped one mile to the north in what is now
called the Old North Vestry. In 1765 this building was carefully disassembled and moved to its current location. Then, in
1834, it was moved yet again, this time to the back of the lot,
to make room for a larger white-shingled structure. Members

sometimes refer to this "new" building, with its iconic white steeple, as the summer church, because the congregation worships in the smaller north vestry during the winter months but shifts to the white building's open, window-lined sanctuary for the warmer, more populated season.

The choir loft and organ are located at the back of the summer-church sanctuary. To reach them you must climb eighteen winding steps of a very narrow staircase. From there, if you wish, you can continue to climb up into our majestic steeple. Although I have never sung in the choir, I have joined many visitors and made the full ascent, visiting the small museum that commemorates the church's history and then climbing further to enjoy a spectacular view of the harbor and the rest of the island.

The choir loft, the first stop on the way to the steeple, affords its own lovely view of the beautiful sanctuary below, but getting there can be a bit of a challenge. Middle-agers who are not in their fittest form have been known to huff and puff a little on the way up. And some of the more mature folks, especially those with joint and mobility issues, can struggle.

What impressed me first about Lilma, who was approximately eighty when I met her, was the grace with which she handled her arthritic challenges. She climbed those eighteen winding steps each Sunday to sing at the worship service, and she never complained—an impressive show of determination and commitment. Besides being a faithful member of the choir, Lilma was also a regular presence around the church—always helping at the annual summer fair and serving as treasurer of the Ladies Union Circle, the oldest continually active women's church group in the country.

Years before, the LUC had recognized Lilma's head for figures and tapped her talent to serve as treasurer or cashier or whatever role involved numbers and money. Lilma was never flustered when it came to that kind of thing. With a sense of calm and dignity, she managed a variety of financial endeavors over the years.

Another thing that nudged me to get to know Lilma better was something she had written in the church's newsletter about stewardship, the practice of giving time, money, and/or talent to support the church's mission. Many churches, during their annual stewardship drives, ask members to share their thoughts about why they give. Lilma was in her eighties at the time, and what she wrote spoke to me in many ways. She talked about her habit of giving, which had begun in childhood, and about her sense of responsibility to the church. But the last and longest part of her essay had to do with thanksgiving. Lilma elaborated on the abundance in her life, for which she was thankful. She closed by saying that she considered it a privilege to give and that she did so joyfully.

How refreshing and uplifting those words seemed to me. This woman had something special going for her: she was engaged in the world, she reached out to people, and she approached her life with a rich sense of gratitude. I immediately set out to get to know Lilma better and learn how she had mastered the fine art of graceful aging.

A Traditional Woman

When I think about Lilma, I see a traditional woman in the best sense of the word—capable and determined, reliable and organized, steeped in faith, love, and gratitude. I see a solidly built woman with softly curled gray hair, sparkling blue eyes, and—more often than not—a broad smile on her round face. A daughter of the heartland, she moved to an island thirty miles out to sea and created a good life for herself, her husband, and her children. And even after her husband of fifty-five years passed away and her children moved off-island, Lilma kept on going—reaching out, singing, and serving her family and the community.

Lilma was born and raised in Iowa, where she faithfully attended church and did well in high school. Most of her childhood coincided with the Great Depression. Upon graduation from high school in 1939, she joined a social and cultural sorority called Delta Theta Chi. But beyond that, "I didn't really know what I wanted to do. . . . College didn't seem to be an option—we just didn't have the money."

Lilma did apply to a nearby teachers' college on the outside chance that she might land a scholarship or the like. But then the phone company came calling—and Lilma answered. She interviewed for a job with Northwest Bell, part of the nationwide telephone network then known as the Bell System. When she was offered the job, she "just decided to take that." In those days, when the nation was still recovering from the Depression, being offered any job was a good thing. But working for the telephone company was considered an excellent opportunity, affording a greater degree of security than many other employment options.

Lilma's career with Northwest Bell provided her with both experience and the opportunity to advance. She first worked at all the operator positions—local, information, and long distance. From there she moved on to clerk positions, then to directories, and finally to the central office, where she handled payrolls and kept track of employee hours, vacation times, and health records. As she proved herself and her skills and dedication were recognized, she advanced in the company.

Enter Fred

When I asked Lilma how she had met her husband, she laughed. "We actually graduated together, but I didn't really know him then." In those days, their high school had midyear graduations. Fred completed his work in time to graduate in January. Instead, he chose to take the next semester off from school to follow his interest in electrical work on his uncle's farm. He then graduated with the rest of his class in June and set off for California to work for Lockheed.

Fred's older sister happened to be in the same sorority as Lilma—Delta Theta Chi. So "when he was home for Christmas [and] asked his sister if she could find him a date," she set the two of them up. And though they were basically strangers, with her keen attention to detail, Lilma recalled seeing him back in high school. "I did remember seeing this fellow on hall duty down at room 101. He had a blue shirt and yellow sweater and was blond. I noticed him, but I didn't have any premonition or anything," she recalled. "But it is funny that I remembered him, though." (The connection really hit her later when she saw him wearing a yellow sweater.)

Lilma told me the date was enjoyable. "We went out to the movies. His sister came along, and then we dropped her off and went to a nice restaurant in town for dinner. It was very nice. Then he left on the next day."

The couple kept in touch by mail, however, and they reconnected in 1942, when Fred came home to register for the draft. Things really clicked then, and they were definitely a couple by September, when Fred was called up to serve in the Navy. "We had a wonderful summer together. I turned down his first proposal, thinking it was too soon, or maybe I was old-school or something, but that didn't last very long."

Lilma's special connection with and memory for numbers surfaced once again when she told me, "But I do have to laugh. I always said, 'We met on the third of the month in 1942, became engaged on the second of the month in 1943, and married on the first of the month in 1945.'"

Letters were the engaged couple's primary method of communication during the war years. At one point in 1942, Fred was in California waiting to depart for the Pacific, and he was given a one-month leave. He called Lilma, and she traveled out west by train. They had a wonderful time together before he had to leave. Then, on her way home, Lilma stopped to visit a friend in Tempe, Arizona. That visit, Lilma explained, "helped to get my mind off focusing on Fred's departure." Fred served in the Navy amphibious forces and participated in eleven major Pacific battles, but fortunately was never wounded. The couple married shortly after his return home.

Getting to Nantucket

Learning of Lilma's Midwestern background, I became curious as to how my island friend had come to Nantucket. I discovered the route was far from direct.

Lilma explained that her husband had been a radio man when he was in the Navy—"He was lucky to be given this assignment since radios had been an interest of his since he was a boy." Then, at the end of the war, on the plane heading home after his discharge from the Navy, Fred happened to talk with a man from the CAA (Civil Aeronautics Administration). The work they were doing sounded interesting, so he signed up for the Capitol Radio Engineering Institute, an electronics school in Washington, DC. Married by then, Fred and Lilma moved there in February 1946 to begin their new postwar life.

Although Fred had been accepted, the school had a waiting list at the time, so he wasn't able to start classes at the school immediately. To fill the gap, he took a job with the Veterans Administration and later began attending school at night. Meanwhile, Lilma was fortunate to be able to transfer from her Northwest Bell job in Sioux City to the offices of another Bell System company, Chesapeake and Potomac Bell.

To her chagrin, she found herself at the "bottom of the totem pole again" and was "assigned nights." That particular assignment nudged her to speak up for herself. "I asked if there was someone I could talk to, someone who was in charge of connecting people to jobs." Someone at the phone company must have been smart enough to recognize Lilma's strengths because "they put me in the accounting department, which is what I enjoyed doing so much." Lilma rose to a management level before she left to begin raising her family.

During their six years in Washington, Fred and Lilma became active in the National City Christian Church, the largest Disciples of Christ congregation in the nation's capital. Lilma had grown up in a Disciples of Christ church in Sioux Falls. Fred had been raised a Methodist, but his childhood church involvement had not been as extensive as Lilma's. So he willingly adapted to this new church and joined Lilma in full participation.

Just about the time Fred was ready to start attending school full-time, Lilma became pregnant. Explaining the telephone company's policy at the time, she told me, "They wouldn't let me work past my fifth month. That's because a woman in my section worked until Friday and then had her baby that night." She laughed. "They said that was too close for comfort."

With Lilma unable to continue working, the family budget suddenly became very tight. I was amazed at how Lilma remembered the fine details of her finances at the time. "I had to go down to the unemployment offices to collect my $21.26 check," she told me. "Our rent was fifty-five dollars, and Fred's salary was one hundred ten dollars, so that was half. It was important that I get that twenty-one dollars."

Lilma and Fred's first child, David, was born in 1949. When Fred graduated from electronics school in 1951, someone from the CAA came to recruit him. He subsequently received a telegram saying, "Report to Nantucket."

Neither of them had heard of Nantucket, but Lilma's mother remembered learning about it in a one-room log schoolhouse back in Linden, Iowa, of all places. Some of the couple's friends in Washington were Massachusetts natives and provided them with more details about the island.

Their actual arrival on Nantucket in 1951 was something of a scattered process. They arrived together, but Fred had to depart shortly afterward for additional schooling in Oklahoma.

By that time, Lilma was pregnant with their second baby. Not wanting to be alone, she traveled to Iowa to be with her widowed mother. There she gave birth to a little girl, Christine. But the baby "was almost a month old before Fred got to see her. He came up for Armistice Day weekend. It was a kind of trying time," Lilma recalled. "We missed him, and he missed us."

Finally they were able to begin their new life together on Nantucket as family, with a newborn and a two-year-old. They would go on to have two more girls, Linda in 1952 and Patty in 1954.

Lilma was now the mother of four children under five—quite a lot to take care of in an unfamiliar environment and community. Her management skills would definitely come in handy over the next few years.

Learning to Manage

When I asked Lilma about the most valuable lessons she had learned in her long life, her family came to mind first. "I think I probably learned patience having four small children—four in five years." Then Lilma thought back further to her time at the telephone company. She had started as an information operator but switched to the more demanding role of long-distance switchboard operator.

In those days, when each call was connected via a physical wire plugged into a board, she had to "overlap those phone wires on the board a lot, handling several calls at a time." She explained that when you had three at a time, "you might be talking to one, but when we had the three-minute cutoff, you had to be sure you kept track and honored that for each call as well." Looking back, Lilma believed that experience had come in handy later when, as a mother, she had to balance multiple priorities and try "to meet the needs of everybody."

Managing the schedules and needs of four little ones definitely required organization, and here Lilma's work experience and practical temperament paid off. She created a system that reduced the hectic nature of getting everyone off to school while helping the children learn to handle money responsibly.

She gave each child a small bank. Then, when she went to the bank to cash her husband's paycheck each week, she requested that the money she received included "eighteen dimes, twenty quarters, and so forth—I had it worked out to the penny." She then filled each child's bank with the exact amount each would need weekly for Scouts, Sunday school, music lessons, stamps, allowance, and so forth. "So I didn't have to go into my purse on a Tuesday morning to see if I had the right change. Each of the children had money earmarked for certain things, and it was up to them to be sure it didn't all get added to their allowance."

Sensing my next question, Lilma laughed. "I'd go to the bank and would almost see the tellers turn around and not want to wait on me. But I had to tell myself, 'They're here to serve me, and I have a perfect right to do this.' And if I had it to do over again I would, because I feel it was a good lesson."

In one of our conversations, Lilma shared a meaningful truth about parenting she'd heard from a minister at Nantucket United Methodist Church: "Once you teach a child to walk, you teach them to walk away from you." Lilma agreed. "What you really do is to raise them to be responsible citizens, to be independent—how to conduct themselves. I've never forgotten that." When talking to me later about the topic, she agreed that being a mother is a complex and lifelong endeavor.

Kids on the Island

Spending three months of the year on Nantucket was a wonderful experience for me. However, I wondered about the challenges that might arise for full-time residents living and raising a family on an island thirty miles off the mainland. Lilma, whose two youngest children had been born on Nantucket, seemed to feel it hadn't been all that difficult.

She mentioned only a few aspects of island life that had affected her.

For one thing, it had seemed like her family was the only one without extended family on-island. The children had their friends but no cousins close, as everyone else seemed to have. "People used to say, 'Be careful what you say about anybody. They might be related.'"

The school situation on Nantucket had also presented a problem, especially for Lilma's two oldest. When their son was about to enter high school on the island back in the 1960s, the Nantucket schools "were in a deplorable situation—families against families, the superintendent hung in effigy. It was just such an unhealthy situation." Lilma and Fred eventually decided to send the two older children off-island for school. "But the youngest girls stayed because the school situation began to improve, and both were doing quite well. They were both valedictorians in their class," Lilma informed me, one going to Wellesley and the other to the University of New Hampshire, where she graduated summa cum laude and was named to Phi Beta Kappa. "So they got an education because they applied themselves," she said. "You get out of something what you put into it." Lilma shared those outcomes with a gentle touch of parental satisfaction.

Back to Work—Making It Work

The better I got to know Lilma, the more she impressed me with her intelligence and ability. So when she told me she had gone to work after her youngest children were in school,

I wondered what her work experience had been like. What jobs would even be available to her considering the locale (small island thirty miles at sea), the circumstances (four children at home), and the times (the 1950s and 1960s)?

Once Lilma started to work again—"not for the phone company this time"—she found jobs she liked to do that could be made to work around the needs of her family. Her first island position was at Butner's, a locally owned small department store on Main Street. "I started in about 1960, and I eventually became assistant manager." She especially enjoyed working with the sales slips and keeping all the records in order.

"Then the librarian at the Atheneum [Nantucket's historic library] stopped me one day and wanted to know if I'd be interested in being a children's librarian," she said. Lilma had been no stranger to the library. "I went in there all the time with the kids to get books." When the new children's room was added, the staff needed someone and thought of her.

Aware of the fact that she had no formal education past high school, Lilma was pleased to have arranged work that coordinated so well with her family life. "When I was at Butner's, I worked ten to two so I could be home for the children before and after school. Then, at the Atheneum, I went in later, and the kids could come there after school or from Scouts or music lessons and do homework." This arrangement assured Lilma that her four "never felt they were neglected or latchkey kids."

Lilma's next position, which would last for sixteen full-time years plus a number of additional part-time years, presented itself when she reached out to help a family in the community. The mother of her daughter's friend was in the hospital, so Lilma invited the girl and her dad over for dinner. "He asked me, 'You wouldn't be interested in working for me, would you, as a bookkeeper?'" He said his current bookkeeper was leaving because her husband had returned from the Vietnam War and would most likely be assigned elsewhere, so the man needed to find a replacement for her.

Lilma had to give the idea of working full- time some consideration. But this offer came at about the time her oldest was preparing to go away to school, so the extra income would be welcome. Soon Lilma was back working with numbers, a comfortable and satisfying place for her.

The work Lilma found for herself on Nantucket allowed her to use her strong math and organizational skills to do something she enjoyed. She'd intentionally created a blend of work and family that suited her values and desires. She told me that she was and had been quite content.

Hard Decisions

That's not to say that Lilma's life was always fun and easy. She shared with me some decisions that had been very hard for her to make. One was the decision to send their son, David, away to school. Concerned about sending him to the local high school, Lilma and Fred explored other options and finally learned about a school some distance away, in Maine.

They investigated to see if it might be a good fit and finally decided to send him there, but not without a lot of thought and discussion.

For residents of Nantucket, especially back then, going away to school was a more significant undertaking than for folks on the mainland. You couldn't just jump in the car and drive there, and the logistics of getting back and forth could be daunting. "I think I cried the whole summer before he left, and I thought about how the girls would miss having their brother."

Lilma remembered agonizing over what to do. "He had never given us any trouble, he was well liked, but we thought he had too much potential to waste." She reminded herself of the additional rationale for sending him away to school: "He had four Latin teachers in one year. They took away that *and* dropped public speaking."

As Lilma sat by me and closed her eyes, I could see her reliving the whole process. "He never said he didn't want to go, but he never said he did." She rolled the pros and cons around again in her head, still questioning whether they had done the right thing. "Sometimes I regret it, but . . ." Refusing to be overcome by doubts, she finally affirmed, "He got an excellent education. He had a wonderful experience, got top honors when he was a sophomore, and was president of his junior and senior class."

Another difficult decision for Lilma involved her church fellowship—not an uncommon issue for people of faith. Over the years I have observed this type of conflict arising when an individual's current worship situation no longer aligns with their deeply held values or current needs. "It was so hard when we left the Methodist church here," she told me. "We were members for thirty-nine years, but we weren't being spiritually fed. My husband would go to church expecting to get something out of it, but because he was chairman of the board of trustees, people would pounce on him—'This needs doing' and 'That needs doing.' And there was never any money to do anything. He was good at what he did, but fund-raising wasn't in his repertoire at all."

But they hung in and stayed a little longer at the church to see if things would work themselves out. Lilma remembered that, as a cost-saving effort, the members met in the lower level of the church to avoid heating the upstairs sanctuary. To make things worse, their new pastor wasn't a particularly proficient or tactful leader.

The turning point came for them at a meeting of a committee on which Lilma served as financial secretary. She spoke up, referring to a disruptive and unnecessary incident during the last worship service. "I just think that our service lacks a measure of dignity. Since we are worshipping downstairs, it makes it hard to capture the feeling of church, so we have to do things better to compensate for what we really can't do financially."

Lilma was stunned by the pastor's response to her, a member who had served the church for thirty-nine years: "Well, if you don't like how we do things here, you can just leave."

They didn't leave—not at that time. But the pastor's comment stuck with Lilma and gave her food for reflection.

Lilma and Fred invested a lot of prayerful thought into how they might resolve their church dilemma. They also discussed the matter with their grown children, who "had been reared in that church." Lilma explained, "We knew so many people and had so many friends. We had a good women's group at the Methodist church. We met in the homes every month and had devotions and programs. I remember the prayer vigil we held, going at four in the morning to pray, and being a Brownie leader. But it just wasn't working overall. After thirty-nine years, to leave was hard, but I have no regrets at all."

A New Church Home

Lilma and Fred made their new church home at First Congregational Church. Finding that fit was important, because church and faith meant a lot to Lilma.

"Whenever anyone asks me for what I am most thankful," Lilma told me, "I say my Christian heritage because I think everything that was so good and wonderful in my life all comes back to that. It gave me the values I was looking for, and I was fortunate in being able to find and keep them. To me that's the greatest thing in my life. Everything follows that."

At First Congregational, as at the previous church, Lilma quickly got involved—and stayed involved. "We've made our contributions: tower duty [conducting tours of the steeple for visitors—a source of income for the church], chair and treasurer of the Ladies Union Circle, visiting committee, choir, taking money at the fair. I try to help any way I can."

As for the actual experience of worship at First Congregational, Lilma was quite satisfied, especially with the quality of the music and the preaching. "Oh, Robby [the music director]—between him and Gary [the pastor], we have a wonderful combination."

We talked a little more about our talented music director, who has a special gift: "He's good at improvisation." I recalled asking him after a service who had composed the beautiful offertory piece, and he replied, "Oh, that was mine—just a little improvisation." Lilma then shared something that had happened while they were still worshipping in the old vestry. "For the postlude Robby played Scott Joplin, and he really got everyone into it. They all clapped. No one was against it, although one could almost say it wasn't appropriate" for church. She grinned. "But with him, anything goes, and it's okay."

On the topic of hymns, we both agreed how important they are to worship. "It can be a very enriching part of the service if you really read the words. There's a story, a sermon, right there." Talking about music surfaced a very sweet memory for Lilma, one that concerned her father. "He didn't sing in the choir or anything, but he had a nice voice and he'd sit me on his knee and sing all the old songs."

Although Lilma cared deeply about church, she remained accepting and nonjudgmental about those who didn't share her affiliation—even those very close to her. "We have a very ecumenical family," she told me. She herself had moved from the Disciples of Christ tradition to the Methodist church before joining the Congregationalist church. And she had family members who were Baptists, Methodists, and Episcopalians, as well as "good and caring people who don't regularly attend church."

With regard to her nonchurchgoing family members, she said, "I would never step in and try to interfere. It could ruin a relationship if you allow it to, and I won't. I feel good about my children, the people they are—caring, good citizens, and responsible."

Remembering Fred

When I first visited Lilma in her home—the house where she and Fred had raised their family—she pointed to the many photos that decorated her walls and shelves. In this way, she introduced me to her family members. Besides all the photos depicting her children and grandchildren, there was a special one of her and Fred on their fiftieth wedding anniversary. "The children had a big party for us," she told me in a contented tone. I could see her leaning back into that warm memory of her whole family celebrating together.

I also enjoyed seeing Lilma's collection of Nantucket lightship baskets. The design of these baskets has evolved over time, and they remain an important cultural icon in Nantucket, reflecting a special part of the island's history. In the Nantucket Lightship Basket Museum,[1] visitors can learn

---

1 To learn more about the lightship baskets, visit the museum website at http://www.nantucketlightshipbasketmuseum.org. Better yet, pay the museum a visit! It's worth your while.

the early history of the baskets, which were initially crafted by coopers aboard the whaling ships and later were made on the lightships for which they are named. Lightships were essentially floating lighthouses, meant to alert ships of the dangerous shoals to the southwest of Nantucket. Their crews spent endless hours offshore, and many spent their spare time crafting the distinctive rattan and wood baskets that became associated with the ships. Museum visitors can view some of these historic pieces, enjoy newer versions created by contemporary artisans, and participate in keeping the craft alive by taking lessons.

Having made two of these baskets over the years, I appreciate the time, skill, and patience they require. So whenever I am in someone's home and see a particular basket, I want to know its story. Admiring one of Lilma's lovely baskets with a specially turned wooden lid, I asked Lilma about it. "Fred made it," she told me. "He didn't start [making baskets] until after he was retired. He made that for me and one for each of the girls, but theirs didn't have lids." She explained that the wood for her basket's base and handle had come from scraps of an old organ. To me, that information added an additional layer of meaning for this precious keepsake because I was aware that Lilma's daughter Linda actually built organs—one of the few females in the profession.

In talking about her husband, Lilma described a resourceful man who had created a full life for himself after retirement. "He was very clever," she told me. "He had been with the FAA [Federal Aviation Administration, the CAA's successor] as an electronics technician out at Altar Rock. He was out there a lot working on the navigational equipment to keep things right. Sometimes he'd have to go out in the night to keep things right for the pilots."

During his time with the FAA, Fred developed a business on the side, installing and repairing boat radios. "He was a month shy of sixty when he retired, so he had a good twenty years of retirement. He had radios lined up all winter long to work on for the spring installation."

But Fred and Lilma's retirement time together wasn't filled with business alone. "We took some nice trips. We went to the Holy Land one year, a train trip through Europe, a western swing through the US, one year to Nova Scotia, and, for our fiftieth anniversary, a trip through the Canadian Rockies." Lilma reeled off the impressive list of destinations with an expression of sheer satisfaction on her face.

Leveraging Memory

When Lilma told me her story more than a half-century after marrying Fred, she expressed deep gratitude for the family the two of them had built together—their four children, seven grandchildren, four great-grandchildren, and counting. She related some stories of how attached one little grandson, Chris, had been to his granddad. In particular, Chris loved to ride with Fred in their big station wagon.

On one of Fred and Lilma's visits, Chris gathered up rocks, placed them behind his mother's car, and declared, "Now that car can't go, so we need to go in Grandpa's station wagon."

But it wasn't enough just to be in the station wagon with his grandpa. "Grandma, do you drive?" the boy asked Lilma. When she answered in the affirmative, he'd followed up with questions about whether she had a license and if she had it with her. Finally Chris revealed his plan: "Why don't you go up and drive, then, Grandma? And Grandpa can come back and sit with me!"

Lilma smiled with contentment as she told the story. "He was so precious. I wasn't hurt or anything. I was just pleased that he loved his grandpa so much."

Lilma was sorry her husband, who passed away in 2000, hadn't lived long enough to see the grandchildren as adults, with kids of their own, because he had enjoyed them so much when they were children. But Lilma wasn't one to remain in a sorrowful mode. Instead she said to me—and herself, "That's life. You just accept it and be grateful for what you did have."

But Lilma was certainly grateful for the memories. Although she remained busy with many functions and activities, she took time to step back and savor her recollections from the past. "I think a good deal about my memories, a lot of those little things—it's a great joy for me, really."

Lilma found that remembering happy times and focusing on gratitude actually enhanced her joy and feeling of well-being. "Life has been good to me," she said. "I have no complaints at all. It's not that you don't have difficulties now and then, but there are all the joys and happiness to kind of slide those bad things off you." When I asked what she meant, she explained, "The joys kind of give you the strength and support you need to handle the other things." Lilma leveraged her good memories and experiences, in other words, to help her get through the bad times. "But," she advised in her sharp and systems-oriented way, "you have to *look* for the good things. So that's what I try to do."

I could see her doing exactly that when she told of a mishap she had had during one of her visits to shut-ins at the island's long-term care facility. "When I fell recently, my face was a bloody mess. But I didn't break any bones. I could have easily with the way I went down. I'm so thankful." She went on: "I might have a little scar on my face, probably negligible, but a small price to pay not to have broken any bones. And nothing happened to my eyes."

Having seen the residual marks several weeks later and spoken to some church friends who were either on the scene or helped her out later, I can testify that Lilma's fall had been a nasty one, especially for a woman eighty-nine years old at the time. But Lilma didn't focus on the negative aspects of the experience. Instead, she spotlighted the things for which she could be grateful. She described how people had stepped up to help, from visiting her at the hospital to taking care of her car to staying with her while she recuperated.

Then Lilma revealed another silver lining, the consecutive visits from two of her daughters. Each one stayed with her for about ten days—"with a six-hour overlap," she emphasized, that allowed "them to visit with each other and go to the beach together. I didn't need constant care or anything, just a little 'family.' I look back on that now and get great joy thinking of them swimming together again at the beach."

Passing the Time

I wondered how Lilma felt about living alone after so many years of full family life, but she didn't express any dissatisfaction. I was also curious about how she spent her time. Some of her answers were predictable, but some I found curious. "When I think back to my first day at Butner's, I liked to fill out the sales slips—anything to do with figures." Reflecting back, she continued, "To this day, I like to do my bank statement. It comes at the first of the month, but I also have other figures to do at different times. The little budgeting that I do—I can hardly wait to get my paper out to do that." (I silently wish I could absorb some of her enthusiasm for such chores.)

"I'm not so much of a TV fan," she added. "Most of what I watch is baseball. Oh, I enjoy the Red Sox—they won last night ten to one," she told me one day, her face lighting up. I didn't ask her any baseball stats, but I suspected she knew more about the Red Sox than the average ninety-year-old woman. She told me she didn't care for the "sexy, violent" TV shows, but "occasionally I watch the old ones like *Andy Griffith* and *Bill Cosby*. Oh, and I never watched *Everybody Loves Raymond* when it was on, but now it makes me laugh. It's just good to sit there and chuckle and laugh out loud."

Music, too, was a frequent pastime. "I enjoy music very much. My daughter gave me a lovely book about hymns and the stories behind them"—a favorite for Lilma to pick up and peruse. "I have this keyboard"—she pointed to an electronic piano-style keyboard sitting on the side of the room—"and if I don't know the tune, I can pick it out. I'm not very coordinated, so putting two hands together, I'm lost." But she could read music, and she loved to sing.

And Lilma was definitely a reader. "I always keep a magazine or a paper next to my chair, and I pick it up and read a little." She expressed a preference for biographies as well as human-interest stories "and a good novel with some mystery." She also enjoyed periodicals. "One of the best Christmas gifts my children gave me was the *Inky Mirror* [delivered] to the door and a subscription of the *Christian Science Monitor* magazine. [But] I had to sacrifice my reading to finish that last quilt, and I [had] promised myself I wouldn't do that again."

Crafting a Legacy

Lilma explained about the quilt: "I made one for each of my grandchildren, and I said I wasn't going to make another." But she had changed her mind and decided to make one for her little great-grandson, who was due to arrive on her late husband's birthday. In order to make something special for this newest member of the family, Lilma was willing to put up with frustration or discouragement when the markings on the fabric weren't clear or when the thread kept slipping out of the needle. "So that will keep me busy," she told me, "getting it finished in time."

Lilma appreciated the family history and legacy that she and Fred had created, and she wanted to be sure nothing important would be lost. The quilts for her grandchildren and great-grandchildren were her way of preserving a sense of connectedness between generations. So were the scrapbooks she had made for each of her children. She made sure to keep the scrapbooks up-to-date and to add "the things the grand-kids had done. And I made photo albums for each of them as well. I like to keep [everything] organized," she explained, to "make things easier for the kids."

But in her typical balanced and practical approach, Lilma had also given thought to getting rid of extraneous stuff to spare her kids the need to do it. Up until recently, for instance, she had kept all the letters from her children. But then she decided that was foolish and tossed the letters she didn't think she would read again. And when each child visited, she had him or her sort through personal items and papers in the attic and decide what to take or toss.

Connected

Living alone, of course, is not the same as *being* alone. I was impressed by Lilma's extensive network of family, friends, and acquaintances. During our visits, we were often inter-rupted by incoming phone calls. The woman was *connected*.

Although none of Lilma's big family resided on the island, she remained in close touch with her children and their fam-ilies. "They may be far away, but they are very supportive," she told me. She enjoyed keeping up with their lives by phone, by traveling off-island to see them, or by welcoming them when they visited her. Lilma's daughters checked in on her regularly and, she told me, "My son calls every Sunday, and we talk for forty-five minutes to an hour. It seems like we keep chatting away." As she thought of these family calls, she sighed, and her eyes filled with tears of gratitude. "I'm feeling so blessed," she told me.

Lilma also considered herself blessed to have longtime friends with whom she enjoyed regular bouts of cribbage and other card games. She especially appreciated June, whose friendship dates back to the time when both of their husbands were still alive and who "stayed the whole night with me when I had my fall." Lilma also expressed gratitude for a neighbor who did her landscaping and flower boxes, something Lilma felt she could no longer do. "I'm very fortunate that way," she acknowledged.

One day when I was visiting, a friend from church called. She had heard about Lilma's recent fall. Laughing, Lilma told me what Sally had said: "I've always admired you and wanted to follow your example, so I fell too—slipped in my laundry room and bruised my face. I thought I'd let you know, and you'd get a kick out of it."

Lilma commented on how thoughtful Sally had been to call. "She didn't need to do that with all she's dealing with"— her own health challenges in addition to her work as chair of the ecumenical harvest fair in the fall. The mention of fairs brought us to talking about the old-fashioned summer fair that the church hosts every year at the beginning of August.

I mentioned that it was one of my favorite summer activities because it brought back warm memories of my own childhood church fairs featuring crafts, baked goods, tasty food, and the wonderful recycled treasures labeled "white elephants." Lilma concurred: "They are fun—a touch of excitement to them." She then told me about the old days of our church fair, when the white-elephant sale—still a popular event but now called "golden elephant"—had been held in Bennett Hall next to the church. Fred had repaired all the electrical items donated for the sale. Back then, on "the day of the fair, people would line up for blocks, and the first place when the doors opened, that's where they'd head," she told me proudly. I guess they knew they'd get reliable items if Fred had checked them over.

Reaching out to others and staying connected was a value for Lilma. "I try to keep up with birthdays and send cards and get-well cards." I could personally attest to these efforts. Caring notes, penned in her distinctive, delicate handwriting and reflecting faith, hope, and gratitude, often arrived in my Virginia mailbox during the winter. When I was going through some health issues, Lilma called to check on me as well.

Lilma also ventured into the world of e-mail and used it to supplement her longtime habit of letter writing. She told me about a time when she had written a very long e-mail. She'd spent over an hour writing it "and then spent another hour trying to find where it had disappeared to when I was editing it." When I shared my own frustrations with technology, she added, "I was angry with both myself and the system, but I wasn't about to give up on it. So I called technical support."

Reinforcing her desire to stay in tune with life and the world around her, Lilma told me, "I certainly can't solve the world's problems, and it's awfully hard to follow all of what's going on and who or what to believe." She expressed discomfort with polarizing political e-mails she received, though she didn't feel knowledgeable enough to give a solid response. She found it hard to accept the comments in those e-mails and said she didn't think they were fair. She speculated that the senders had been going through tough times and had developed a negative perspective on things. But she refused to do the same, doing her best to keep a healthy and balanced view of the world around her.

Reaching Out

Lilma did not always stay at home, of course. In fact, she was still driving in her nineties and had even ventured to Alaska on a trip with two of her daughters. "I'd always wanted to do that," she told me.

Most of Lilma's out-and-about time, of course, was spent in Nantucket—and most of that time involved caring for others. For instance, she served on the church's visiting committee, an outreach to those who are homebound or at home recovering from surgery or hospitalization. "I visit along with my partner or I go alone," she explained. One particular woman on the island was able to keep up with local happenings because of Lilma. "She can no longer read," Lilma told me, "so I read the paper to her."

When I asked if she ever went to the Saltmarsh Senior Center—a popular gathering spot for retirees—she said she stopped by occasionally for lunch. "It depends on the menu. But I am a Star Stuffer."

I had to ask. "A what?"

"I help with getting out the newsletter," she hurried to explain.

Referring to her position as Ladies Union Circle treasurer, she said, "It's not a hard job at all. I like to work with money. I guess that's why I enjoyed setting the children up with their banks." She laughed. "My bank balance is to the penny. And I have a statement of accounts that keeps track of everything." But working with money was not the only draw of the LUC position. "I enjoy being treasurer. There's not that much work, but there's the responsibility of it." Lilma had hit upon one of the areas that folks often struggle with in retirement—having a purpose and bringing value to others. Lilma had mastered this in several areas of her life.

Brainwork

When I remarked on how sharp Lilma was for her age, I asked if she did anything in particular to preserve her faculties. She thought about it for a little bit and then replied, "Well, there is something I do—it's something I like to do. I say the books of the Bible frontward and backward and alphabetically." (I remembered learning to recite those as a child, but wasn't sure I could still name them in order. I did know I could never recite them backwards or alphabetically at any time in my life.) "I do the presidents alphabetically and chronologically," Lilma continued, "and I do the states and capitals geographically and alphabetically. I do this, all this memory work. I guess it helps my brain, but it's just something I enjoy."

Lilma did have a caution concerning her brain-stimulating work. "Sometimes I get to the end of the day and say, 'I haven't done the presidents for a while,' so I do them and get my mind straight, like how many *B*s there are. But I have to watch myself, because if I do it last thing before I say my prayers, it might keep me awake."

At one point I had the opportunity to hear Lilma think aloud about an area for self-improvement or personal growth. She was analyzing a recent bout of stage fright she'd suffered while giving the sermon on a Sunday when lay church members led worship. It had happened on another occasion when she presented a Good Friday reading she had written. And she was annoyed with herself. She remembered many previous times when nervousness had not been a problem—"all my experiences as Worthy Matron in the Eastern Star, doing long and numerous recitations. I had also sung solos and prayed before that I would be singing for the glory of God, so as not to be nervous."

Analyzing the circumstances, Lilma then developed a theory. When she performed the works of others, she did better than when delivering her own words. "I'll just have to think about that." And she expected to do some praying about that theory as well.

Like Jane, Lilma liked to challenge her brain with puzzles, but unlike Jane, she wasn't much for Sudoku. "I don't do so well with that. But before you came, I was working on a word puzzle, which I had set aside because making that quilt got top priority over everything."

"I Can Accept Things"

No life is without its setbacks. I was curious about how Lilma dealt with hers, particularly the physical changes associated with aging. This issue was heightened by Lilma's fall, which had affected her ability to do some of her favorite activities. The fall, for instance, had made it impossible for her to sing with the church choir—because of those winding stairs to the choir loft in the summer church. "I think my body took a real jolt," she told me. "Probably I could [get up there] again, but I think I owe it to myself and others not to take a chance. In the autumn, I can go back full-time when we're in the old vestry," where the choir loft is only a few steps high.

While we were discussing this issue, the lawn folks came by, and the sound of their mowers drowned out our voices. The temperature was mild that day, so we decided to close the windows. I offered to pull them down so Lilma wouldn't have to get up. "It's hard sometimes," she told me. "Like your closing the windows—I used to be able to get right up, but now I have to struggle or depend on the good graces of somebody else to do it. But you accept that's the way it is. I guess I'm a little stubborn; I want to do it myself. It's just hard to give up that independence. But, you know, that's part of age.

You have to accept it and look at it [like] 'I've been there, done that. It's somebody else's turn now.'"

Lilma told me she felt blessed to have so many good friends and neighbors who helped her with things she could no longer do, such as strenuous chores around the house. Walking with a walker also posed some logistical challenges, especially when getting in and out of vehicles. Here, too, Lilma had many offers of help. But while she appreciated the generosity of those who offered and didn't want to seem ungrateful, she also wanted to keep doing whatever she could. This occasionally led to discomfort when someone offered help she didn't actually need. "Whenever a person's there to help you, you can't push them off. It's awkward to tell them, 'I can really do this myself.'" She concluded, "It all comes down to not wanting to lose your independence."

Then Lilma made an interesting point about accepting help from folks. "Honestly, people are so good. People just seem to rise up to meet a need. It makes me wonder whether I have my eyes open to help someone in need."

A conversation about visiting the beach uncovered another area where Lilma felt a sense of loss. "I'm sorry I can't go [there much] anymore. I always took the kids and enjoyed it so." In recent years, she had gone regularly with friends from church, accessing the water near Cliffside Beach via the boardwalk. But parking in that area had become difficult to find, and Lilma found it difficult to maneuver her walker— necessary since her fall—over the sand. These barriers probably could have been overcome, but Lilma was reluctant to put any of her friends to the trouble. "I wouldn't enjoy it for the effort—not that I'm afraid to put forth effort, but I wouldn't want to jeopardize the others."

When her son came to visit, he usually set aside time to take his mother to the beach. She told me that she loved to watch him in the water because he was a wonderful swimmer. But she confessed, "I don't know how it will be this year with the walker. I don't think I'll be going to the pops concert either. So there are some things that I have to give up that I wish I could do."

Even so, "I can accept things. I don't want to be a burden on anyone, and I don't want to make people feel sorry for me. There are some things I can do and enjoy doing, so I concentrate on those." In that vein, Lilma told me, "I want to go to Robby's concert this Sunday at church." Even as she faced losses in her life, she pulled herself forward, focusing on the positive and enjoying the possible.

Lilma also broached a topic that, as a life coach specializing in retirement issues, I've found I sometimes have to nudge my clients to consider: "What will you do when you can't live alone anymore?" Lilma was thinking out loud about her options, running through them in her typical systematic fashion. As she ticked them off, she explained some of them. She loved one daughter very much but knew that their living together wouldn't work for either of them. She had been invited to live with another child, who had recently retired, but she hesitated, not wanting to intrude. She expressed her thoughts and options honestly but remained sensitive and not judgmental.

"I don't really know what I'll do," she finally told me in a calm voice. "I guess that's my prayer work, to figure that out."

By the 1914 summer season, Lilma had finally made her decision. After undergoing surgery to install a pacemaker the previous spring, she'd decided to move to North Carolina that fall to live with one of her daughters. She would be sorely missed at First Congregational Church and in the Nantucket community at large.

Her Works Bring Her Praise

Lilma and I talked often about how we as individuals can choose the perspective and attitudes that prevail in our lives. During one of those conversations, Lilma mentioned someone she knew who tended to look at life in dark, more restrictive terms, whereas she tried to focus on the aspects of her Christian faith that emphasized redemption, love, faith, and grace. I believe she was successful in that attempt because no one would describe her approach to life in dark or negative terms. In fact, I believe those who knew and loved Lilma would recognize her in this passage from the book of Proverbs in the Bible she relied on for guidance and strength:

> She is clothed with strength and dignity;
>   she can laugh at the days to come.
> She speaks with wisdom,
>   and faithful instruction is on her tongue.
> She watches over the affairs of her household
>   and does not eat the bread of idleness. . . .

Honor her for all that her hands have done,
and let her works bring her praise at the city gate.[2]

Lessons from Lilma

Seeing Lilma at age ninety-two participate in life with generosity and intention—living to the fullest extent she possibly could—was quite an inspiration for me. She continued to reach out and give of herself to her church and community through her voice in the choir, her mind for numbers at the women's service organization, her welcoming heart when greeting visitors for the steeple "tower tours," her compassionate visits to the homebound, her gift of reading the newspaper to a woman who couldn't see, and her team spirit in serving as a Star Stuffer at the senior center. She used everything she still had to remain active and involved despite her age, and did it all with a servant's heart, focusing on others' needs more than on her own. And this list doesn't include the ways she loved and served her family.

Like others her age, Lilma had experienced significant losses and diminished physical capacities, all of which were difficult to bear, but she had developed strategies to cope and keep herself positive. Just as she had loved to set up systems in the workplace and organize her home, she developed systems of managing the challenges of old age.

Gratitude was key to these effective systems. Lilma lived and served with a grateful heart. Not only did others benefit

2 Proverbs 31:25–27, 31, New International Version.

from this approach, but she did as well. By choosing to be thankful for all she had, Lilma fed her mood and her spirit. Her gratitude motivated and energized her to do what she did for family and others. As a result, she saw her work as a joy, not a burden.

Lilma was not just grateful for what she had, however. She also made a point of *using* what she had. I loved her way of leveraging the good to deal with the bad, consciously focusing on the good things to "kind of slide those bad things off you."

Lilma also knew what she needed and made sure she did what was necessary to take care of herself. She kept her mind sharp with those prodigious memorizations—presidents, books of the Bible, and so forth—and challenged herself by doing puzzles. And she made a point of staying current with local and national events by keeping up with her reading.

Remaining connected with others is very important for well-being in the later years. Lilma accomplished this through her volunteer activities as well as by conscientiously maintaining friendships through visits, phone calls, e-mail, and snail mail. Her island church family also provided vital support and social opportunities. One summer I met her son, David, who was visiting from Tennessee, and he commented on how well people in the church had cared for his mother after her fall. He expressed his appreciation to those involved, and their response made it clear that they appreciated Lilma's contributions in their lives as well.

Living alone in the house where you raised your children can be comforting but also potentially lonely. But Lilma's use of memory helped keep that loneliness at bay. She didn't live in the past, but she did lean back into the past to glean the pleasures found there, recapturing the feelings and using them to enhance her present. But she was intentional about how she did this. Instead of dwelling on hurts, disappointments, resentments, and regrets, Lilma focused on her positive memories, savoring the good thoughts and feelings associated with them. She used the past to enhance her mood, not drag herself down.

Living alone can also push older folks to spend large amounts of time in front of the television. Lilma recognized this possibility and refused to succumb to mindless watching. She used the television intentionally to support her well-being. She watched lighter comedies and laughed out loud—a recognized form of therapy. Being a keen baseball fan, she had fun following her Red Sox. And though she tried to keep current, she chose not to immerse herself in the angst of the sensationalist news cycle.

Creativity is a positive outlet at any age, and Lilma found creative expression in putting together memory albums for her grown children and crafting quilts for the growing number of grandchildren and great-grandchildren in the family. Lilma enjoyed not only the creative process itself, but also the sense of completion and purpose that came with a finished project and the satisfaction of knowing she was leaving something worthwhile behind—a legacy. Of course, her most important legacy was the way she modeled positive and engaged living.

During the later years, especially, those who need help and those who provide it can find themselves walking a fine line of sensitivity. Lilma demonstrated a high degree of wisdom on this topic. She understood both the dignity of independence and the grace of accepting assistance, and she did her best to maintain a healthy balance between the two.

Despite Lilma's talent for systems and order, I also saw in her a healthy flexibility and tolerance for others. While remaining strong in her beliefs, she granted to others the right to hold different views. Maybe this attitude stemmed from her understanding of love and dignity, or maybe it evolved from the strong faith that guided her. Wherever it came from, her combination of organization and flexibility had served her well, enabling her to move forward in life with extraordinary grace.

To me, the most powerful aspect of Lilma's example of healthy living was her insistence on seeking out the positive side of any situation. Even after that serious fall, she talked a lot about how people had helped her, but very little about her aches or pains, which must have been considerable. She stressed the help she had received, not the annoyance of needing the help.

"You have to look for the good things," Lilma told me more than once. "That's what I try to do."

I only hope I can be half as successful as she was at this endeavor.

LILMA'S GALLERY

Lilma as a young woman in
Iowa (before World War II).

Lilma attending a church
visitation committee
meeting (2013).

Lilma on tower duty at First
Congregational Church (2014).

CHAPTER 5

❧

Estelle Cordoza

"I can make do."

ALTHOUGH ESTELLE, LIKE LILMA, was a member of the church I attended, my first encounter—and my first meaningful conversation—with her happened at the hospital thrift shop. This attractive, blue-eyed, fine-featured lady was working in the women's "better wear" room. With pencil and pad in hand, large eyeglasses in place, she would add up the purchases and hand each customer a small slip to take to the cashier stationed at the top of the stairs. But issuing sales slips was only one part of Estelle's contribution as a thrift shop volunteer. The other was to bring smiles and a feeling of welcome to all who passed her way.

Once I read Estelle's name tag and her voice registered in my mind, I recognized her as the person who had phoned me soliciting baked goods for the church's country fair. She had overseen the bake table for thirty-odd years.

Business was slow that afternoon, so Estelle and I had time for a delightful conversation. "For a while there," she told me, "I was very shy . . . and lonely. But once I worked on that and reached out with humor, I found I'm not lonely anymore."

I suspect this "shy" period came after the loss of her husband of fifty-seven years, Arthur. As I got to know Estelle better, I recognized that they'd experienced that special partnership that can develop when a couple does not have any children but derives a unique and special strength and closeness with each other. By the time I met her, however, Estelle had moved passed her shyness—way past it. She related an anecdote to illustrate her newfound boldness.

She had entered church one Sunday and, across the narthex, noticed a tall fellow she knew. She made a beeline over to the man and embraced him in a big bear hug. Because of her petite stature, her face landed her in the middle of his chest. When she looked up to meet his eyes, she was aghast to realize the man she was hugging was not the man she knew. She apologized profusely. "Oh, don't worry about that," he said. "I sure enjoyed that hug."

Telling the story, Estelle grinned at me with a pixie glint in her eye. "See? I'm not shy anymore." I found myself wondering just how blind that hug really was.

Purpose and Faith

In a conversation later that summer, Estelle shared with me that she had a life purpose—words that are always music to a life coach's ears. Since my work often involves helping retirees and empty nesters identify a new sense of purpose and focus for their next phase of life, I was eager to hear what Estelle had defined for herself.

"Well," she explained, "I was reading about how laughter and joy have a very positive effect on your body—and that negativism can be harmful even to your organs. I figured that I didn't want that negativism to be playing its music on my organs. So the best thing for me is to bring laughter to people whenever I can. That's my life purpose." I saw evidence of this in Estelle's conversation, which was peppered with little puns and humorous remarks.

One year when I was saying farewell to Estelle at the end of the season, she told me that she, too, would be going off-island—to Massachusetts General for breast-cancer surgery. She delivered the information as casually as if she were telling me that she was catching a ride home from the thrift shop with a neighbor. My face must have reflected my concern because she serenely responded, "Oh, I'm sure things will be all right, dear. You see, I have this splendid ability to remain calm and sort of get out of my body and watch what's happening. So they will do their work, and I'll just calmly watch. Then I'll be OK—I'll just need a little mending. I don't know. I guess it's just faith."

I knew Estelle well enough by then to know she wasn't describing an actual "out-of-body experience" or an episode of what psychologists call disassociation. She just wasn't into stewing, fretting, or angst. She seemed to have this marvelous ability to relax, trusting that the doctors would do their job and God would do his.

In that same conversation, Estelle also mentioned with a wide grin, "You know, I'm turning ninety-four soon."

The thoughts were streaming through my head. First, *can Estelle possibly be that old? Next, what are the doctors thinking, operating on a ninety-three-year-old woman? Can the discomfort and disruption possibly be worth it?* Then I argued back to myself: *I know people forty years younger who are not nearly as full of life as Estelle. So why not?*

And yet I couldn't help wondering, *When I return next summer, will she still be with us?*

So on my second day back the next summer, I was relieved to see Estelle at a luncheon decked out in a becoming suit and crowned with a stylish straw hat. *Sparkling* was the word that came to my mind when I saw her—a sparkling lady with an air of the magical about her. I realized Estelle could teach me a lot about aging positively, so I would have to seek out her wisdom.

Tough Beginnings

No one could claim that Estelle had an easy start in life. Born in 1912, she'd grown up in a stark mining town in Michigan. And even before that, hardship had seemed to define the very fabric of her family's experience.

Her mother, Ellen, had roots in an area along the border between Sweden and Finland, with family residing in both countries. After being abandoned in tragic circumstances by her own mother, Ellen was shuttled around from place to place in the poorest areas of Finland before a local church program sponsored her emigration to the US at the age of twelve and arranged a job for her. Ellen, who spoke Swedish and Finnish but no English, would be working for a British family with five children.

Leaving her family was a wrenching experience for Ellen, but what truly broke her heart was having to leave little Leonard, her beloved three-year-old brother. Over the years as she grew up, married, and raised a family in Michigan, she always dreamed of reuniting with him. Later her daughter, Estelle, made a promise: she would take on the mission of reuniting her family.

Estelle described her early life with a degree of compassion and lightness that defied the harsh realities and challenges her family had faced. She fully acknowledged the tough parts, explaining them to me in terms that showed a complete realization of how stark and painful they had been. Yet somehow she managed to soften their impact by putting them into a context of the times, the place, and the circumstances. She did so without blame, rancor, or regret. She seemed able to mine gentle and joyful memories from even the grimmest of situations.

Times were indeed lean in the mining town of Amasa, Michigan, where Estelle spent the early days of her childhood. Her dad worked in the iron mines. He labored to shelter and feed his five children while his wife did her best in their humble surroundings to make a warm and happy home for the family.

When Estelle described her early home to me, she did so in terms of the intangibles—of being together with her older brothers and of her father and mother's deep concern for them. She was also especially sensitive to her mother's sense of loss due to having to leave her family—especially Leonard—behind in Finland. Inspired by her mother's faithful practice of writing home to her family abroad, Estelle began her own lifelong habit of letter writing in order to stay connected to loved ones separated from her by great distances.

When Estelle and I were together, our conversations often turned to Estelle's family. She slipped easily into what I came to call her "thinking back" mode and recalled the time she'd spent with her father. "He didn't have a lot of time for cuddling. But I remember one day when I was up on his lap. He had his flannel shirt on, and he chewed Copenhagen tobacco. I can still remember that smell of flannel and Copenhagen. I felt so small and comfortable and safe."

Another remembrance involved a time when Estelle's mother went into the cellar with her pan to get vegetables. "It was a root cellar." She looked at me and asked if I knew what a root cellar was. I did, so she continued. "[Mom] told Ruby, who was a few years older than me, to 'watch 'Stelle.' But Ruby got distracted and, sure enough, I toddled over to the edge and tumbled right through the hole. My mother caught me in her enamel pan. I got banged up a little—my lip was cut, but not too badly. The photographer came to our town the next day, and my mother got a picture of us made, but it wasn't the nicest of me, I can tell you. My hair needed a trim, and it was hanging in my eyes. My 'didee' was hanging down in one corner, and I was standing up on a chair scared of the photographer—I never saw him before."

Estelle also vividly recalled a time when her mother showed an independent streak. "That was the day when my mom saved my father's life," she said. "Annoyed at him for something, she decided he'd have to wake himself up for work. Her failure to wake him meant he missed work." Given their financial circumstances, this would ordinarily have been considered a grievous lapse on her mother's part. But as it turned out, that was the fateful day of a tragic mine disaster. Eighteen men were trapped in a shaft and died. "The story told was that the miners weren't able to use the escape door because it had been locked by the owners to prevent the miners from leaving their shift early. That might be a story," Estelle continued. "It might not be altogether true. But whatever the cause of that disaster, I feel like I can still hear that wailing whistle, announcing tragedy."

Warm Memories from a Cold Place

Her father escaped death that day. But only a few years later, when he was just thirty-two, he succumbed to pneumonia. Estelle was five years old. "There was no work for women then in that town," she explained. "So we moved to Sault Ste. Marie, where Mother could work in the leather factory."

Estelle remembered being distraught at leaving behind a little neighbor—her first friend, Margie. "I was determined to keep in contact with her, and I wrote to her for eighty-seven years. She passed on three years ago." Estelle also regularly sent letters across the Atlantic. She said she had managed to learn enough Swedish then, "with my mother's help." Estelle's Swedish "wasn't perfect," but it was good enough that she could write to her Uncle Leonard, the brother her mother held so dear. Through her letters over the years, Estelle kept alive the hope of a reunion for the family.

Situated on the frigid Upper Peninsula of Michigan, Sault Ste. Marie offered Estelle a variety of life experiences. Winter temperatures hovered around zero, and for folks of modest means, keeping warm could present constant challenges. But in remembering that place, Estelle chose to recall the adventure and magic that land of cold offered. In one February note to me, she recalled evenings spent with her two younger sisters, "dragging a toboggan a mile from where we lived, just to go down *once* from a soldier's prac- tice ski jump at the top of the hill, then dragging it back home another mile."

Estelle's reminiscences of times spent with her family during this time are especially poignant. When she and I talked on the phone one Thanksgiving Day, she told me that the approach of the holidays reminded her of her Christmases growing up. "There was no Santa Claus for us. We had so little," she explained, "but that didn't really matter. I can still see that tree and all of us stringing popcorn and singing carols together. It's just too much these days. It's really about the warmth of loved ones, not all these *things*."

While Ellen worked at what Estelle called the "leather factory"—perhaps a tannery or processing plant—the children took care of one another, and all eventually worked at the factory themselves. "We all got our education in that factory," she remembered. Her mother later "made a marriage, not suitable," and three more girls were born into that marriage.

Because she was experiencing some health difficulties, Estelle was sent south for a while when she was about twelve or thirteen years old. Under the good guidance of the town doctor, she traveled miles away from her family for medical treatment and some rest in Michigan's Lower Peninsula. Her regimen included lying outside in the sunshine. Eating well, she put on some weight and was told she "looked like butter cream and eggs" by the time she returned home.

In keeping with the practice of the time, Estelle was never told the exact nature of what was wrong with her. She recovered quite well but was haunted by the idea that she might have had tuberculosis—a significant concern of the time. Trying a tactic rare back then, that of patients acting as their own advocates and posing questions, she finally asked the doctor point-blank. Handing Estelle her records to view, the doctor confirmed their contents: Estelle had not had TB.

Because she had been away for treatment, Estelle only finished school through the sixth grade. She had performed well in school before then, but circumstances made it impossible for her to continue. For the rest of her life, this lack of education would be a source of embarrassment for her—although anyone who met Estelle and spent some time with her would see her not as a woman of limited education, but as a clever woman who liked to stay informed. At ninety-six, she was still relating the top stories in the *Inky Mirror* to me.

Working Girl

In the midst of the Great Depression, with jobs scarce and money always a nagging need, Estelle moved to Detroit to take a job in a bomb factory. She worked the graveyard shift—eleven in the evening until seven in the morning. She was now making better money, so she was able to send some home to her mother. (This sounds a bit different from today, when parents so often are sending money to their children.)

According to Estelle, the bomb factory was an intense place with a pervasive sense of danger. World War II was brewing, though the United States had not yet entered the conflict, and Estelle's factory was manufacturing and shipping bombs to support allies who had already begun to fight.

Because the country was not yet at war and men had not yet been called up for service, Estelle was one of only a few women working in the factory at the time. Then she lost her job when the stove factory across the way shut down and many of its male employees moved over to take the jobs at the bomb factory. So Estelle moved back to the leather factory in Sault Ste. Marie, where she rejoined her sisters working from nine at night until four in the morning.

One Saturday Estelle and a sister took the streetcar into town and, for a treat, stopped for lunch in a hotel dining room. They saw a friend who was in the Army—a so-called "peacetime soldier"—and he sat down to chat with them. "Then, from kitty-corner across the room, this other soldier was trying to catch my eye, finally walking across the room to us. I was puzzled; I didn't give him any come-on or anything. But then he said, 'Hi, Tom' to our friend, and we realized that they knew each other from the Army."

Estelle and her sister welcomed this young soldier, Arthur Cordoza, to the group. They had two brothers in the Army at the time, and Estelle found herself hoping that, wherever they were, someone was being kind to them as well. (Her brother Carl would later serve in Germany and be awarded the Purple Heart, and her other brother, Leonard, would die at Normandy.)

Reflecting back on that first meeting with Arthur, Estelle told me, "Little did I know on that day that I would marry that boy." She also pointed out that, from their chance meeting place, they could look out the window and see the roof of a church near the railroad tracks. Arthur specifically asked about the church, and Estelle explained that it was the church her family attended. And, as it turned out, it was the one where she and Arthur would marry.

With Arthur's unit stationed in tents at the nearby fairgrounds, they were able to see more of each other, and a friendship developed. He would occasionally come for supper, walking the two miles each way. "We were just friends," she told me. "There was no romance. And he didn't have any money for entertainment, so we'd have picnics or go to the beach where we could see the shores of Canada."

Arthur went on leave to visit his family in Boston, and while he was gone, the war broke out. The friendship between him and Estelle continued to grow after that, but by necessity it was through written correspondence alone.

Enlisted

With the country at war, Estelle and her sister had the idea of enlisting in the Navy. "Maybe doing this would help," they said to each other. Estelle wrote to Arthur to elicit his opinion. She thought she might receive a negative response because women's military service was a relatively new phenomenon and people made unflattering assumptions about it. Some held to stereotypes about the "type of woman" who would sign up, and others felt that the military might change a woman in unfortunate ways.

But Estelle was pleasantly surprised by Arthur's thoughtful and supportive feedback. "There are a lot of benefits, and it might be good," he told her. "It's up to each person to decide. Whatever girl you are, you will remain because you have a level head."

Reassured, Estelle signed up for the WAVES. Shortly thereafter Arthur was shipped out to the Philippines, and Estelle boarded the train headed to boot camp in the Bronx, New York. Her journey lasted several days, the train stopping often along the way to pick up other prospective WAVES.

Upon her arrival in New York, Estelle navigated the interview process with some finesse—until an interviewer asked, "How did you get in? You need to have at least completed tenth grade." Estelle had been concerned about this herself. However, she had recently learned about the results of some tests her principal had given her around the time she went to the Lower Peninsula for medical treatment. She had tested at the eleventh-grade level. So Estelle told the interviewer about the principal's test and added, "I liked school, I'm not dumb, I'm learning all the time, and I like to do it."

She was inducted into the WAVES.

At first Estelle was a bit sensitive about her slight build. But she completed boot camp successfully and, ironically, her first assignment turned out to be security. I admit it gave me pause to hear her speak of "guard duty." It was difficult to envision this slip of a woman—barely five feet tall—defending a perimeter or presenting an imposing physical deterrence. As far as I could tell, however, the Navy found a place where this little woman could serve the cause.

WAVES on Dry Land

Estelle's next duty station was a base in Crane, Indiana, that served as an ammunition depot. She held the rank of seaman first class and was assigned to the quartermaster command, helping to make sure that the troops had the supplies and provisions they needed.

Thinking that Indiana was an odd place for a Navy base, I asked whether the base was located on Lake Michigan. She replied, "No, there was no water nearby at all. The only water around us was in the pool, where I thought I would drown."

She went on to explain, "One Sunday I was sitting outside sunning myself, as we did in those days, when a young sailor came up and swooped me up into his arms. Holding me, he ran and then jumped into thirteen feet of water—and I couldn't swim.

"I can still feel myself clutching and clutching at the water and thinking, 'This is the end.' Then I saw something long hanging into the pool, and I grabbed onto it. It was the long arm of a redheaded sailor who had seen it all [happen]. He was hanging over the edge trying to pull me up. After I got my wind again, I asked what happened, and he told me the other sailor wanted to get acquainted with me. That didn't happen. And I can say I'm [still] not a good swimmer—to this day, I'm afraid of the water."

I guess that must have been the extent of the drama in Crane because Estelle said of her time there, "Well, it was not the most exciting place to be, but you were doing your work."

She did tell me of an incident that happened one day at lunch. One of the girls was intending to go shopping at the PX and asked Estelle, "Want to go, kid?" When Estelle said she wasn't going to do any shopping, the girl asked, "Do you have any money?"

Oh, this is where it starts, Estelle thought, worried she would be tapped for the little money she had. She was still sending a regular allotment to her mother. Her youngest sister, who had learning difficulties and had contracted polio, required extra care, which meant additional cost. On top of that, Estelle was required to pay for her own life insurance and was saving money for a visit home. So there wasn't much money left for more than the basics.

But Estelle's fears were allayed when the girl said, "I have some if you need it. I was the secretary to Leopold Stokowski [a famous conductor of the period, who had married a Vanderbilt]." Estelle never took her friend up on the offer, but she also never forgot her generosity.

"I Don't Know What's Going to Happen to Your Haircut"

Estelle continued to write to Arthur during the rest of her service in the Navy. She was one of the first to be discharged at the end of the war because her family needed her at home. So Estelle, unaware of any other options, headed back home to resume work at the factory in Sault Ste. Marie. But she attended beauty school while working and eventually took a job at a friend's beauty salon. She found the work to be quite agreeable—a big change from the factory floor.

Describing for me the general mood in the country after the war was over, Estelle explained that there was a great deal of emotion in the air, with some people jubilant over the return of their loved ones and others distraught at the loss of theirs. But "for whatever reason," she told me, "I felt like a stone—there was nothing. It was so strange, but I couldn't explain it." A bit like being in limbo, I would guess.

At five o'clock one morning, Estelle received a phone call from Arthur, who had been wounded and received a Purple Heart. He was calling to say he was back on US soil and would be coming up to see her when he could. Estelle was thankful to hear that Arthur had survived. But not knowing his timetable or his intentions, she went on with life and busied herself with her new profession.

Then one day, while the owner of the shop was gone and Estelle was busy cutting a customer's hair, she heard a knock at the salon door. "I figured it was a salesman, so I called out to tell him the owner wasn't there. He then stepped toward me and said, "Stelle, don't you recognize me in my civilian clothes?'"

Estelle's comb and scissors fell to the floor and, as she remembered it, "I went to pieces. I told the customer, 'I don't know what's going to happen to your haircut now.'" No more limbo for Estelle.

Estelle invited Arthur to her family home, where he was a familiar face from before the war. But Arthur was not there just for a visit. After a prewar friendship and a wartime courtship via mail, Arthur was convinced that Estelle was the woman he wanted to marry. He proposed to her, and she accepted. Then he returned to Massachusetts to see his family and share the news with them.

Arthur's family, unfortunately, was not terribly keen on his plan to marry Estelle. The various members seemed to have had their own plans for him right there in Massachusetts. But

Arthur prevailed, and in 1946 he and Estelle married in that little church they had viewed through the window on the first day they met.

The Help

The newly married couple moved east to Massachusetts so Arthur could look for a job. Unfortunately, Arthur's family was still not happy with the union and gave Estelle a less than warm welcome. Housing was hard to come by after the war, especially for those without a job, so Estelle and Arthur stayed for a while with one of Arthur's sisters, whom Estelle described as "halfway decent to me compared to the others." Then, in the course of his job hunt, Arthur came upon someone who made a valuable suggestion: Why not look for a job as a couple—one that included the benefit of housing? When Arthur asked Estelle if she wanted to give it a try, she agreed. "I didn't want to stay on so long with his sister, as it wouldn't be fair to her."

They interviewed for a joint position as "help" for an older couple, the Williamsons,[1] who were eager to hire them. Soon Estelle and Arthur were taking the train for the couple's home in Concord, New Hampshire. Estelle would work in the house while Arthur served as driver and handyman.

Telling me this story, Estelle confessed that she'd gotten "the worries" about this adventure right about then, especially since she had not been trained to cook. But Arthur had

1 Not their real name.

said something funny and had helped diffuse her stress. She'd figured that the combination of his sense of humor and hers might serve them well as they moved forward.

Upon arriving at the house in Concord, Estelle was surprised by the significant size of the property. When she and Arthur introduced themselves to their prospective employers, the elderly woman of the house asked if Estelle had ever held such a position before. Estelle answered honestly, "No, ma'am, I haven't." The woman smiled and said, "I think you and I will do fine."

That assessment proved to be prophetic. Estelle told me Mrs. Williamson was a sweet and interesting woman who came into the kitchen each morning to share stories about her travels abroad. Estelle loved hearing about the many places the couple had visited in Europe. For her it was like taking a journey, something she hoped to be able to do on her own one day. She still dreamed of fulfilling the promise she had made to her mother to one day visit her Uncle Leonard.

The days were full for both Estelle and Arthur. Estelle, who was no stranger to hard work, found herself quite busy taking care of not only the elderly couple, but also their two sons, a daughter-in-law, one son-in-law, and a three-year-old—"all of them," she told me. But Mrs. Williamson was quite complimentary and supportive. She often made a point of coming back after a meal to say, "That was lovely, Estelle." Estelle beamed when she told me about that. "That was really something. Nothing I was used to before, and I loved doing it— being with them."

Mr. Williamson, however, was a slightly different matter. Though he was a very fine man "in back of it all," as Estelle put it, he was also somewhat "bullnosed." He would tell them how to vote, for instance, an employer's expectation that was quite a new experience for the couple.

Estelle and Arthur considered themselves fortunate to have a place to live rent-free, but their quarters came with a touch of mystery. The previous occupant, a chauffeur who worked for the family before the war, had been found dead in the garage. As a result, their room "felt kind of scary" to Arthur and Estelle.

One night Arthur got up in the middle of the night to use the bathroom located down the hall. Estelle, half asleep, decided she would follow him. She was always reluctant to go into the hallway at night alone, but in this case, she thought she could tag along behind her husband. She followed him without saying a word, so Arthur was unaware of her presence—until he sensed someone behind him. "It must have been the hairs standing on the back of his neck that caused him to let out a bloodcurdling yell as he realized what was happening. Shaking, he asked, 'My God, 'Stelle, why didn't you tell me you were coming? You scared the daylights out of me.'"

Perhaps Arthur's reaction was a carryover from his wartime experiences in the Pacific, just as his periodic malaria episodes were. Estelle had to help Arthur through them, going to the doctor for his medication and washing and hanging his pajamas out to dry when they were soaked by his malaria-induced sweats. This, of course, was on top of doing her regular work for the family.

"Arthur was really very ill at times. It was rough. But I always told myself, 'I can make it.'"

And she did.

New Territory

All in all, working for the Williamsons suited Estelle and Arthur well, and they were grateful to have the jobs and a place to live. But this kind of employment meant they had no real time off, no time just to themselves. Given their wartime separation and their newlywed status, the arrangement was hard on the young couple.

One day, Estelle told me, the mistress suggested they go to church on Sunday so they might have a chance to meet some other young people. "What Sunday?" she protested to me. "Between making breakfast and then turning right around to prepare lunch for all of them, there was no Sunday time."

After two years on the job, Estelle and Arthur realized they were too young to be tied down in such a way and decided to leave their positions. They traveled back to Michigan, where Arthur managed a golf course—"Never did that before," Estelle said before I could ask about his experience in the field. She had maintained her license as a beautician and began working in salons again.

They had one especially painful experience while back in Michigan. All the men at the golf club were talking about a wonderful bank and how "even when all the banks failed years before, that bank had stood and remained solid." This was a privately owned bank, and the gentleman who owned it had a "good name," as Estelle told it. So Arthur decided to put the couple's money in that bank. But, as she explained to me, the owner "had loaned a heck of a lot of money to a son-of-a-gun without any collateral, and it wound up breaking the bank when he didn't repay."

When I asked about FDIC insurance, she said, "Yes, the bank across the street had it, but Arthur took the advice of the men at the club, and we lost all but 35 percent of what we had. Now, that wasn't all that much because we hadn't saved very much. And then I didn't know enough about those things to be making the decisions." This was new territory for Estelle, but she learned from it.

The Human Connection

I asked Estelle the question I asked all my golden ladies: "What brought you to Nantucket?" She told me her Massachusetts-raised husband had been the primary influence. "Arthur kept telling me about Nantucket this and Nantucket that and how I would like it." The place had the blessing of Estelle's mother as well because of its relative proximity to places she had lived when she first came to America—Springfield, Massachusetts, and along the coast in Gloucester and Rockford.

"And I did like it," Estelle confirmed, "It was very simple when I first saw it in the '50s, calm and not fussy, needing repair work here and there." Smiling, she added, "I got to know a lot of nice people."

Once on-island, Estelle and Arthur continued their careers in various service positions. Arthur worked as a bartender and she continued as a beautician. In those days, Nantucket already had a seasonal population, and many wealthy and socially prominent families summered there. Estelle and Arthur became part of that experience, working for "the rich people," as she called them, in Nantucket during the summer and then following their clientele to Florida for the winter.

Mrs. Morrison,[2] a woman whom Estelle counted among the nice people she knew in Nantucket, had a "special place" in Palm Beach when Estelle and Arthur were living in nearby Delray Beach. One day Mrs. Morrison called to ask if Estelle could come to do her hair. Estelle told her she had no transportation because Arthur was working. Mrs. Morrison told her not to worry; she'd send her chauffeur.

"This was the chauffeur we had met in Nantucket, and he drove up in—oh, what's that big, fancy car?" she asked, trying to recall the name of it.

"A Cadillac?" I ventured.

"No, much more than a Cadillac."

I tried again. "Rolls-Royce?"

"A Rolls-Royce—that's it. And nobody in the neighborhood was out to see me step into that vehicle!" She shook her head and chuckled at that lost opportunity.

---

2 Not her real name.

As Estelle continued her story, I could see how she had deftly navigated the social order of the time, employing her special blend of humor and charm. "I had luncheon with Mrs. Morrison and her companions and then did their hair and nails. When it was time, the chauffeur came to drive me home in the family limo. On the way back, driving along the walk in Palm Beach, I saw the beach-bus driver from Nantucket standing beside the limo he was now driving." (Apparently he too had come south to Florida for the winter.) Estelle asked the chauffeur who was driving her to pull up alongside her Nantucket friend.

"He knew the fellow as well. Everybody knew the beach-bus driver. So the chauffeur pulled up alongside him, and I said, 'Hi, Armando.' And Armando stammered, 'Hi, 'Stelle! How's Art doing?'"

She gestured to indicate her luxurious ride and replied, "You can see for yourself, can't you?"

Armando burst out laughing. "I always knew that son of a gun would make good."

Estelle told Mrs. Morrison that story the next time she saw her—"And did she ever laugh." Telling me, she fell to giggling again herself.

Hearing that story, I was struck by Estelle's lack of self-consciousness and the ease with which she moved among both service folk and socialites. She managed to maintain a delicate balance between the two worlds, drawing out the common human connection that exists between all people but isn't always revealed or nurtured.

"I Don't Know Where I Got the Nerve"

One year when Estelle returned to Nantucket for the season, she was approached by the owner of a gift shop located on Main Street. The owner's sister had been managing the shop but was leaving town, so he wondered if Estelle would take the position. She said yes, choosing once again to tackle a new challenge.

"Well, that was no picnic," she remembered about that job—"moving long ladders, carrying the boxes of merchandise, getting help—all new to me, this thing." She and Arthur lived "right down at Steamboat Wharf and Easy Street" in quarters that came as part of Estelle's compensation agreement. "We shared the building with an art gallery of a then well-known artist. We were right by the Skipper," a popular boat-cum-restaurant that unfortunately is no longer part of the Nantucket harbor scene.

Estelle soon found that her new boss was "not a real business manager type." One night she was invited to his house for dinner, only to find piles of unpaid bills "like a haystack of papers" on his dining-room table. In addition to owning the gift shop, he also rented out accommodations, but he failed to handle the reservations properly. So people who arrived expecting accommodations often found confusion instead.

One day Estelle's boss, whom she described as "something of a schemer," pulled her aside to tell her he wanted her to hire a woman from off-island to be cashier in the shop. He also said the woman wasn't familiar with the cash register and warned Estelle to watch her because she was "a drinker." *That's all I need,* she thought.

When the woman arrived at the shop, Estelle was pleasantly surprised to find her to be a seemingly normal, nice-looking woman. But that evening, when Estelle counted the money for the day, her heart sank to find that some money was missing. She mulled it over in her head and wondered, *what will I say to the help? I have to put it nicely.*

The next morning she said to them, "Girls, in doing the books last night, I discovered I was twenty dollars short. I don't want anyone to jump to any conclusions that I am pointing a finger, but I have been worried and have no answer."

Then the new girl stepped forward to say that when she worked in a gift shop in Boston, they had put the twenty-dollar bills under the cash drawer to help keep them safe. Looking under the drawer, Estelle exclaimed, "Thank you very much. You taught me something—that's exactly where it is."

In reflecting on the experience, Estelle told me earnestly, "You have to be very careful what you say to people." And then she added, "I felt good. I was in charge, and I really tried to do a good job."

Doing some mental calculations, she told me, "I think I was [at the gift shop] three summers—and then back into hairdressing." Estelle and Arthur still went to Palm Beach in the winters, and she continued to hold a beautician's license in Michigan, Florida, and Massachusetts.

Shaking her head, she acknowledged the irony of her profession with a smile: "I always wore *my* hair plain."

When I commented to Estelle on the range of things she had taken on with no prior experience and the fact that she seemed to approach challenges without hesitation, Estelle thought a bit and smiled. "Yeah, right. I don't know where I got the nerve to do it. But I thought, well . . ." She shrugged.

"Something Clicking Here All the Time"

Estelle and Arthur's last off-island experience before retiring to Nantucket was working for a wealthy older couple who lived in one of the resort communities of Palm Beach. They worked for them for three seasons. Estelle began the story, "We got along fine, had some time off there, a place to live, and a salary. But we had a dog, and at the beginning we anticipated a problem." Estelle proceeded to tell me an amusing tale that illustrated her talent for persuading people to make changes Estelle believed in.

As they drove through the neighborhood to the initial interview, Estelle and Arthur noticed folks walking dogs along the sidewalks of a community filled with beautiful homes. That must have reminded Arthur of their own dog, because he suddenly remarked, "'Stelle, they may not want a dog. We may need to put him in a kennel just to get the job."

Leaning over to me as she told this story years later, Estelle explained in a soft voice, "I knew how Artie loved that dog." She pulled herself straight up. "And I did too."

She giggled, thinking back. "I kind of educated Arthur on what to say and what have you." If at the end of the job interview they were offered the position, Arthur was to say mildly, as if it were an afterthought, "We have a dog."

It all went as planned—almost. The owner did extend the job offer, and Arthur did mention the dog. But the woman responded by saying, "Oh dear. Dogs are not allowed on this island."

Estelle and Arthur knew this was untrue—they had just seen evidence to the contrary walking down the street—but they could hardly call their future employer on the lie. "Perhaps you can put him in a kennel," the woman suggested, and Arthur responded respectfully, "We've never had to do that before, but we can give it a try."

They arranged to board the dog for the winter and began their work. But as Estelle told me, "Arthur missed that dog terribly—a sweet collie, he was." So again Estelle assured her husband, "Leave it to me."

The next evening, as she was helping the mistress get ready to go out to dinner—"I helped her dress and everything"— Estelle broached the subject. "I understand that our dog is not cooperating at that kennel and not eating. We're kind of worried about him, and I think we'll have to go and get him."

"But then he'll be more lonely when you and Arthur take him back," commented the lady.

"Oh, but Arthur misses that dog terribly," Estelle told her, "and so do I. And we're worried about the dog's health."

The lady just said, "Well," and nothing more.

As soon as her mistress left for the evening, Estelle rushed to tell Arthur, "Let's go get the dog." Eyes wide, Arthur asked, "She told you we can have him?"

"Nooooo," Estelle responded. "But I didn't hear her say no."

As she talked to me, Estelle drifted back into that shining place of memory. She smiled and then laughed. "The look of heaven on his face . . ." I can see she was there with Arthur, sharing his feeling of pure joy.

The morning after they picked up the dog from the kennel, the husband came outside to see Arthur with the collie. "I see you have the dog," he commented.

"Yes, we were afraid we couldn't leave him in the kennel any longer," said Arthur, with perhaps a bit less confidence than Estelle might have shown.

He was surprised when the husband said, "Well, say, I have an old quilt in the attic." He pointed to the yard. "I'm going to put it under the bushes, and your dog can lie there and not be in the hot sun."

Then the woman of the house came down. "Estelle, I see you have the dog." Estelle nodded and explained they couldn't leave him in the kennel. After a long pause, the mistress said, "We'll see." Then, settling into the idea, she continued, "Now, when you go out shopping or driving, I want you to leave the dog here. I will water him and feed him. I don't want you to have that dog with you in the hot car." She finished off the conversation by telling Estelle, "Don't worry. The dog will be fine with me."

As we both laughed at the story's fortuitous outcome,

Estelle pointed to her head and said to me, "There's something clicking here all the time," and we both laughed some more. She got no argument from me on that score.

Keeping a Promise

Although there had been one particular instance in Michigan when Arthur took banking advice from his golfing buddies and the situation turned sour, some other advice from Arthur's buddies had borne much sweeter fruit. Still wishing to fulfill the promise she had made to her mother to visit Uncle Leonard in Finland, Estelle had continued her correspondence over the years, but at one point during the seventies, she decided something more was needed.

All her life, when Estelle had a goal, she took actions that set things into motion to achieve that goal. In this instance, she explained to Arthur's Nantucket golfing buddies how much she really wanted to visit her uncle and asked them to encourage Arthur to go along with her plan. They agreed—and soon Arthur did too. "With a hurricane threatening, we managed to get off Nantucket on the last boat, and we were on our way."

Estelle's face showed a mixture of delight and serenity when she described her Finland trip to me. "I had the most wonderful feeling of closing the circle by seeing Uncle Leonard, Aunt Esther, and my cousins." On top of that, she had the warm satisfaction of keeping the promise to her mother.

A Kind Man

When Estelle and Arthur finally retired, they didn't have an employer's retirement plan or a defined pension and benefit package that had accrued over the years. But they did have each other. And Estelle and Arthur were devoted to each other. They had created a strong partnership that lasted until Arthur's death in 2003.

Even after that, Estelle continued to hold him close in her heart. One day she related to me another story that illustrated Arthur's kind and generous spirit. The couple was on a trip to see Estelle's recently widowed sister in Michigan. The sister was expecting a fourth child, and she and her children didn't have a place to live.

"Arthur took my mother and sister and went out looking for houses," Estelle told me. "When he returned, he asked me to give him the checkbook to make a down payment on a house for them. He told them they didn't have to pay us back right away, just whenever they could."

She smiled proudly. "I thought Arthur was pretty wonderful."

Wrestling with Reality

After Arthur passed away, Estelle remained in the house they had retired to together, a neat cedar-shingled cottage located in Brant Point, a low-lying part of the island convenient to town. But in 2009, after she underwent serious hip surgery and rehabilitation off-island, her house of many years had to be sold. She returned to a new home, an assisted-living apartment in a newly built senior facility on the island. She hadn't quite expected to make that change, but managing her home had become too much for her, and the threat of flooding in the area where she lived always loomed.

Located at a point between Nantucket Sound and the harbor, Brant Point is vulnerable to hurricanes and the dreaded nor'easters that bring abundant rain, higher tides, and coastal flooding. Estelle described her last experience during the flooding in the 1990s: "Five-and-a-half feet of water in the yard and two feet in the house—oh my! What a mess." She pointed to the legs of her wooden chest. "You can still see the water stains on my furniture."

Estelle had loved her Brant Point home and still missed it. But at the same time, she recognized that the burden of being a homeowner, especially in that particular location, was greater than a ninety-six-year-old widow should have to bear.

When I visited Estelle in her apartment and asked about some of the things she enjoyed doing there, she told me about her painting. "This morning I was working on a painting of the Mona Lisa—a big project. Nothing like copying the Masters," she joked with a touch of mischief in her eye. "They have a little art class downstairs," she explained, referring to the activities program at her assisted-living residence. "But that one up there," she said, pointing to a wonderful, colorful depiction of Nantucket's historic Main Street, "I painted that from memory in 1975. That's how Main Street looked the first time I saw it."

I had noticed the painting when I first entered the apartment but had assumed it had been professionally done. I was impressed by the way Estelle had been able to capture the color and vibrancy of that familiar summer scene. She told me she liked to depict real subjects, "not a bunch of imagined things" (her description of abstract art). "I want to paint life, action—where something's going on." And she had done just that.

Indestructible

I was aware that Estelle had faced significant health challenges all her life, including her breast-cancer surgery, so I brought the subject up on a visit. Unlike folks who dwell on their maladies, Estelle had to be coaxed before she would even admit to any. Even then she told her stories in a matter-of-fact, "isn't this the way it is everywhere?" manner. Her overall view of herself was that she was healthy and whole. Actually, she talked about her entire life that way, mentioning any "incidents" as just routine little tasks to be dealt with along the way.

"When I was in the Navy, I fell off a bike—I was trying to learn to ride. And they had me up on crutches and back to work the next day. No babying there," she said. The Navy's approach didn't bother her. In fact, it bore great similarity to her own way of addressing things medical. When she fell off a motorcycle in Michigan and broke her arm, she dealt with it on her own. A week or so later, she was encouraged to visit the doctor, who advised her to have an X-ray. Not thinking it necessary, she deferred to the doctor out of respect. The

X-ray showed her arm had been broken, set in place, and was healing well.

"See!" she exclaimed, throwing back her head and laughing. "I'm indestructible."

When I pressed her a little, she finally admitted, "Well, there were a few little things. I had a pacemaker." She giggled as she owned up to that one. "And then there was the broken hip. Oh, and I did have that one breast removed." (She said this with an air of "It's only one, but who's counting?")

Only when called upon to enumerate her many health issues did Estelle really even consider them as such. "I guess I *did* have some serious things," she admitted.

Referring to one of her heart procedures, Estelle said she hadn't realized exactly what was going to happen. "But I wasn't worried in the least. I went in, probably they sedated me, and the next thing I knew someone was pounding on my chest to keep the fluids from building up. It wasn't until later that I found out that they had taken my heart out and put it on the table."

"I Didn't Bother" to Worry

Estelle had undergone a coronary bypass in 1988. She told me that before the procedure they'd had the patients "watch something on the TV—some preliminary knowledge," as she called it, about the process. But she had been more concerned with the young girl who sat there crying and the woman next to her who kept asking, "Aren't you worried?" But Estelle *wasn't* worried. "I just felt, I don't know—it's just something you have to go through, and that's it. I'm not the bravest person in the world, but I felt there was nothing I could do by worrying, and I didn't bother."

As we sat in Estelle's apartment many years later, I commented that her ability not to "bother" with worry was a trait many people would like to have. Thinking about that, she nodded. "My mother was the one who was behind it all, and it just built up in me without knowing it. I don't feel pains or limitations. In fact," she added, steering the conversation to the present, "I'd like it if we had more outdoor exercise here."

Elaborating on the topic, she pronounced, "I feel healthy. We were doing yoga yesterday, and I do exercise a couple of times a week, but there's not enough standing. I would like to walk briskly, but they make me use my cane. But without the cane I can still do it," she insisted. To support her assertion, she added, "When I first arrived here, the porter said, 'You walk so straight, not like this.'" She stood up and demonstrated to me how he walked bent over and wobbly. "I hope I don't have to be in a wheelchair, dependent upon others to move me around." (She got her wish for a while, at least. She made it to age ninety-nine before finally having to resort to a wheelchair.)

"I'm Not Alone"

Despite her sense of wellness, Estelle did wrestle with the realities of not living independently in her own home, especially the need to balance privacy and security. Like many in an assisted-living environment, Estelle felt the tension between the two acutely. "Other people have the keys" is the way she described it to me.

She expressed the feeling that nothing was safe from "intrusion" and suggested opportunities for such: "when I go to church, to lunch, and so forth." I heard her rational brain kicking in when she reminded herself, "Of course they need to come in to clean, and if I needed help, of course." But a shade of uneasiness remained as she pondered the dilemma.

Then the topic of what she termed her "stuff" came up. Although her home had been small, she'd had enough space for her things. Now, with much of it "packed away," she missed being able to look around and take "mental inventory." She grew a little agitated as she wondered where certain items were and if they were still with her. I was reminded of that feeling I've had after one of our many moves, when things were upside down at home and I was looking for something important. I've known that frantic sense of *it's not here and I have no idea where it is.* So I could relate to what Estelle was telling me.

But again Estelle bolstered herself by saying, "When I try to get it sorted, I start, and then I get interrupted. I'm called to a class or to lunch or such. There's so much going on, I don't try anymore." Putting things in an even broader perspective, she reminded herself and me: "It could be worse."

When referring to some of the other drawbacks of her current living situation, such as minor slights by a staff member or perceived favoritism toward other residents, Estelle again dug deep. "I just make do as best I can," she said. "I'm fine, and I can get by." From there she launched into a description of what a great chef they had at the facility and how much she liked the new activities director.

When I called Estelle on Thanksgiving a few years ago, I inquired about her holiday dining arrangements. She told me that the other residents in her assisted-living complex had dined out with family, but her dinner had been served to her in her apartment, and she had eaten it by herself. "They all worried about me being alone, but I'm fine," she said with finality. "I'm not alone, after all. A friend like you has called me, and we're having a wonderful visit."

We chatted about food, and she commented that her Thanksgiving dinner was good but that the artichoke dish was not up to par. "They left those tough parts in there, which is not how you do it," she exclaimed. "Now I have a wonderful recipe for artichoke appetizers that I used to make for the rich people. Would you like it?"

I responded in the affirmative, and the following Tuesday the recipe and a lovely note appeared in my Virginia mailbox.

Drawing on the Past

As Estelle related her life journey to me, she frequently mentioned her mother. She believed that her mother's example had inspired her own strength and fortitude. Anytime she needed to wrestle with new challenges, she would reflect on how her mother came to America "at that young age, all alone, to work for an invalid woman with five children, not understanding their language nor they hers." Estelle used that vision as an inspiration: "I say to myself, 'I can do it. I can do it.'" She explained to me that both her mother's experiences as well as her own had "built my character to be strong."

Estelle's familial experiences continued to serve her in the form of memories—warm destinations she could visit in her later and less active years. When she reminisced her head would tilt, her eyes would peer into the distance, and her lips would curve into a gentle smile. I could literally see her gliding back in time, engaging all her senses as she relived the moments—tasting, hearing, smelling, and feeling it all.

To her great credit, Estelle could tease out and savor the good times from the breadth of her life memories, even the tiniest moments of joy in the harshest of circumstances. When she described those meager Christmases of her childhood, she chose to focus on what had made her happy. When I talked to her during one holiday season, she told me she was thinking about her childhood. "Just the other morning, while still in bed, I sang those beautiful songs and it brought me back there. It was wonderful."

Estelle's artistic bent, I learned, was a family trait as well. "My mother, sisters, and brother all liked to draw. My sister Helen could work on a car and get it to go and then come back inside and do some of the finest embroidery and lace I've ever seen. They all sewed so well, and I can't sew worth a darn." With a set chin and note of humorous defiance, she added, "And I don't care."

Stopping to clarify, she went on. "What I liked most to do

was to entertain—make my family laugh, regardless of the hard times. There was always something I would do to make them laugh. Sometimes I'd go a little too far." She didn't elaborate on that last confession, and I didn't ask. But her revelation didn't surprise me. People who knew Estelle in earlier days had already told me she'd been a superb cook and an engaging hostess.

Not Plain

When I asked Estelle what she considered to be her current fun activities, she said she really liked to go for drives out and around the island. A friend of hers, Louise, was kind enough to come and take her out for a spin from time to time. Estelle had been particularly enthused to receive an invitation to the wedding of a friend, the brother of the chef at her assisted-living residence, that took place out at Miacomet Pond on Nantucket's south shore.

"We had to cross over all these sand dunes," Estelle told me. "That's tiring when you are an old lady like me. And I made it," she sat tall and exclaimed, although "the next day I did have cramps in my legs." And she added, "They showed me a good time."

On the topic of outings, Estelle also told me, "I used to go for rides with a friend who had a companion who drove us. Come to find out, the companion cleaned my friend out for $26,000, and she had no idea." And when Estelle mentioned a recent newspaper article about embezzlement at the

Steamship Authority by someone who "really did a job," I realized that, at ninety-seven, Estelle was still keeping up with the local news and read the paper regularly.

In contrast to her friend's experience, Estelle emphasized, she had received dependable and honest help managing her affairs from Chuck Soule, a fellow member of our church. "He's such a smart and good man. He and his wife have been so good to me—even came over to the rehab center off-island [where Estelle was recovering from surgery] and brought me back safely."

When I inquired about her philosophy of life, Estelle summed it up as "Make the best of it. Give it a try. Take a chance. If it doesn't work out, something will come up. Try not to be harmful or do hurtful things."

She went on to say, "I don't really want things or need things. I never really desired frilly stuff. I'm very plain—plain old 'Stelle." She smiled over at me, and I smiled back.

But she wasn't plain, of course.

She was complex, brave, smart, funny, and wise—but not plain. Not at all.

To me, Estelle was a true golden lady.

Saying Good-Bye

At age ninety-nine, no longer able to navigate on her own any longer, Estelle moved from her assisted-living apartment to Our Island Home, Nantucket's long-term-care skilled nursing facility. I visited her there shortly after she arrived and found her much more subdued and in a wheelchair. She seemed glad to see me, and I enjoyed her familiar smile. But she seemed somewhat distant, not as engaged as she once had been. There was a faraway look in her eyes, as if she were viewing and living in the memories of her family and her dear Arthur. She barely spoke.

On a subsequent visit she continued to be rather quiet, so I decided to tell her some of her own stories, ones that she had generously shared with me. She smiled a little more brightly, and I saw serenity and contentment appear in her eyes.

I went to see her again at the end of the summer. "You have to excuse me," she said after we chatted awhile. "I feel very tired these days." Then she gave me one more of her precious, gracious smiles.

On November 30, 2012, Estelle's many friends on the island—seventy-five, they tell me—gathered for the grand celebration of her one-hundredth birthday. I regretted that I was unable to attend that party, though I sent a card and thought of her that day.

Five months later, on April 28, 2013, Estelle found her final rest.

I miss my visits with my friend and golden lady, Estelle.

Wisdom from Estelle

To this day, thinking of Estelle conjures feelings of lightness and inspiration in me. In my profession, I have studied about resilience, strength of spirit, and positive aging and found these topics fascinating. But Estelle gave me a vibrant, in-the-flesh example of all three. These qualities played out across her long life and supported her in old age as well. I am grateful to her for showing me the possibilities for maintaining well-being over the course of a long and sometimes difficult life.

In her early years, Estelle overcame so much that could have easily broken or discouraged her but did not. Instead, she developed positive survival tools that she would continue to hone and use throughout her life.

Listening to Estelle, I could see clearly that her connection to and identity with her family were powerful and significant factors in her whole life. Both her mother's story and her own experiences played a key role in molding her character and informed her philosophy, her actions, and her reactions to adversity. Those early days nurtured her positive perspective, her heartfelt gratitude for what she had, and her healthy ability to distinguish between the need to simply accept one particular situation and to take decisive action in another.

From an early age, Estelle identified her mother as a mentor. A model of determination and resiliency, Ellen continued to serve as a touchstone and inspiration throughout her daughter's life. When Estelle faced challenges, she often compared them to difficulties her mother had faced, and this perspective empowered her to prevail over adversity. Whether facing a health challenge, the loss of a job, or the need to leave her beloved home, she didn't succumb to self-pity. Again and again as she related parts of her story to me, I heard the refrain, "I can make do."

Estelle mined the good from even the grimmest situation, and she stored those little gems carefully in her rich memory bank to withdraw and use when needed. Even when revisiting difficult times in our conversations, she acknowledged the stark realities but didn't linger on them. Instead, she managed to float above the pain, pulling the joy in the moments along with her.

Estelle's sense of gratitude for all of her life—easy and difficult, happy and painful—helped her stay positive. She measured life by the intangible and not the material, focusing on her family and the good hearts of people who had made a difference in her life. She also managed to keep things in perspective, a key to well-being. "It could be worse," she often told me when relating a difficult situation.

Estelle was nothing if not game. When a job or life circumstance didn't work, she tried something else. She took risks and tried new things. How many times did she tell me, "Well, that was a first" or "Never did that before"? She possessed a flexibility that enabled her to move forward or step to the side instead of getting stuck in tough situations. The variety of her jobs and the number of her moves testify to this.

And like a good Nantucketer, Estelle used whatever she had to accomplish her goals. She employed her creativity in problem solving as well as in her artistic endeavors. I'm reminded, for instance, of her clever strategies for persuading her Florida employers to allow the dog and for getting Arthur to facilitate the reunion with Uncle Leonard.

Estelle never had a life coach. But she developed some techniques on her own that coaches often use to help clients move forward through difficult times, take on something new, or calm themselves during distressful situations. For instance, Estelle used self-talk to encourage, soothe, and move herself past challenges. "I can make it" and "I can do it" were phrases she told herself often.

Visualization is another coaching technique that Estelle developed on her own. She used her mind's eye to summon wonderful memories or envision good outcomes. During lonely times at the assisted-living facility, for instance, she deliberately revisited the good moments of her life, adding to her sense of peace and well-being. And when faced with surgery or a medical procedure, she pictured things going smoothly in a serene atmosphere. She then intentionally let go of worry and leaned on her faith—yet another life tool that enabled her to live positively and with grace. (Her personal faith often served to lighten her load.)

And I can't forget to mention Estelle's sense of fun and humor, something that spanned her lifetime and added a level of lightness to her life. That lightness diminished some after Arthur's death, but only for a while. Estelle was a person who strongly believed in the power of her own self-agency. So she drew from her well of humor and redesigned herself as a widow with a life purpose of spreading joy. In my view, she achieved that purpose splendidly.

For some reason, when I think of Estelle, I picture one of those inflatable "bop bag" toys with a weighted bottom.

Whenever you push one down, it pops up again—and again and again.

That was Estelle, my funny, resilient, creative, and not-at-all-plain golden lady. Summers in Nantucket just aren't the same without her.

CHAPTER 5

ESTELLE'S GALLERY

Estelle in her WAVES
uniform (1940s).

Estelle dressed for an evening
out with Arthur (about 2001).

Estelle celebrating her
one-hundredth birthday (2012).

CHAPTER 6

❦

Maggie Meredith

"What a fantastic world I can create."

FLAIR, COLOR, VIBRANCY, ACTION, and a touch of drama that defied her ninety years—all come together to create the vision of Maggie I hold in my mind's eye. My initial exposure to this golden lady came solely through her artwork. I had seen her paintings in various shops around town over the years and had admired her unique style. I think her work caught my eye because it seemed to blend a sense of comfortable approachability with a hint of mystery.

Maggie painted a variety of subjects. But because I am a cat lover, I was captivated by her whimsical cat paintings, which I thought captured the essence of a cat's nature—endearing yet independent. This sense of mystery and spirit permeated each of her pieces. The more I saw of Maggie's art, in fact, the more I liked it. But I didn't know anything about the artist.

My golden lady Claire Dwyer was the one responsible for introducing me to yet another aspect of Maggie's talent. After one of our lovely lunches, Claire dug into her stash of books and pulled out a book called *Not Beyond Recall: Poems by Maggie Meredith*.[1] At Claire's request I thumbed through the book, came upon a poem called "Waste Not," and began to read aloud. The poem ended with the observation that we waste so much of our precious time, and the poet charged the reader to recognize that we only have the present moment.

I was hooked. After reading some of the other poems, I asked Claire if I could borrow the book, and after I'd read it, I was certain I wanted a copy of my own. I searched the island's bookstores, the museum shop, the variety and news stores, but since the book was more than twelve years old, it was no longer on the shelves. I shared my disappointment with Claire. "Call Maggie and get one from her," she said. "Just call her up."

So I looked Maggie up in the phone book, called her, and asked about buying a copy of her book. "I have some copies here in my studio," she responded. "Come on out."

"Well, it's just past five. Is it still okay to drive out now?" I asked.

"Oh sure, honey. Come on out." Despite the friendly, upbeat invitation, I had no way of anticipating the pleasant surprise awaiting me.

---

1   Maggie Meredith, *Not Beyond Recall: Poems by Maggie Meredith* (Nantucket: October Press, 1989). Published poems quoted in this chapter are used by permission of Chris Meredith, executor of Maggie's estate.

Carefully watching for the house number, I slowly drove down Maggie's tree-lined sand road. Spotting the number, I turned into a driveway and saw Maggie's cottage-cum-studio nestled behind a grove of trees and surrounded by a lovely garden. I approached her porch and was greeted by a friendly painted wooden kitty perched on a rough bench. Then the screen door swept open, and Maggie was welcoming me with a broad smile, outstretched arms, and a hearty "Hi there. Come right in."

She escorted me inside, saying, "I was just going to have a glass of wine. Won't you join me?" I accepted a drink and sank into her white sofa, then spent the next ninety minutes enjoying the most interesting cocktail hour I've ever attended. Sitting in her space was like being in a cozy, private, and charming gallery accented by a beautifully arranged collection of perfectly fitted pieces and grounded by a collection of colorful hand-hooked rugs.

By the end of that conversation, after experiencing that environment of beauty and creativity, being entertained by a vivacious hostess, and then learning that Maggie was, in fact, eighty-five years old—she looked sixty, tops—I decided one visit would not be enough for me to tap into her recipe for positive aging.

Getting to Know Maggie

Maggie, like my other golden ladies, was a washashore and a widow. She and her husband, Stan, who had been gone fifteen years when I met her, had raised two sons: Greg, who had died in 1978, and Chris, who lived next door to her on the island.

Whenever I visited Maggie, I was struck by the way her dynamic qualities merged with the warmth and coziness reflected in her surroundings. Her brightly lit studio was filled with the trappings of an artist—brushes, paints, pencils, a large worktable with a small easel set on top of it, and shelves running across the studio's back wall. On my first visit, I noticed the book I wanted to purchase perched on display along with others she had written more recently. Above those was an array of postcards, small painted boxes, and plaques decorated in her unmistakable style.

A stand filled with colorful prints of Maggie's paintings marked the entrance to her living room. But the originals hung on the walls in glorious display. I recognized her signature cats, each one imagined as a unique character dressed in appropriate outfits and sporting stylish headgear—everything from fisherman cats to flapper cats. And filling the remaining spaces were paintings of whales. In its heyday, Nantucket was the whaling capital of the United States, and the whale is a traditional Nantucket icon. But Maggie's whales were far from traditional. They were a busy bunch—dining elegantly, playing cards, painting, or engaged in other leisure pursuits.

I discovered the roots of Maggie's talent as she pointed out items to me in her home. "Over the fireplace there is a picture my father painted. He was an artist." Shifting direction, she showed me another painting hanging over the threshold to her studio. "He did that one too."

Getting up, Maggie walked over to a long table that created a visual boundary with her dining room and retrieved a large, heavy, coffee-table book. Browsing through its glossy pages, she explained, "This was the companion book to my brother's exhibit at the Metropolitan Museum in New York." She went on to tell me they "had a big sign on the steps for the show of his work. Richard Pousette-Dart was his name. Unfortunately, he's dead now."

Maggie then guided me over to a wooden cupboard that her late husband Stan had built for her. She showed me a variety of items, including a sweet little book about a bear that her son Chris had made especially for her when he was a boy. Resting alongside it were photos of Stan as a child, a pair of her mother's old-fashioned button-up shoes, and other keepsakes that represented various aspects of her rich and eventful past.

"It's been a fun life," she told me. "Not the illness part of it, of course." She laughed. "But honestly, I've had a wonderful life. Wonderful."

Given this upbeat assessment, one might expect Maggie's life story to reflect mostly lightness and levity. What I heard instead was an intriguing candor about the various experiences she had faced in life. She said what she thought without any candy coating, presenting her personal challenges and difficulties quite openly and vulnerably. But there was no expectation of pity or sympathy. She simply wanted to tell her truth, her story.

An Artistic Upbringing

Maggie Pousette-Dart grew up in Valhalla, one of the afflu-ent Westchester suburbs of New York City. With her mother a poet and her father an artist, Maggie grew up surrounded by culture. She was particularly fond of her father, Nathaniel, who seemed to balance his love for Maggie, her sister, and her brother with his love for art and the beauty of nature. He gave of himself, and she felt unconditional love from him. On the other hand, Maggie told me, she wasn't at all close to her mother, Flora. "I found her very cold and unresponsive—intellectual. She was one of those child geniuses, and all the older people used to drool all over her. And she was an *only* child—ugh."

At some point in Maggie's young life, Flora moved to the third floor of their house to immerse herself in her work, and she made it clear she was not to be interrupted. Maggie's grandmother then stepped in to provide a mother's warmth and nurture in Maggie's young life. "Most of the years when I was growing up, [my mother's] mother lived with us, and I adored her. She was the one who was there for me, not my mother."

When I asked about Maggie's education, she confessed, "I quit high school, much to my grandmother's distress. I think I walked out and told the principal to go—you know. I was a very incorrigible child, no question about that." When asked whether she had had any formal art-school training or attended an art college, she offhandedly replied, "A couple of months at fashion school, but I didn't like it. No, college wasn't my thing. I did sell some designs for jewelry to Lord and Taylor—I think I was in my teens then."

That, as far as I could tell, summed up Maggie's formal education and training. However, her artist profile at the Artists Association of Nantucket provides a fascinating peek at how Maggie spent those formative years. She might not have been in school, but she was learning a lot.

> In High School I sang with a number of dance bands, and later in New York City I won a Deb singing contest at the El Morocco, a very elegant nightclub for several summers, and then decided that it was not the kind of life that I wanted. I spent a season at the Waldorf Astoria, dancing with a handsome partner in the Rainbow Room, until my parents met him, and that was the end of that adventure! Next I worked for my Father, who had an Advertising Agency in New York. It was fun for a while and then ceased to interest me. I traveled to Hollywood to spend some time with my [brother's ex-wife] who was under contract to Paramount. We were great friends and it was an eye-opening experience, but it didn't take me long to know that it was not the place that I wanted to be.[2]

Although Maggie is a contemporary of the other ladies, her experience of the two great events of her generation, the Great Depression and World War II, was very different. In a letter to me she wrote,

2   Quoted in "Maggie Meredith," artist profile, Artist Association of Nantucket, https://www.nantucketarts.org/index.php?q=meredith-maggie.html, accessed September 30, 2014.

I have no recollection of being affected in any way during the Depression—I was very fortunate. My brother was a conscientious objector—from his high-school days, not newly thought up when the purpose arose. My life was fortunately never affected by war! Although I do remember when my family let go of . . . a couple [who worked for us and] lived on the third floor. I was fifteen at the time—and every summer I would drive to visit them for I dearly loved them and they felt that I was their child. To me they were "Mammy and Uncle Willie."

"That's for Me"

Romance surfaced for Maggie when she was quite young. She married a man named Buddy, but the marriage was short-lived and ended in divorce. "He had this fantastic house—I think I fell in love with his house more than I fell in love with him. He was twelve years older," she added, laughing nervously.

The real and lasting romance in Maggie's life arrived while she was visiting with an artist friend named Connie—"She was old enough to be my mother. I adored her." This friend lived with her photographer husband in a part of upstate New York that Maggie described as "the woodsy, woodsy."

On one memorable visit, Maggie was out sunbathing in the meadow—"nude as always," she told me—when she heard a car coming up the drive. "I threw my clothes on, ran into the house to put makeup on, and that was when I met Stan." Stan, she learned, was a photographer as well. He and a colleague "had been shooting old churches in New York State and exploring their basements" and had decided to drop by.

Maggie was immediately smitten. "All I did was sit and look at him across the room, and Connie made breakfast." Maggie went on, with drama filling her voice and excitement lighting her face. "I took one look at that guy and said, 'That's for me.' There was no question. I thought, 'I'm going to get him.'"

Maggie expressed her feelings about Stan to her brother, Richard, telling him, "I fell so madly in love with him I can't stand it. I want to marry him. I want him for the rest of my life."

"Well, then," her brother said, "go and tell him just exactly how you feel."

"That was his advice," she told me. "So I did. I said, 'Listen, I'm madly in love with you.' That was that."

When I asked what Stan said, she responded with a look that said I must be blind to the obvious. "Well, we got married." Apparently Stan was a man of action as well as a man with a camera.

"Very Unconventional"

My given name is Margaret, and many Margarets—including my grandmother—are nicknamed Maggie. So I asked Maggie if she was a Margaret too.

She replied with eyes wide, "No. Helen Elizabeth. God, if that isn't ugly—ugh! Hate it. I can't remember when I became

Maggie. I think I named myself that—it just stuck. I feel like a Maggie."

With that answer in mind, I wasn't thrown—much—when I received the answer to my follow-up question: "Now, is Meredith your husband's last name?" Maggie replied, "As a matter of fact, Stan was some—I'm trying to think—of Polish background, and I can't remember what his name was when I met him. Some kind of Polish or foreignish name. So before we got married, we went to the phone book and"—she demonstrated how their fingers had circled around in the air and then landed on a spot on the page—"Meredith. So I became Maggie Meredith, and he was Stan Meredith."

My amazement must have transferred from my mind to my face, because Maggie nodded. "Very unconventional life," she said, and I quite agreed. I was learning that the unexpected was to be expected with Maggie.

During the first years of marriage, Maggie and Stan lived in a cottage on the grounds of her parents' home in Valhalla. Then they bought their first house in Pleasantville, New York. They had two little boys, who joined Stan in becoming what Maggie called the "loves of my life." During this time, Stan was working as a cameraman in the motion-picture business.

On one of our visits, Maggie leaned over and pointed to Stan's picture on the wall. I could definitely understand what she saw in him—he was a very handsome man. When I asked if Stan had been fun as well, she smiled. "Oh yeah. All of the gay guys adored him too. I had a lot of gay friends in the art community. Peter and Paul were our dearest friends."

The Salt of the Earth

One of the fascinating experiences that Maggie told me about happened when she joined Stan on location in New Mexico for a film called *The Salt of the Earth*. Her boys were little at the time, and Stan's parents were kind enough to take them to their home in Florida for the duration of the shoot. Maggie adored being with Stan and found the whole experience of being on the project fascinating.

"I had the most terrific time in my entire life," she told me, her face bright with enthusiasm. "While there, I became the script girl on [the film] because the one from Hollywood didn't show up, and I didn't know anything about it, but I took to it like a duck to water—I adored it. I worked directly with Herb Biberman, the director. . . . He liked the little sketches I made on the scripts."

Maggie and Stan stayed in New Mexico a few months, filming with the whole crew and living in a big castlelike lodge on the top of a hill. "Working with Herb Biberman was great," Maggie told me. "I even got a special letter from him. I'll have to show you. He took me to lunch and said he 'kind of fell in love' with me. But I said, 'Sorry, I can't make that trip. I'm in love with my husband.' Wonderful. I loved it."

Realizing how personally memorable this experience had been for Maggie, I became curious about the film, which I had never heard of. I suspected it might prove to be obscure or hard to find, but it turned out to be neither. In fact, *The Salt of the Earth* is both notable and historic. The Netflix website film write-up says this about it:

Director Herbert Biberman's prescient drama incited a furor upon its release with the political overtones in its story about the Mexican-Americans who went on strike to protest unsafe conditions and unfair treatment at New Mexico's Empire Zinc Mine. Presaging the civil rights and feminist movements, the 1954 film—the only one blacklisted in American history—paints a thought-provoking picture of the struggle by the miners and their families.[3]

With this unexpected revelation, I wanted to check back with Maggie, since she had been in the midst of its dramatic production in 1953. "Maggie, you were working on a historic and highly controversial movie—in the middle of the McCarthy era. *The Salt of the Earth* was the only film that was blacklisted for political content in American history. The film landed Biberman on the blacklist, and he was investigated and had to testify before the House Committee on Un-American Activities." I guess I thought I was telling her something she already knew but perhaps didn't appreciate. "Wow," I concluded, out of breath.

Maggie just laughed and emphasized again what a great experience she'd had working on it. She concurred that the movie was controversial and that it caused a great stir, but she assured me that Stan's career had not suffered at all because of it. She did tell me, however, that "toward the end . . . it got pretty scary and we had to get out of there—we were worried for our lives."

3   Netflix film blurb, http://dvd.netflix.com/Search?v1=%27Salt%20of%20 the%20Earth, accessed September 30, 2014.

An Island Artist

When I inquired as to what had brought Maggie to the island initially, she told me that her parents were the first in the family to buy a house on Nantucket. "Stan had a plane," she told me, so he would fly Maggie and the boys over for visits. They moved over to the island as their primary residence when Maggie was about thirty-five.

By that time, Maggie had been painting in earnest for about five years. When the family settled in Nantucket, she "quickly became part of the artists' community—didn't plan it or anything." She even placed some of her work in a Nantucket gallery and was amazed when her first painting sold.

"My youngest son came running home to say, 'Mom, somebody bought your painting.' I had seventy-five dollars on it; it was a watercolor. And I said, 'You must have made a mistake, honey.' 'No, no!' he yelled. He was so excited. After that I had another showing at the Little Gallery and then moved over for a number of shows to George Vero's."

Whenever I sat in Maggie's living room, I had trouble keeping my eyes off the vivid array of cleverly designed rugs scattered on her pine floors. "Did you make these?" I asked.

"Oh yes, of course," she told me. "I design and make at least one rug a year. It's a wonderful hobby, a great craft—useful too. In fact, Claire Murray was a good friend of mine in the old days. I taught her how to make rugs." Pointing to a few of the rugs, she said, "This is all her wool. She was selling it then."

(For those who don't know, Claire Murray started her business on Nantucket featuring hooked rugs that depicted "scenes and styles" of Nantucket life. Over the past twenty-five or more years, her business has expanded into an international retail and wholesale enterprise offering a large variety of home fashions.)

Pain and Poetry

In our various conversations, Maggie often brought up Stan's name in some way or other. "I had a wonderful, terrific, sexy husband," she often told me. "We had a great marriage." But their life together came to an end on their fortieth anniversary, when death showed up as an uninvited guest. Years later that "frozen moment of horror"[4] would still be etched in her memory.

"He died on one of our anniversaries—almost," she told me. "I mean, he's sitting across from me, and all of a sudden he went back and pffft." She fell silent for several breaths, remembering the shock of that moment. "They had to get the ambulance," she went on. "He died a few days after that. . . . And that was the end of him," she finished with a nervous laugh. But although Stan died in 1988, he remained alive in Maggie's thoughts, her speech, and in her writings.

Whenever Stan's name came up in conversation, Maggie always reiterated that "he was the love of my life" and that she had "adored him." She described their many years together as "forty short years." She also made it clear that he was her "dearest friend" and that his death meant losing a part of herself.

4 This quote and the "uninvited guest" idea are from Maggie's poem "October 30, 1988" in *Not Beyond Recall*, 38.

A loss of such depth and intimacy can be extremely difficult to overcome. But Maggie discovered something that would ease the struggle. A while after Stan's death, a good friend of Maggie's invited her to join a creative-writing class on the island. Having been an artist her entire adult life, she didn't view herself as a writer of any sort. But her friend persisted and encouraged her to get her feelings down on paper. Poetry soon became not only a creative outlet, but a way to process her pain.

Facing the first spring after losing Stan, for example, Maggie used her new poetic voice to capture her devastation in a poem called "Spring Returns":

> New beginnings everywhere—except within my heart
> there lives a cold and bitter silence.[5]

She went on to describe her feelings of profound loss in numerous poems, some of which she would publish in her subsequent books. In time, the process of writing about her loss would become a powerful tool for healing, her own words a bridge that carried her from sadness and tragedy into a new phase of life.

Searching for Answers

Losing Stan wasn't Maggie's first encounter with a devastating loss, however. Thirty years before I met her, she had suffered through one of the most wrenching experiences a

---

5 Meredith, *Not Beyond Recall*, 40.

mother can endure—the death of a child. Losing her older son, Greg, a talented musician who died young, was a devastating blow to Maggie.

Even many years after his death, Maggie's grief was still evident in her conversations with me and in her writing. "I think he did it himself," she told me, adding that she and Greg had conversed days before about his attempt to find answers for questions that haunted him. "He seemed to feel that it was much better there, wherever he was going. It was a shock."

The family contemplated leaving the island, but eventually decided against it, perhaps because so many came by to express their respect and love. "The whole island showed up," Maggie told me, clearly taking comfort in the memory. "Everyone knew Greg."

Hard put to understand what had happened, Maggie continued to look for answers over the years. This quest is also captured in her poetry. She found a measure of hope in the seasonal cycles of nature, for instance, hoping that somehow he would return to her. She included a poem entitled "Greg," which further explored this process.[6]

Maggie also tried to cope with losing Greg by turning to his favorite book. She held it in her hands and wrote about it, noting that Greg had searched there for answers and that she would search for them as well within its pages. During this quest Maggie found a connection with the "riches and

6 Ibid., 36.

beauties of life: love, friendship, and nature." In so doing, she found what she considered to be her answers. She described the process in her poem "A Much Loved Book."[7]

When dealing with their losses, many people find comfort in their faith or in religious rituals. I asked Maggie whether she held to any particular spiritual practice. "I wasn't brought up in any religion—my parents didn't belong to any religion. No, I am not affiliated." But then, almost as an afterthought, she commented, "All my dearest women friends are Catholic." She shook her head as if wondering how that fit together, then added, "And I've been writing the last four years to a rabbi. We became great friends. Young guy, thirty-eightish or forty. I have bags of his letters. He wants to be a doctor—that's what he's headed for. Sweet guy."

She also shared, "Mother was a hand reader. I sat and watched her read many, many, many hands. I sit here and think, 'Damn, I wish she was here.' So I got a book on palmistry. There it is," she said, pointing to a book on a nearby table. She never mentioned later whether she had mastered the art of palm reading.

In Touch

Maggie described herself as "a people lover," and I saw evidence of this every time we met. Our conversations were filled with the names of friends on-island and off, living and deceased: "She was in real estate." "She was so talented." "I

---

7 Maggie Meredith, *Footsteps in the Sand* (Nantucket: October Press, 1998).

wrote to her for years." She often finished these references with "She's gone now" or "We lost him." She told me, "They're dying one by one."

However sad that might have been, Maggie seemed to enjoy acknowledging the people who had been in her life and their notable qualities. She spoke with a combination of resignation and nostalgia, acknowledging nature's course and commenting, "You can't do anything about that."

Maggie enjoyed staying in touch with her friends through visits, phone calls, and letters. She maintained a connection with people she cared about, even those who lived far away. A faithful and enthusiastic correspondent, she had cultivated some of her pen pals for decades.

I was always delighted to receive a letter from Maggie. Discovering an envelope from her in my mailbox, addressed in her dramatic, flowing handwriting, always lifted my spirits. And then, tucked in the envelope, I often found a special bonus—perhaps a poem or a sketch that brought additional color and joy to my day.

In a letter to me with the very specific date of December 7, 2010, 7:20 a.m., she enclosed a newly minted poem entitled "A Bit of My Life." Beneath the typed copy was a brief handwritten note: "Thought you'd get a kick out of this! Love, Maggie Meredith."

> But I am happy to note that I do
>   get a lot accomplished.
> Printing out all that I have written—
> My thoughts, my feelings, my

happiness, my pain—
Turns into verse so I can't complain—
'Cause this is my life and I live it
the best that I can—
And I really don't do that badly—
Considering that I now live my life—
Without even a man!

I had to smile when I read the last lines of that poem. It reminded me of a conversation we'd had one fall when I was preparing to leave the island. All of Nantucket's seasonal residents (like me) return to their off-island homes before winter arrives. If they can, many of the year-round residents also retreat for a short time during the winter to somewhere warmer and less remote. I asked Maggie if she would be staying the winter. "Oh yeah, I'll be here. Chris and Linda [Maggie's son and daughter-in-law] might go. Maybe I'll try to find someone to come and keep me company. I'll find some tall, dark, and handsome man. I miss a man in my life, I can tell you—I really miss a man. Something about a man." She laughed. "Nothing can imitate it!"

In the spring of 2011, I received a darling picture that Maggie had rendered in pen, ink, and pastels on a letter-sized piece of typing paper. One of her dashing cats filled the center of the page, dressed—as all of Maggie's creations were—with special flair. This particular kitty wore a blue scarf, fancy beads, and a pink flower pinned to her lapel, and her wide-brimmed hat was decorated with a blue band and yellow spring flowers. Surrounding the cat portrait were the words,

"I am the beginning of spring 2011, Love, Maggie Meredith." What a creative way to stay connected with friends and celebrate spring, a season that is always welcome after the gray and windy winters on Nantucket.

Another envelope contained a sketch of her bluebird of happiness—a signature design element almost as well known and loved as her cats—and a slogan: "Love, Love, Love—My Crazy Bird of Happiness Is Always with Me." The accompanying letter reflected my friend's amazing creative energy: "I might hook a rug of this [design] this winter."

Yet another note from Maggie informed me, "My computer gave up last week. I am now learning how to use the new one." I think we can all relate to tackling that life challenge. It's not for the faint of heart. And whatever Maggie Meredith might have been, fainthearted she was not.

Aloneness and Loneliness

During one of my visits with Maggie, I learned that an old friend of hers was staying as a houseguest and would be with her until a summer rental became available. Maggie described her as a "great gal, but a chatterbox." Then we talked about the special pleasure of being with friends but also the necessity of having time alone.

Maggie explained, "She understands me, which is good—necessary" in a friendship. "We are both early risers. In the morning, of course, I listen to the news and the market"—Maggie enjoyed keeping up with the stock market—"and I do a lot of writing then."

Shuffling through her papers, Maggie pulled out a poem she had just written. Entitled "My Life Today," it addressed the topic we were just discussing. She read it aloud to me:

> Aloneness has become part of who I am today.
> I live in a silent world, and some I can create.
> Mornings, mainly I wear my thinking cap,
>> deciding what the day will offer
>> in terms of new ideas or paintings.
> It's a silence I have grown used to;
>> it has nothing to do with the love of my friends.
> I need them just as much as always, just on my schedule.

She then commented, "I need to be alone. I'm used to it." And she told me that it was during her alone time that she tapped into her muses. "I write about most everything that goes on—how I feel, what I view."

Aloneness, of course, is not the same as loneliness. But aging often means the loss of lifelong partners and dear friends, and dense feelings of loneliness can blanket those who survive.

Maggie was no exception. She told me that loneliness was "a real presence in my life" and addressed the topic in several of her poems.

But in speaking with Maggie and reading her poetry, I could see she used her solitary time to do the necessary work of self-reflection and creative thought. And when loneliness did cross her threshold, Maggie chose to step into the pain, using her alone time to shed her tears, mourn, and express anger. In the poem called "Tragedy," for instance, she spoke to the idea that "everyone must confront their tragedies alone."[8] And in "Pain" she affirmed,

> So everyone needs
> time alone
> to allow their
> pain to escape.
> To let their tears flow.[9]

For Maggie, however, this place of solitary mourning was not a destination, but an expected stopover along the greater route of life. Even within the context of the loss, Maggie eventually stepped back into her active, busy, and creative routine, recognizing that she had "so much living still to be done."[10]

In fact, Maggie often used her alone times to engage in what she called "getting myself together," so she could figure out what she wanted to do next. She referred to these times in "The Puzzle," which concludes with the line, "I search for the pieces that might make me whole."[11]

Fun, Work, and Happiness

When I asked Maggie what she liked to do for fun, she replied, "Fun? Hmm." She contemplated briefly, then responded with enthusiasm, "Fun. Seeing people I like, having the studio, fun

8 Meredith, *Not Beyond Recall*, 21.
9 Ibid., 12.
10 Meredith, "Being Alive," *Footsteps in the Sand*, 31.
11 Ibid., 27.

painting, fun writing—whatever I do is fun because I only do what's fun for *me*. I'm very fortunate. I know that."

That statement confirmed what she had written about her work in a letter to me: "The days just aren't long enough. I have been doing *a lot* of writing and also started a new cat painting. No question that the creative paths that we create for ourselves keep us the happiest."

Maggie was a firm believer in work as a resource for dispelling fears or worries, and I saw that dynamic at work in one of our last visits. Her eyes shone as she described some of the projects she was working on at the time. Because she had previously mentioned the idea of a "cat book," I asked about it. "That's one of the possibilities," she responded. (That book came to fruition. Published by October Press in 2010, it was entitled *Maggie's Cat House*.) She then told me about some of the other book ideas she was contemplating, including "*Life Like a River,* with paintings I have done over the years on each page."

Unfortunately, she told me, technical difficulties had made the quality and clarity of the pictures an issue in terms of publishing. Not discouraged, she began rifling through her pages of poems she had dashed off, telling me, "I write and write and write—I can't stop." Reading aloud to me, she said, "Here's one I wrote this morning while sitting on the deck."

> Thoughts run through my head,
>   silent endless packages of thoughts in my head.
> No time, no days, no years separate them.

They remain all together
and I'm able at any time to find them again.

Though Maggie's work often offered her opportunities for fun, it held more than merely enjoyment for her. In her book *Footsteps in the Sand,* two poems clearly present what meaningful roles work can play in a person's life. In a poem actually entitled "Work,"[12] she included a reminder to herself and a suggestion to others about its value in overcoming fears and displacing tears. And in the poem "Sometimes," she stated that work can serve as an antidote to the negatives of life and become a source of happiness.[13] She even delivered a little pep talk to herself in that poem, explaining that her happiness emanated from her work, that her work was capable of filling her current voids, and that it would grant her perspective and displace the unimportant.

This view of work was congruent with Maggie's firm belief in self-agency—that is, taking responsibility for ourselves and being willing to initiate necessary action. In particular, she felt each of us is in the driver's seat when it comes to our own well-being. With Maggie there was no blaming anyone else, no sense of victimhood. In her poem "Get a Life," she expressed it this way:

We alone are the keepers of
our own happiness—
And only we can provide ourselves

12 Ibid., 12.
13 Ibid., 53.

with new exciting ways of
thinking, and living creatively.[14]

In other words, as the title to yet another of her poems summarizes, "It's Up to You."[15]

Savoring the Moment

The theme of time wound throughout Maggie's mature narrative, both in print and discourse. She often compared moments to raindrops with respect to their penchant for slipping out of sight as well as our inability to hold them.[16] Her personal advice to me was to savor what moments I had as I was experiencing them, for "they will not return." And she demonstrated her own capacity for savoring precious moments—not only in the present, but in her memory as well. I witnessed her spirit's uptick when she reminisced and shared some of the wonderful moments she had with Stan. On those occasions, I felt her energy increase and her warmth expand.

Maggie's acute sense of the finite nature of time was always present as a backdrop to our visits. When describing time she had spent with a friend, she remarked, "Boy, how the time does fly." She also expressed that concept in her poem "Dwindling" as she visualized the hands of her life's clock

Picking up speed
hour by hour—

14 Maggie Meredith, *Within the Silence* (Nantucket: October Press, 2006), 45.
15 In Maggie Meredith, *Capture the Fireflies* (Nantucket: October Press, 1995, 53.
16 Her poem "Time" expresses that concept beautifully. See Meredith, *Not Beyond Recall,* 2.

> Leaving smaller
>   and smaller
>   amounts of time
> In which I have left
>   to live my life![17]

I could relate to that feeling. It's a common sensation for all of us as we age. But Maggie's main concern was not the quantity of time available, but the quality of time spent. "Don't be careless with your moments," she urged me. "Make each moment count."

Poignantly aware of the fleeting nature of beauty around us, Maggie once told me about seeing her daughter-in-law's horse walk by and fearing "for the day when he will no longer be here."

Then she burst out laughing. "Come to think of it, neither will I."

Sustaining Gifts

To most of us, home is an essential element in sustaining our well-being. Finding the right living arrangement can be crucial to well-being in our senior years. The ideal situation is one that allows us to fully engage in and enjoy life, permitting the optimal balance of freedom and security. Maggie's son, Chris, had helped her secure just such a situation. He

---

17 Meredith, *Footsteps in the Sand*, 26.

encouraged her as she worked with an architect to codesign her lovely studio/cottage combination, which was situated on the property adjacent to his home. Maggie always spoke with deep affection and love for her son and his wife, Linda. In glowing superlatives, she told me of how wonderfully they took care of her while respecting her independence.

Maggie had not always enjoyed the fullness of health, and on one of our visits we talked about some significant medical challenges she had recently faced. Recalling one serious incident, she exclaimed, "Linda brought me back to life! I had been eating some peanuts and began choking, leaning back in my chair. Linda saw me as she was taking care of all my plants. Linda gave me artificial respiration, and they got me to the hospital. Most incredible woman I have ever met," she said emphatically. "I adore her!"

Maggie told me the choking incident was her fifth hospitalization in four years—she'd been in for pneumonia, babesiosis, and a mastectomy. "It's been one damn thing after the other," she laughed. Then, exhibiting her skill for putting life into perspective, she reached behind her to pull out an unpublished poem she had written about her mastectomy experience. Bottom line for Maggie—it was all about putting one breast in the perspective of her total life and that her life had a purpose. The last lines read,

> So life goes on and what will be, will be,
>   for I'm not ready to see the end of me!

Then in a later letter she wrote that "when needed—I can be strong," referring to the choice she had made to have additional surgery. She did so, she said, in order to "have a few more years of living a joyful, creative, and happy life."

A Perfect Legacy

Late in the fall of 2012, I received an upbeat note from Maggie announcing her latest news. *N* magazine, Nantucket's outsized glossy publication, had done a feature article on Maggie entitled "An Artist at Ninety." I immediately hopped onto the magazine's website and located the article about Maggie. Wanting my own hard copy of this tribute to my friend, I called the offices of *N,* and they generously mailed me a copy.

In the midst of the excitement, I had almost overlooked the new return address Maggie had put on her letter—no longer her usual home address, but an independent and assisted-living property on the island. Her note made no mention of what had precipitated her move. After failing to reach Maggie by phone, I wrote a letter to congratulate her on the exciting magazine spread.

That was my last communication with Maggie. When I didn't hear back, I expected she might be busy or was dealing with a medical issue. Then I was faced with my own health issue during the spring and was unable to keep in touch. However, I kept abreast of the on-island news via the *Inky Mirror,* and I looked forward to connecting in person with Maggie when I arrived on Nantucket for the summer of 2013.

Not long after I arrived on the island, I was dashing down Center Street one day and noticed some of Maggie's distinctive work in the window of the Nantucket Artworks gallery. I returned a little while later when I had more time to enjoy the exhibit. When I inquired about Maggie, the gallery owner broke the sad news. Maggie had died on December 18, 2012.

In keeping with Maggie's wishes, there had been no ceremonies or formal obituaries. Instead, her son and daughter-in-law had placed a small notice in the *Inky Mirror* that included one of her poems about love. And I had missed it.

I was shocked and saddened at the loss of my vivacious friend. But I agreed completely with Chris and Linda's choice of a poem for the notice. It sums up Maggie's outlook on love and the realities of moving on—the perfect legacy poem from this talented golden lady of mine.

To Love Enough

> How lovely to believe
>   that every day we leave
> A part of who we are
>   with someone
>   who will remember
>   the moments that we share.
> How lovely to believe
>   that when we move on
>   the memory of us
>   will not be gone—
> But remain alive
>   in the thoughts of those

who cared enough—
who loved enough—
To make us last forever.[18]

Gifts from Maggie

With her characteristic flair, Maggie provided me with a hearty dose of inspiration for vibrant aging. She modeled for me numerous life-affirming strategies that I can apply in my later years. Maggie faced many of the difficulties that accompany a long life, and she earned my respect not only for her endurance, but also for her insistence on living fully and exploring life in all its shades of color and range of shadow. I'm grateful that she shared her journey with me.

We all encounter change and loss in our later years, and Maggie certainly faced her share: the loss of her husband, the death of her young son, and multiple health issues in her last years. But Maggie wasn't intimidated. She took on the challenges with courage and energy, and I loved her feisty spirit. I also found it interesting to see how she was able to accept the realities of aging and not waste precious energy fighting them, as so many people try to do. Instead of fighting her circumstances, she used her energy in constructive and creative ways to enrich her life as it was.

Maggie taught me something of the power of celebration. Instead of letting her losses get her down, she chose to celebrate a past filled with beloved people who were no longer with her. But she celebrated the present too, acknowledging

18 Meredith, *Not Beyond Recall*, 53.

all the good things she still had. In her poetry and her conversations with me, she expressed her courageous intent to live life fully. Refusing to let herself stagnate, she acted on whatever possibility she saw, whether it was writing a new poem or designing her next rug or painting a new picture.

Maggie was a strong woman who took full responsibility for her own happiness. She believed in personal agency and never saw herself as a victim. She had retained the personal power she possessed in her earlier life, and she deliberately tapped into it as a source of strength for the course ahead of her.

Maggie also had a good understanding of who she was and what she needed to survive and thrive. She grasped the importance of self-care—another aspect of self-agency, and something we coaches continually address with clients. She also drew on her artistic and poetic talents to develop powerful skills for self-nurture. (Building on your strengths and values to reach your goals is foundational in life coaching.)

Maggie illustrated this process when she frequently accessed the many wonderful memories she and Stan had made together. Tapping into her memories, she used her imaginative skills to create and enjoy a place of peace and happiness in her mind, a place where she and Stan could "visit together." In so doing, Maggie was able to provide a soothing and serene experience for herself at any given moment—a kind of portable mood enhancer. She described this eloquently in a poem called "Stan":

There are times
when I disappear
into the past and
I find you
waiting there for me.
I suddenly see
the whole of you again
Just as if you'd never left!
What a fantastic world
   I can create—
And through my imagination
   bring you back again.[19]

Maggie's deep and joyful sense of gratitude surfaced in nearly all of our visits. She was always telling me in some way or another how fortunate she was or what a good life she'd had. She acknowledged her good fortune without taking it for granted or making herself sound entitled. That exercise in gratitude also provided her with those warm, positive feelings that nourish the soul.

Time was an important commodity for Maggie, as it is for those in the final third of life. She often spoke and wrote about time, reminding both herself and others to make the most of what time we had and cautioning us to not squander it. She also practiced and emphasized the importance of savoring the moment—sage advice from a wise and experienced woman.

Maggie applied that wisdom as she navigated the realities of being alone at this stage of life. She understood and leveraged the roles both solitude and loneliness could play *for*

19 Meredith, *Within the Silence*, 1.

her, not just *against* her. She used her solitary hours to grieve or work through the difficult issues she felt she needed to process by herself, but she also employed those alone times as creative vessels for planning, writing, or painting. I found it quite interesting to observe the artist as pragmatist and the dynamic results of her creative realism.

Maggie also recognized the importance of balancing solitude with socialization. She put effort into remaining in touch with old friends, actively socializing locally, and maintaining her studio/shop, all sources for the different levels of the stimulating social contact she wanted and needed.

As an artist, of course, Maggie had long ago mastered the art of perspective—not just in her painting, but also in her view of life. When a conversation took a negative turn, she always seemed to counter with positive views. I witnessed this habit during the instances when she talked about the difficult experiences in her life. She was always careful to offset her frank discussion of pain with an expression of gratitude or humor or by pointing to the gifts and joys she had known or could anticipate. When the glass was half-empty, Maggie would shift her perspective to make it half-full.

She also taught me something else about perspective when she described how she kept life's little annoyances from growing into worries and obsessions. Her solution was to get to work or to create something. Once her focus shifted to work, she said, her perspective would shift as well, and she'd see that those petty distractions were unimportant in the greater scheme of things.

That's not to say that Maggie ignored or denied reality. Quite the opposite. She named her difficulties candidly or, as she put it, "real, rich, straight, honest." But she always followed her acknowledgments of pain with a spunky "Buck up, girl—you can deal with this!" self-lecture. Then she seemed to nudge herself back into action, moving forward and not retreating.

"You have to tackle the tough stuff in life and not let it get you down," she once told me. How very inspiring to have both your own special recipe for resilience and the fortitude to use it.

Here's the familiar pattern for living that I saw in Maggie: look at life, acknowledge the rough parts, mourn if needed, give yourself a pep talk, acknowledge the gifts that came with the pain, and keep on living life as fully as possible. With exquisite panache she lived out the words she spoke to me one day as a special benediction: "Life is about keeping busy, honey—and involved, interested, and appreciative."

When my mind turns to Maggie, I see a guide for facing my own aging challenges, and I am grateful she became one of my golden ladies. In fact, I am convinced that Maggie and her work could embody the curriculum for a course on positive aging and well-being. Her poetry could serve as a rich resource and text. If only Maggie could appear as the guest instructor, it would never be a boring course!

MAGGIE'S GALLERY

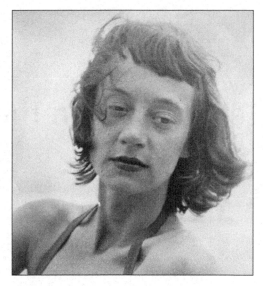

The young, intriguing Maggie (1940s).

Maggie's charming spring
greeting to me in 2011.

Maggie in her cottage
studio and home
(early 2000s).

CHAPTER 7

Reflections on the Journeys: My Thoughts

As this book project evolved, I found it interesting to explore how my personal experience—as an aging baby boomer and as a friend of my golden ladies—has interacted with my professional one—as a life coach specializing in retirement issues.

My connection with the ladies started out as personal, of course. We met and became friends. Then I was struck by the way their lives could shine light on my professional studies. I became immersed in talking to the ladies, listening to the recordings of our conversations, rereading their letters, observing their lives and actions, and comparing what I learned from them with what the experts say about positive aging.

Meanwhile, the world turned a good many times, and I continued my own aging journey. Over time I found myself gaining a new appreciation for the privileges of being a first-hand observer of my ladies' lives—the depth of their spirits and their examples of how to remain in a place of well-being despite so many challenges. This experience grew into more than simple friendship and a professional enhancement for me. It became a profound source of inspiration and application.

I and so many of my fellow baby boomers (born between 1946 and 1964) have always tended to see the future spread endlessly before us. That's how it felt, at least. Then, via either a dramatic incident or a slow creeping into our consciousness, we realized that those distant horizons were no longer far away. The great expanse of options we had always anticipated seemed to shrink somewhat, and for the first time we found ourselves needing to deal with certain limitations, some feelings of diminishing control or decreased potency.

At the same time, our society's culture of youth—which began with our own generation—tended to reinforce negative perceptions of aging. We were not programmed to seek the positives in growing older. As a result, many of us have bought into old paradigms and limiting assumptions that don't allow for the fullness of possibility in our later years.

All of this negative energy can create discomfort and raise a lot of questions. How are we going to manage this looming transition? Is it really possible to grow old with grace and positivity, to look at aging honestly and still find the silver linings?

In both my professional life and my experiences with the ladies, I have come to believe the answer is yes. A broader, balanced, and more positive view of aging does exist, and the reality of it is definitely achievable. My golden ladies demonstrated by both their actions and their attitudes that it is possible to keep their personal life ledgers tilted to the positive side and, just as important, that growth and positive change don't have to stop with retirement.

Recent brain and behavioral research bears this out. Studies in neuroplasticity—the ability of our brains to change and to open new neural pathways even as we age—give reason to believe that the choices we make can have an influence on how we experience later life.

In his book *The Mature Mind,* renowned psychiatrist and gerontologist Gene Cohen introduces the term *developmental intelligence* to describe what he sees as "the greatest benefit of the aging brain/mind."[1] According to Cohen, "developmental intelligence reflects the maturing synergy of cognition, emotional intelligence, judgment, social skills, life experience and consciousness . . . and, as with all intelligence, we can actively promote its growth."[2]

Cohen goes on to explain that "the brain actively grows and rewires itself in response to stimulation and learning" all through life.[3] In other words, with such stimulation and

1 Gene D. Cohen, *The Mature Mind: The Positive Power of the Aging Brain* (New York: Basic Books, 2005), xix.
2 Ibid.
3 Ibid., 7.

learning, our brains can change even in our later years, as can the attitudes and actions impelling us forward. This means the possibility exists to shift to more positive and optimal living no matter our age.

That's not to say that growing old is always a pleasant experience. The physical changes that come with age—decreased strength and mobility, diminishing senses, decline in energy, age-related health problems—can be difficult or even painful. So can related changes in circumstance such as the loss of friends, family, or independence. Nevertheless, the consensus of both my ladies and the experts in the field is that a "negative only" perspective is shortsighted, counterproductive, and simply untrue. Much potential for positivity exists in the next season of life. Whether or not they are golden years, these decades can indeed have silver linings.

The women in this book did not deny negative realities. They faced them, they mourned them or worked through their anger about them, and then they chose to let the negative go. When they could, they expressed gratitude for what they'd had and lost and also for what they had now that might be lost in the future. But then—and this is key—they widened their perspectives and explored new possibilities.

As Lilma so astutely observed, "You have to look for the good!" That is what my ladies chose to do time and again, and they taught me it is possible to do just that. For me—and I hope for you too—they have served as invaluable guides on a path we all must take.

The value of mentors and role models[4] has long been recognized in our society. When we enter a strange new territory,
it is always helpful to be able to look to others who have been
where we are going and can provide some tips and tools for
navigating our own unique journeys.

The importance of following such guides is particularly
recognized and emphasized for the life stages of childhood
and adolescence. We all want our children to have good role
models to follow and mentors to support their development.
Perhaps you can recall people in your early life or at the start
of your career who might have shared their expertise and
showed you how to operate in unfamiliar environments.

Businesses, educational and religious institutions, and civic
organizations have long accepted the concept that one-on-one
modeling can be a powerful way to impart important attitudes and illustrate possibilities for navigating a particular set
of tasks, a job, or a phase of life. Only recently, however, have
we begun to recognize that the importance of mentoring and
modeling doesn't stop with early adulthood or middle age. It
also applies to the more recently recognized developmental
stage of mature adulthood and to old age as well.

It should be clear by now that I consider my golden ladies
to be stellar models and mentors for later life. I created this
book (with their cooperation) so that their stories might help

---

4   Technically, there is a difference between a role model and a mentor, though
    both can serve as important guides. A role model is a person who inspires
    us, someone we aspire to emulate. We may or may not know that person.
    Mentoring, on the other hand, always requires a personal and intentional
    relationship. Mentors share their experience and often offer specific guidance.
    The women described in this book filled both functions for me.

others as well. It is not intended to be a comprehensive guide to the later years. But I hope my ladies' words and examples will help start your own internal conversation about enhancing the next stage of your life.

What qualities do these ladies model that can help those of us who are following in their footsteps? I've touched on them in the individual profiles, but here I would like to explore these qualities a little further from a coaching perspective. All are amply recognized in the professional literature as important in promoting well-being and positive aging.

Self-Knowledge

All the ladies, by the time I had met them, had a good handle on who they were, what their needs were, and what was important to them, but they also realized the necessity of revisiting these areas and redefining or reprioritizing as their situations changed.

At age ninety-two, facing significant health issues, Claire decided she needed to make herself her own number-one priority—in contrast to the years when she actively mothered her ten children. She continued to be a mother, of course, but she saw the need to shift some of her efforts toward herself.

Maggie did a similar thing when she orchestrated her days to balance alone time with the social time she needed. Her understanding of the need and her ability to make sure that need was met required a keen degree of self-knowledge.

Whenever I take on new retirement and transition clients, I begin the coaching process with activities designed to foster self-knowledge. I invite the clients to introduce themselves to me and, more important, to get to know themselves better by clarifying their *values* and acknowledging their *strengths*. Values play an important role in defining personal goals and providing energy and motivation to reach the goals, while strength identification supports the development of strategies to attain those goals. So recognizing them both is key to helping clients define, align, and execute their plans for the next life stage.

Commitment to Self-Care

Claire's decision to make herself a priority also pointed to another foundational component in the philosophy and practice of life coaching: self-care. This is not the same thing as selfishness, and collapsing the distinction between the two can lead to misunderstandings, guilt, and blame. Self-care is a vital component of health and well-being.

One of the best real-life examples of this concept can be found in the safety instructions flight attendants deliver before takeoff. Those traveling with a small child or someone else in need of assistance are told to put on their own oxygen masks before helping the dependent person, ensuring that they can effectively function and take care of the other person. That is not a selfish act.

Selfish means taking care of oneself to the exclusion of others' well-being. *Self-care*, on the other hand, means taking care of oneself in order to function properly and be available to attend to others if needed.

The practice of self-care can be looked at from other perspectives as well. Jane saw self-care as a way to honor the God who had created her and therefore to bear witness to her faith. Maggie believed that each of us is responsible for our own well-being and that we all need to attend to that task without guilt.

What did my golden ladies do to care for themselves? Maggie knew she needed her alone time to regroup, to refresh, and, when needed, to mourn her losses. She made that happen. Both Claire and Lilma chose to limit their television and reading choices in order to maintain their sense of well-being and deflect unnecessary stress. Jane told me that she modified her diet to reflect her health needs, choosing not to eat some foods she liked because they tended to cause her physical distress.

Healthy self-care does not preclude getting assistance from others when it makes sense to do so. After all, getting the help you need *is* self-care. I was impressed by the way all my ladies handled this sometimes delicate balancing act between maintaining independence and seeking the help they needed, whether from family, from friends, or in an assisted-living situation. They did what they could for themselves but faced the reality of what they could no longer do and took responsibility for arranging help.

Adjustable Perspective

The ability to look at a situation from more than one angle can be a powerful tool for facing the future. I saw my ladies make good use of this tool again and again. They chose to take a broader view of their circumstances and tried to see the positive as well as the negative, the big picture as well as the details. So when something upsetting or awful happened, they were able to escape the narrow trap of viewing it as personal, permanent, or pervasive. They did not paint the picture with the broad brush of "disaster only."

Claire, especially, was intentional about this kind of perspective adjustment. When she talked of turning "a page in my book of life," she was really putting each experience in the context of a larger whole. Seeing the situation as merely one page in a very long book helped her move on from her troubles and acknowledge that, on the whole, "life is good."

Focus on the Good

For one reason or another, my golden ladies had learned to look for the good in all their circumstances—focusing on the beauty and blessing that touched their lives, drawing on these good things for a sense of warmth and well-being, and leveraging the good things to help them cope with the inevitable bad that came their way. This is the essence of gratitude, and it's an essential skill for positive aging.

Each of the women had health issues, for instance, but they chose not to dwell on them. Claire told me that specifically one day after ticking off the parts of her body that no longer worked right: "Ah, but you don't focus on that." Instead, she and the other women expanded their positive feelings by focusing on the many things for which they were thankful—

the good things they'd enjoyed or were still enjoying in their lives. This practice has been shown to have positive benefits for both mental and physical health and well-being.

Healthy Use of Memories

My golden ladies developed an excellent way to preserve their positive energy, lift their mood, and enhance their feelings of well-being: they regularly "visited" their good memories. They also laid groundwork for these memory journeys by savoring their present good experiences. Appreciating and enjoying life in the present helps imprint and lay down strong positive memories for the future, actually creating stronger neural pathways in the brain. The ongoing practice of retrieving those memories only reinforced the positive pathways.

All of the ladies made frequent memory "visits" and in so doing found warmth and peace. Thus, Maggie had wonderful times with her Stan, and Estelle heard, smelled, and felt the joy of Christmas with her family in frigid Michigan. They tapped their senses, employed visualization to paint the pictures in their minds, and used the good feelings of the past to enrich their present.

But although the ladies used their memories frequently and intentionally, they also used them *selectively*—specifically choosing the remembrances that would serve them in a positive way and refusing to dwell on the negative or painful ones. They remained grounded in reality, not living in the past, but using memories for present enhancement.

Willingness to Let Go

If you were planning a long hike, you would gather your gear and carefully consider what you wanted to take with you—what would be useful and what would just add weight. Then you would leave behind anything that might slow you down and impair your journey.

Lightening one's mental and emotional load can also be a significant and ongoing process in life, and these five ladies executed it with grace. They chose to leave behind or let go of negative memories, draining or nonessential activities, unnecessary possessions, and so forth to conserve their energy and make their ongoing life journeys a little easier.

But letting go is not just a matter of clearing out the extraneous and nonessential in our surroundings, our schedules, and our lives. It's also a necessary component of dealing with involuntary loss—and most people find that such losses increase in number as they age. Through no choice of their own, these ladies had been forced to let go of loved ones, friends, full health—all of which they would have loved to have retained. But their chosen response to such involuntary loss was to acknowledge it, mourn it, adopt a grateful attitude for what they'd had, and then eventually let go and move forward.

They were not living in denial, nor did they forget. They honored those loved ones they had lost and fully acknowledged the role each had once played in their lives. They were grateful for the beneficial aspects of their lives that were no longer there, and they kept a part of what they had loved and lost tucked inside their hearts and memories. But they still made the choice to move forward, looking to the present and the future for other possibilities that might fill a void or provide for any needs that would arise. As for regrets, Claire's advice was to the point: "Cremate the past, but take a lesson."

Use of Self-Talk and Visualization

All of my ladies had discovered an important reality: we can all be our own ever-ready cheerleaders through the use of self-talk and visualization. Whether we do it out loud or internally, we can actually talk ourselves into a better attitude or positive action, and we can enhance our feeling of well-being by picturing ourselves where we want to be.

Claire, especially, was the queen of positive self-talk. She'd started giving herself little encouraging talks when she was a child, and these talks continued into her nineties: "If you go through life telling yourself you can't, you can't, you can't—you can't!" Maggie did this too, frequently reminding herself to "buck up" and not feel sorry for herself.

The women also employed visualization, not only for their memory visits, but also to picture a good outcome for themselves in the next steps of their lives. Estelle employed that technique when she faced medical procedures: she would ease her mind by visualizing calm and positive outcomes. I am convinced it was her willingness and ability to do so that helped her to enjoy such a degree of well-being well into her nineties.

Resilience and Adaptability

Estelle was a prime example of someone whose attitude and approach to life reflected both resilience and the ability to adapt to life's changes and demands. "I can make do," she told me repeatedly. This didn't mean that she "settled." It meant she was proactive and persistent in addressing her problems but flexible in the way she addressed them. Again and again when life knocked her down, she got back up. If something wasn't working in her life, she tried something else.

Many people believe resilience is an inborn trait—if you didn't get it at birth, you won't have it later. Not so. Studies by such psychologists as Al Siebert, director of the Resilience Center, and Robert Brooks, a faculty member at Harvard Medical School, show convincingly that resilience can be developed and strengthened.[5]

Cultivating open thinking (wider perspectives) and being willing to adjust one's views or plans as necessary are important components of resilience. On the file cabinet in my office, I have a magnet that says, "We cannot direct the winds, but we can adjust our sails." That is what these women did. They didn't expend lots of energy shaking their fists at the wind when adversity hit. Instead, they set to work adjusting their sails. The optimistic overall attitude they adopted also contributed to their resilience.

5 See Al Siebert, *The Resiliency Advantage: Master Change, Thrive Under Pressure, and Bounce Back from Setbacks* (San Francisco: Berrett-Koehler, 2005) and Robert Brooks and Sam Goldstein, *The Power of Resilience: Achieving Balance, Confidence, and Personal Strength in Your Life* (Chicago: Contemporary Books, 2003). Both books contain exercises and activities to help readers develop resilience.

Self-Agency

Self-agency is the willingness to assume responsibility and take the initiative in one's own life. The ladies all continued to do this in their later years; they didn't lean exclusively on others to make things happen for them.

Maggie was a firm proponent of this approach, claiming, "We are the keepers of our own happiness." Claire moved to the island in her eighties. Jane made the quick decision to move into the Homestead when she realized the time had come. And Estelle's advice was "Take a chance. If it doesn't work out, something will come up." Even at their advanced age, these women were the drivers in their own lives.

Taking the initiative, however, did not mean the ladies were opposed to accepting help. Maggie relied on her son Chris and his wife, Linda. Claire leaned on Wizza and her other children. Lilma relied not only on her children and neighbors, but on her church family. Jane and Estelle eventually moved to places where they could receive support on a regular basis. But even then, the ladies retained their willingness to take initiative when appropriate. Often, in fact, choosing to accept limitations and seek out help can be a manifestation of self-agency.

Social Connection

Old age can easily lead to isolation. But each of my golden ladies was intentional about maintaining social connections that both sustained them and allowed them to sustain others. Such interaction is considered an extremely important factor in maintaining a sense of well-being in later life.

The ladies' social interactions could span the continent and cross the ocean via mail, e-mail, and phone calls, or they could remain within the closer ranges of residence, church, and community. Either way, these connections allowed the ladies to exchange ideas with others, to serve and be served, and to be fed intellectually, spiritually, and emotionally.

Humorous Outlook

Humor involves so much more than being funny or cracking jokes. It's an attitude, a coping mechanism, and a deliberate choice not to take life or oneself too seriously. It is also widely recognized as a significant enhancer of well-being at all ages and a quality associated with healthy aging. My ladies relied on humor to lift their moods and move them forward. They were often ready with a laugh and an outlook that included humor.

Estelle and Claire were the comedians in the group, of course, employing witty repartee or puns to entertain themselves and others and to keep things light. As I have mentioned, Claire's gift for humor in particular was a great inspiration for me and showed me a lighter way to cope with my own challenges.

But Jane and Lilma also showed good humor in their readiness to smile and their tendency to point out amusing happenings within the community, their churches, or their families. They might not have generated the fun, but they saw it, shared it, and used it to lighten their own spirits and those of friends. In Maggie's case, humor often took the form of whimsy, captured in her clever paintings of whales and her beloved cats.

Creativity

Maggie, of course, was a talented and imaginative professional who kept creating poems and paintings until the day she died. But all the ladies participated in numerous creative outlets: painting, drawing, quilting, needlework, poetry, scrapbooking, rug hooking, baking, music, dollhouses, letter writing, and decorating their homes. They also approached life creatively, seeking out new or unique ways of addressing problems and resolving issues. They beautifully illustrated Dr. Gene Cohen's claim that engaging in generative activities— those that involve creating something new—can have positive impact on mental and physical health.[6]

Commitment to "Use It or Lose It"

"Use it or lose it" is more than a casual phrase, especially as we age. Exercising our mental and physical abilities not only adds to our sense of mastery and well-being, but also helps keep our minds and bodies functional.

Jane certainly counts as someone who used her mind well and wanted to learn more. She continued her study of the Bible both alone and in organized Bible studies. She also intentionally exercised her brain through puzzles, games, and reading— not to mention studying nanotechnology at age ninety-one!

Jane was not alone in her quest for learning, however. All the ladies were curious about people, events, and the world

---

6   Cohen addresses this in *The Mature Mind* and focuses more specially on the subject in *The Creative Age: Awakening Human Potential in the Second Half of Life* (New York: HarperCollins Quill, 2000).

around them; they were avid readers and eager learners. Even Estelle, who never went to high school, sought out ways to improve her mind. Lilma kept her own mind sharp and "in shape" by the mental exercises of reciting her memorized lists of Bible books, presidents, and states. She also satisfied her hunger to learn by reading books, magazines, and newspapers. And Claire was always a wealth of interesting new items for discussion. She kept informed about current events, nature, and the arts and remained ever eager to learn and understand more.

Although the physical aspects of maintaining health have not been a main focus of our journey with the ladies, it is important to point out that they continued to use what physical abilities they had for as long as they could. They did their best to enhance and support their physical well-being through exercise, use of assistive devices where applicable, and learning new ways to stay active when they could no longer do what they used to do. I am convinced this "use what you have" focus is one of their most important secrets for remaining vital well into their nineties.

Sense of Purpose

No matter the stage of life, having a purpose—a reason to be—is important. In the later stages of life, with professional life often behind us, purpose becomes even more important. This is something I address with clients as they work to redefine themselves during their transition to retirement.

For Lilma, reaching out to others provided a rich sense

of purpose. She read to someone who was no longer able to read, visited the homebound, sang in the choir, and kept the books for the Ladies Union Circle. Despite Jane's more restricted environment, she led exercises and encouraged her housemates through positive conversation.

In the later years, our purpose might need to be refashioned given the realities we face. We saw Estelle redefine her sense of purpose after losing Arthur, redirecting her energies to bring humor to others and to help her thrift shop customers feel welcome. And Claire, when she could no longer work at the thrift shop, shifted her purposeful efforts to making phone calls or writing notes of joy and encouragement to friends and family. She also touched many with her intercessory prayer.

In these later years, especially, many people find purpose by focusing on what they want to pass along to future generations—what they want their legacy to be. Legacies can be either tangible or intangible, though most contain elements of both.

Maggie's body of created works represented a tangible legacy, but her art and poetry also provided an intangible legacy of hope and understanding to many. Jane's tangible legacy, her delicate artwork, coincided with an intangible legacy of inspiration for her granddaughter's artistic pursuits and her example of pursuing learning at an advanced age. Lilma's homier tangible legacy of photo albums and quilts for family members went hand in hand with her intangible legacy of faithful service to and love for family. I must add that I hope this book perpetuates the legacy of these women who taught me so much about living well.

Spiritual Connection

Faith, spirituality, religion—all of these words refer to a belief in or a connection with something beyond what the senses can perceive. Most of my ladies identified themselves as Christians, and although their specific religious affiliations varied, their sense of spiritual connection played a significant role in their lives, providing meaning, comfort, purpose, and direction as well as a sense of community with others who shared their faith.

Lilma enjoyed listening to spiritual music, and she loved singing hymns with the church choir. Estelle leaned on her faith when facing difficulty. Claire prayed for and meditated about those she cared for, including the earth itself. Jane studied the Bible and saw her faith as something to refine and grow. Rituals, prayer, music, Scripture studies, fellowship, and communion with the transcendent through nature enhanced these women's sense of well-being and security while also serving as a link to God, other people, and the whole of creation. Even Maggie, who claimed not to be "affiliated," found herself drawn to people of faith.

In his most recent work, *Flourish*,[7] eminent psychologist Martin Seligman draws on extensive research—supported by the National Institute of Mental Health, the National Science

7   Martin E. P. Seligman, *Flourish: A Visionary New Understanding of Happiness and Well-Being* (New York: Free Press, 2011).

Foundation, and others—to identify the signature strengths for well-being. Included among them is the general category he calls "Spirituality/Sense of Purpose/Faith/Religiousness," referring to the higher purpose and the sense of meaning, comfort, and being a part of something greater than self that faith often represents.

Dr. Harold G. Koenig, a faculty member at Duke University Medical Center and the co-director of Duke's Geriatric Research Education and Clinical Center, has studied and published extensively in the area of spirituality, theology, and health. In his book *Medicine, Religion, and Health: Where Science and Spirituality Meet,* he cites research from a large number of studies and concludes,

> Religious involvement, particularly attending religious services, is associated with a lower risk of mortality based on reports following subjects for up to three decades. . . . Effects on mortality have also been observed for prayer and meditation but primarily in those without health problems. Religious struggles, however, predict greater mortality. These findings suggest that religious involvement is generally associated with lower mortality, particularly when religious beliefs are without conflict.[8]

The landmark Harvard Study of Adult Development, on the other hand, did not find a direct association between positive aging and spirituality or religious adherence: "It was

---

8 Harold G. Koenig, *Medicine, Religion, and Health: Where Science and Spirituality Meet* (West Conshohocken, PA: Templeton, 2008), 145.

hope and love rather than faith that seemed most clearly associated with maturity of defenses [coping mechanisms], with successful aging, and with Generativity [giving to others and legacy]."[9] But for most of my ladies and for many other people as well, that sense of hope and love is inextricably linked with their personal faith and spirituality.

Use of Inspiring Models

Estelle was the prime example of consciously relying on a role model throughout her life. When circumstances became challenging, she looked to her mother as an example of someone who had survived the direst of difficulties with strength, determination, and faith, someone who had proven the possibilities. Estelle leaned on that resource and, using it as a touchstone, found courage to press forward herself.

Lilma, too, looked to her mother for inspiration and guidance, although she didn't specifically refer to her as a role model. In one of our conversations, Lilma shared with me what an upbeat, caring person her mother had been—a leader in the PTA and at church, someone who handled administrative matters well. I don't think we have to look further for Lilma's role model.

Mentoring and modeling can be a "pay it forward" proposition, and it certainly was for my golden ladies. They learned from those who went before them, and they in turn became

9   This study, directed by Dr. George Vaillant, is discussed in Vaillant's book *Aging Well: Surprising Guideposts to a Happier Life from the Landmark Study of Adult Development* (New York: Little, Brown, 2002), 259.

role models and mentors for younger women—including me. In addition to my own dear mother's example of strength, faith, compassion, persistence, and positive attitude, I was blessed to find these golden women who enriched my life by modeling well-being in old age.

They have given me so much. Yet I like to think I have given them something as well, something that adds an important dimension to the mentor relationship. I have acknowledged them as wonderful human beings and shown respect for their guidance. I have remained in contact with them and prayed for them. And, of course, I have written this book to honor them.

My remarkable role models, in other words, have become a part of my life treasure of friends. It doesn't always happen that way, nor does it need to. But I'm so grateful that in my case it has. Befriending my mentors has enriched my life immeasurably.

During the process of writing this book, I have sadly lost two of my ladies. Given the ages of the remaining ones, I must expect to lose others as well. But, true to what I have learned from my golden ladies of summer, I will celebrate them and be grateful for their presence in my life. I will slip into memories of them to enhance my mood. I will keep my eyes and heart open to more golden ladies as they may cross my path. And, as I look forward, I will aspire to be a golden lady myself—one who points out the silver linings for those who come after me.

CHAPTER 8

Reflections on the Journeys: Your Turn

NOW THAT YOU HAVE gotten to know my golden ladies, seen them as models of positive aging, and witnessed the practices and attitudes they adopted, I invite you to take the opportunity to reflect upon what you have read and how it might apply to your life. If you, like me, are a baby boomer facing your retirement years, now is the time to develop a strategy for positive aging. And even if you are younger, developing positive habits and perspectives can only enhance your life journey.

I have designed the following exercises and applications from my experience and training as a life-transitions coach. So even though what we will be doing in these pages does not constitute actual coaching, it might be helpful to clarify just how the coaching process works.

The relationship between a life coach and a client, designed to secure change on the part of the client, is called an alliance. The coach offers discovery-based approaches and frameworks designed to enhance the client's learning and facilitate her actions. In actual coaching relationships, the coach may offer follow-through and accountability functions as well. But the client's agenda is foremost in any coaching alliance. It is understood that clients are able to generate their own solutions and strategies for creating and managing change, and the choice about how and whether to proceed is always the client's. In other words, a client who does not want to answer a question or complete an activity is always free to say no.

I invite you to keep that dynamic in mind as you read through the various prompts and applications that follow. You are in the driver's seat—the expert on you. You always have the option of whether or not to participate in a particular exercise, and you can choose what you think would be most helpful to you and your situation. And, as in a coaching alliance, you are responsible for generating your own outcome.

It may help you to know the various kinds of questions coaches use when we work with clients. I have included a variety of them in this chapter. Sometimes we ask specific questions that might encourage the client to view something in a different way so as to gain clarity or a fresh perspective. Other questions, called "inquiries," are intended to encourage the client to think deeply over a period of time about a concept, feeling, action, or outcome—to ponder rather than give an off-the-cuff answer. Finally, there are application exercises that might include some information and direction drawn from the coach's experience and expertise. With any of these questions, once again, how—or whether—to answer remains the client's choice.

An actual coach-client alliance includes the back-and-forth dynamic of conversation, which obviously is impossible in this context. But my hope is that you will derive some benefit from exercises in this chapter by engaging your mind, making some plans, and taking actions that you feel could enhance your aging journey. You might also find it helpful to write down your responses, observations, and commitments so that you can revisit them later. Some clients keep a journal or notebook or create an electronic file for this purpose.

As you read through this chapter and reflect on your life, keep in mind that we live in a hectic world and that quality reflection time tends to be at a premium. It's often necessary to take an intentional step away from our current pressures and duties in order to relax, think, and feel. When conducting workshops on life balance and retirement transition, I emphasize the importance of creating "stopping points" to recharge ourselves. Such times can be invaluable for reflection and refreshment, for designing plans and nurturing our resolve.

What form these stopping points take depends on your situation. They can range from "still points," the kind of one-minute retreats identified by Dr. David Kundtz,[1] to a more organized full-day, weekend, or weeklong retreat designed to help you reflect more broadly and deeply. Such retreats are offered at many church and spiritual venues as well as through women's organizations, educational institutions, community groups, and lifelong learning centers.

Even if a formal retreat will not work for you, you can create a retreat environment for yourself. Decide on a day (or more), clear your calendar from responsibilities (enlist help if needed), prevent interruptions by turning off your phone and all electronics, and find a special corner inside or outside—whatever makes you feel relaxed. Then focus on yourself and on how you want to fashion and find support for your journey in aging. (When my clients hedge about taking time for themselves and need a bit of a nudge, I often remind them, "You are worth it. In fact, you owe it to yourself.")

Once you have been through this chapter, you may be interested in working one-on-one with a life coach. If so, please see Appendix B to learn how to connect with a certified coach who can serve you either in your own area or remotely. Many coaches operate routinely by telephone, and some use video chat applications such as Skype or FaceTime.

---

1 See David Kundtz and Steven Harrison, *Quiet Mind: One-Minute Retreats from a Busy World* (York Beach, ME: Conari, 2000). These daily mini-retreats were designed to help the superbusy develop an appreciation—and a daily habit—of taking time out for reflection.

Now, let's look again at the qualities the ladies displayed that enhanced their well-being in their later decades and explore some ways you might develop these qualities in your own life.

Self-Knowledge

I often use the following set of activities with clients to help me get to know them and, more important, to help them reaffirm for themselves who they are. This is the starting point from which all future learning, change, and action flow.

My experience working with clients has shown that the better we recognize our values and align ourselves with those values, the more integrity we'll sense in our lives and in the goals we have set. In addition, the process of tapping into values will help provide energy and motivation for working toward those goals. Almost every client I have worked with has told me that this process of clarifying their values was powerful and important.

The same is true of recognizing our strengths and our preferences. The more clearly we recognize our strong points, the more effectively we'll be able to employ them to achieve our objectives. And the better we know our needs and desires within the context of the values we have identified, the easier it will become to define our goals.

My golden ladies were pretty good at knowing who they were and what they were about. How good is your self-knowledge? I invite you to take some time to explore with the help of these activities.

1. Create a list of twelve of your most important *values* and describe what they mean to you, then rank or prioritize them from the most important to the least. The resulting ordered list can guide you as you make plans and move forward. Revisiting it from time to time to reprioritize as needed or adapt to changes in your circumstances can be helpful as well.

2. List your *strengths* (physical, mental, spiritual, social, and so on). If you find this difficult, think of each decade of your life and consider what you achieved, what you are proud of, and what brought you the acknowledgment of others. What qualities helped you in these achievements? Now is the time for honesty, not modesty. Don't hesitate to enlist the help of close friend or loved one to help you formulate this list. You can use it as a reminder of what you have to work with as you move forward, tapping into these abilities when you encounter new opportunities for growth and reminding yourself of past successes/strengths when challenges arise. Remember how Lilma leveraged the good to deal with the bad? Here you would be leveraging your strengths to reach your goals.

3. Create a *preferences* list to remind yourself of those people, places, activities, and lifestyle amenities you already like and want more of as well as those you don't have in your life but would like to have. You might want to divide this list into needs (what you believe is essential to your

well-being) and wants (what you would enjoy or like to do or have). These preference lists can be helpful to keep on the table as you plan your future and to revisit if circumstances change.

Commitment to Self-Care

Many people spend years of their adult life caring for others. Women especially tend to be familiar with the caretaking role and have developed the tools to fulfill it. They may be reluctant, however, to engage in self-care. I encourage all my clients to practice self-care throughout their lives, but especially in later years, to better cope with the changes that often accompany older age.

1. What do you see as the necessary components for your personal self-care? List what you think you need to live a functional and fulfilling life. (Remember, there is a distinction between a want and a need.) An example of how this might look:

> Optimally, to function, I need enough rest, appropriate socialization (not too much or too little), mental and intellectual stimulation, access to healthcare when needed, spiritual support on a regular basis (Bible study, prayer group, or church at least once a week), the ability to do my reading and some creative craft or needlework, a suitable exercise option, ability to eat the things that are good for me and that agree with my system, the ability to explore some new places, and some alone time.

2. What current attitudes, assumptions, or habits might prevent you from caring for yourself in a way that will enhance your experience of aging? Some barriers my clients have experienced are listed here:

   - Thinking that taking care of yourself would be selfish.
   - A family refrain: "It was always done this way."
   - "I won't have the energy after taking care of _____ [husband, parent, cousin, or so forth]."
   - "I don't know how to _____ [cook, handle finances, take care of cars, or so forth]."

3. Brainstorm some ideas for overcoming the barriers you listed. For example, in response to the first excuse listed above, you might say, "I will be better able to care for others and be my best self if I take care of myself and make sure my needs are met. So self-care is *not* selfish."

4. Think about the self-care needs you identified in question 1. Outline what you can to do to meet the needs you have identified for optimal self-care. An example from the sample list might be: "In order to get enough rest, I will try to get to bed by eleven. I will nap on the days I feel tired or have an evening function. I will say no to people or activities that drain my energy."

5. How do you think flexibility and adaptability apply to the idea of self-care? In what ways might you need to be more

flexible or to encourage flexibility in others? How might perfectionism sabotage your self-care efforts?

6. How can you best communicate your self-care plan to others to elicit supportive, respectful understanding of your need for self-care? Sometimes having friends remind us to take care of ourselves or establishing a mutually supportive relationship can be helpful.

Adjustable Perspective

As we saw in chapter 7, our willingness and ability to adjust our perspective can make a big difference in our later years. In particular, being able to look at the big picture and take a broader and longer view of our lives and circumstances can help us see the possibility of good and avoid the trap of thinking our problems are too personal, permanent, or pervasive for us to manage.

You might be interested in honing this ability. When clients come to me with something they are stewing about, I often engage them in various activities that encourage them to shift their way of viewing things and entertain other, more positive, possibilities. As you think about a particular situation in your own life, the following exercises might help you find a fresh perspective.

1. *Time Travel.* Like Claire, consider tapping into the context of time. She saw her life as a large book and her problems

as confined to pages in that book that could be turned and left behind. So each setback Claire experienced fell into the much broader context of time and experience. You can do something similar by considering how the situation you are dealing with might look to you in a week, a month, a year, five years, and so forth. Within the varying time frames and contexts, what is the significance of that situation for you?

2. *The Debate Game.* Sit down at your kitchen or dining room table and list everything that troubles you about the given situation. Then move to the other side of the table and review the situation from a different or opposing viewpoint. (You can do this in your imagination, but try doing it physically as well.) What can you learn by viewing the situation from this new perspective? You may even want to do this several times, moving all around the table, sitting in different seats, and gaining a variety of perspectives.

3. *Call the Consultant.* Enlist one trusted person or several to give you their honest take on the situation. Soliciting the views of others can broaden your own perspective, help you entertain other ideas, and give you some hints for the next time you get stuck. But do make it clear that you are seeking perspective, not advice—and don't feel bound to follow any advice you do receive.

4. *The Prospector.* When facing a difficult patch, try asking yourself, "Where's the gold here?" Stretch your mind to dig for unexpected benefits, valuable lessons, and other ways to do things.

5. Brainstorm what positive possibilities could grow from the various perspectives you explored in these exercises. What can you take from the exercises to use in your journey forward?

Focus on the Good

In coaching we often say, "That on which you focus expands." The overall focus for all of my golden ladies was not on what was bad, missing, or diminished in their lives, but on what they had to enjoy or be grateful for. Such a positive focus comes naturally to some people at some times, but it can also be intentionally nurtured. In difficult or challenging situations, "counting blessings" can become an important survival tool for anyone.

I learned this for myself after my mother passed away. I vividly recall that November and the gray winter that followed. My daughter had grown and left the nest, and my husband was commuting to Chicago for work, coming home to Virginia only on weekends. Despite my own work, those weeks were long and lonely, the gray days cold and dreary.

During this time I chose to keep a gratitude journal, charging myself to find a minimum of *six different* things each day to be thankful for. To be honest, I found that very difficult at first, and many of my entries felt forced or seemed trivial. But as I kept at it, seeing the good in my life got easier. Keeping the journal enhanced my ability to recognize blessings because I was actively looking for them. As I became more attuned to what was good in my life, my mood and my sense of well-being gradually improved.

None of my golden ladies kept a formal gratitude journal, but they were all adept at focusing on the good in their lives and counting their blessings. Consider the following ways to enhance your own gratitude response:

1. What do you consider the richest blessings in your life? Create a list of the top five or ten and keep the list where you can see it every day: on your phone, on the bathroom mirror or the refrigerator, even embroidered on a pillow. Photo displays and mementos can also help keep your blessings in sight.

2. Consider keeping your own gratitude journal for a period of time. A common approach is to write down one item a day in a notebook, but there are many other possibilities. One woman set a goal of noting "one thousand gifts."[2] Others have posted their thanksgivings daily on Facebook or Instagram. However you keep your journal, reading through it regularly can remind you of all the good things in your life.

2 Ann VosKamp, *One Thousand Gifts: A Dare to Live Fully Right Where You Are* (Grand Rapids: Zondervan, 2011).

3. If you are a person of faith, beginning your prayers with thank-yous on a regular basis might help keep the practice of gratitude out front for you.

4. To enhance your capacity for seeing the good, play a "silver lining" game. For every "dark cloud" you can think of, purposely look for something good connected with it, even if that something seems small or mundane. If you have children in your life, playing this game with them might be a way to teach them gratitude skills while improving your own.

Healthy Use of Memories

My golden ladies developed an excellent way to preserve their positive energy, lift their moods, and enhance their feelings of well-being: they regularly visited their good memories. They handled their negative memories in a positive way, not denying their past pain, but deliberately choosing not to dwell on it. Consider the following possibilities for enriching your own life with positive memories:

1. Practice now to savor those moments that will one day be rich memories for you:
   - When you experience a rich, happy, or beautiful time, try to be very present in that moment. Engage fully, and don't allow yourself to be distracted or drawn away.

- Consciously engage all your senses so that you capture the whole scene in the fullest way possible. Note the sights, sounds, and smells as well as the emotions of the moment. Doing so will help you firmly imprint this experience in your memory.
- Consider intentionally choosing a sensory cue—an object, a scent, a sound—to prompt future memories of this good time. For example, "Every time I see that box, I will think of the carefree days I spent in Hawaii."

2. Don't wait. Deliberately revisit your happy memories in the near future to enjoy the good feelings but also to strengthen those neural pathways. Obviously, it would be counterproductive to live exclusively in memories, but do use them to enhance the present from time to time.

3. Based on the ladies' examples, what are some possible healthy strategies for dealing with unpleasant or negative memories? What has worked for you in the past?[3]

4. Consider writing a memoir. It doesn't have to be a major tome—just tell a few stories about times that stand out in your mind. You'll probably find that the very process of

---

3 Handling recurring painful memories is beyond the scope of this book and my role as a life coach. If you find that simple measures like shifting perspective, looking for the good, and letting go are insufficient to keep you from dwelling on negative memories, I highly recommend that you seek professional counseling.

telling these stories brings more to mind. Besides adding pleasure to your life, you'll be leaving a tangible legacy for another generation. (If writing just isn't your thing, consider making an audio or video recording of your stories.)

Willingness to Let Go

As we saw in the preceding chapter, letting go is a necessary component of the grief process, an important step in handling the involuntary loss that all of us experience, especially as we age. Handling such losses in a healthy way involves acknowledging them, mourning them, then choosing to move on while holding them in our hearts and memories.[4]

But letting go can also involve a deliberate lightening of the load, the intentional release of those involvements, relationships, and "stuff" that no longer serve a purpose or enhance life. I call this process "proactive letting go." Learning to release the extraneous—or sometimes simply shifting our perspective on it—can facilitate a more unencumbered life journey. The following exercises offer different perspectives on letting go as well as some ideas for doing so.

1. Make a list of relationships, involvements, or "stuff" that you feel might be weighing you down or interfering with your progress toward a positive and fulfilling life ahead. Maybe it's your involvement in a group that no longer

---

4　Again, if you find yourself stuck, unable to move beyond a loss after a reasonable amount of time, I encourage you to see a grief counselor for professional support.

interests you, a relationship that seems to bring only negative energy, or that heirloom table of Aunt Nellie's that has been taking up space and gathering dust.

2. Read through the list you made. What would it take to divest yourself of each item?

3. If you feel overwhelmed by "stuff," consider what you could do to lighten your load by simplifying and decluttering. Most people find it less overwhelming to do this in stages, working in one room at a time or for a limited period each day. For each item, you might ask the following questions:
   • Do I need this?
   • Does having it enhance my well-being and/or my environment?
   • If I choose to get rid of it, what would be a good home for it? (Finding good homes for our possessions can ease the letting-go process.)

   If you find this process too difficult, consider enlisting either a trusted friend or professional organizer to assist you.

4. Think about your daily or habitual activities and their role in your life right now:
   • Which of these tend to give you energy and build you up?

- Which sap your energy or weigh you down?
- Which are not in line with your current values and purposes?

If an activity or habit is important to you and consistent with your values, consider how you might alter your involvement to reduce its energy drain on you. If it's *not* important or aligned with your values, what is keeping you from jettisoning it altogether? What alternative might weigh on you less?

5. Are there people in your life who drain your energy or prevent you from being your best self? Brainstorm and list ways you could gracefully end that connection, significantly reduce your contact with the person, redefine your relationship by setting boundaries, or limit the energy you allow him or her to drain from you.

Use of Self-Talk and Visualization

We heard several of the ladies talk to themselves in order to help themselves either get back on track or stay there, and I'm sure other conversations happened internally. We also saw them employ visualization, creating mental images to soothe their emotions and picture a positive future. (Estelle was particularly good at doing this.)

Both self-talk and visualization can be effective motivating strategies, but the *content* matters. Positive self-statements (such as Estelle's "I can make do") are powerful motivators and encouragers. But negative statements (for example, "I'm such a ditz") can easily turn into self-fulfilling prophecies. The same is true of visualization—what you picture in your mind can influence your emotions and motivate you either positively or negatively. See if the following exercises can help move your "self-conversation" and visualizations into the constructive zone.

1. Try to take notice of what you typically tell yourself when you encounter challenges, enjoy success, or need to get moving. Jot down the situation and the words that form in your head—your *scripts*.

2. Examine the content of the scripts you noted. Is what you are saying to yourself accurate? Helpful? Hopeful? Realistic? Affirming? Do the scripts reflect what you currently believe or want, or are they relics that don't serve you?

3. Take a stab at rewriting one of your scripts. Consider a typical situation you face—a challenge, success, or call for action—and ask yourself, "What would be the most helpful, truthful, and energizing message for me to hear?" If you are struggling with the words, think about what someone with no vested agenda (such as a coach) might tell you in your situation. Write your new script on an index card, a sticky note on your bathroom mirror, or a notice on your computer or phone. Practice saying it to yourself to motivate you and maintain your well-being.

4. If you have never practiced visualization, you might want to begin by picturing in your mind something you already know. Close your eyes and take a deep breath in, then slowly exhale. Picture in your mind the most beautiful and serene place you have ever been—a happy, safe, and comfortable place. Notice the colors, smells, and sounds, and relax into that picture. Stay there for a bit and keep on slowly breathing. Once you open your eyes, notice how relaxed and calm you feel.

5. Once you have mastered the process of visualizing known scenes, try picturing an outcome or situation you want in your future. Follow the steps above, answering the questions about how it looks, feels, the colors, the scents, the sounds, and so forth. Capture that picture in your mind's eye. Remain in that place for a while, breathing and absorbing the feeling of possibilities.[5]

Resilience and Adaptability

My ladies were excellent models of adaptability and resilience, both vital components of positive aging. These qualities can be cultivated and enhanced in anyone's life, but doing so can require time and intention. The activities below suggest some places to start the process. If you feel you need more

---

5 Visualizing a desired outcome won't necessarily make it "come true," but it can enhance feelings of well-being, help with relaxation, and, for some, provide a form of motivation to work toward a goal.

help in this area, I suggest you visit some of the resources on resilience listed in Appendix B at the end of this book.

1. Identify where you saw resilience in the lives of my golden ladies. In your opinion, which of their attitudes and actions played a role in their ability to be resilient? What similarities do you see between what they did and what your usual approach to life's challenges is? What are some differences?

2. What aspects of your typical reaction to change and challenge do you wish were different? What would you like your reaction to look like? Be specific.

3. Try to visualize yourself as a more flexible, adaptable, and resilient. How does that mental image differ from your life right now? What benefits might enhanced resilience and increased flexibility bring for you?

4. Think of a time (preferably recent) when your life changed significantly. What was your response to the change? Now picture yourself being more flexible and adaptive in that same situation. What possibilities might have been generated from your more resilient reaction?

5. What modifications in your current or typical thinking can you make to enhance your adaptability? Building on

your new thinking, what actions can you take in order to become more adaptable?

6. Refer back to questions under the heading "Adjustable Perspective" earlier in this chapter. In what ways could adjusting your perspective help you become more resilient and adaptable?

7. What do you need to tell yourself in order to develop more flexible attitudes and perspectives? (You might want to revisit the earlier section in this chapter headed "Use of Self-Talk and Visualization.")

Self-Agency

Self-agency, remember, is the willingness to assume responsibility and take initiative in one's own life. It involves making decisions for oneself and taking action instead of just waiting for life to happen or for others to watch out for us. Inertia and procrastination can be powerful forces at any stage of life, but seniors especially can be prone to postpone important decisions that require a lot of energy or involve unpleasant realities. The trouble is that not deciding is a decision in itself and can sometimes translate into letting others manage our lives. The following questions can help you explore the idea of your own self-agency and how you want to manage it going forward.

1. In what way(s) were you inspired by the ladies' initiative and willingness to "get into action" in critical times in their lives?

2. In what area(s) of your life do you think you might need to take action or make decisions soon in regard to your future?

3. What do you see as typical roadblocks for you when it comes to taking action? What feelings, assumptions, or circumstances tend to hold you back? What changes can you make that would help you move past these roadblocks?

4. What have you done in the past that successfully motivated you to take initiative and get things done? How could you apply that strategy now?

5. What do you need to tell yourself to keep the process moving forward? (See the earlier section in this chapter headed "Use of Self-Talk and Visualization.")

6. Do you believe there are times in a person's life when "inaction" could actually be a positive action? Why or why not? Where have you seen this in your own or someone else's life? Under what circumstances might choosing *not* to act serve us best?

Social Connection

Every person's social needs are different, but we all need some form of regular social interaction to maintain a sense of well-being throughout our life spans. Social interaction can take many forms, as we saw with the women. Consider these questions to help you reflect on your own social needs and strategize ways to remain connected with others in your later years.

1. How would you describe your current level of social engagement with respect to its quality, type, and quantity? How satisfactory do you find your social life? What changes might you like to make? What are some first steps you might take to facilitate those changes?

2. Looking forward, in what ways do you see yourself socially engaged as you age? What challenges do you anticipate? What can you do now to increase your chances having your social needs met in the later life stages?

3. What things can you learn from the way the ladies modified their social engagement as they advanced in age?

Humorous Outlook

The old adage "Laughter is the best medicine" certainly applies as we age—it costs little, goes down easily, and does wonders to help us meet the challenges we encounter. Intentionally looking at the humor in situations can be a wonderful strategy to nourish and support our good health. Consider:

1. What aspects of the ladies' stories made you laugh? What other uses of humor in a broader sense did you see in their stories?

2. In what ways, if any, does humor help you deal with the tough changes in life and the bumps on the pathway? How would you like to use humor in the future?

3. What steps can you take to encourage more uplifting laughter and humor in your life? Think in terms of people you associate with, books and media you consume, and the way you approach various issues in your life.

4. If you don't consider yourself a naturally amusing or humorous person, consider that intentionality does play a role in incorporating humor in your life. Remember how we discussed looking for the good in a challenging situation? What do you think you could do to help yourself find more humor when you encounter difficulties? (You might find it helpful to ask yourself what your funniest friend might have to say.)

Creativity

Some folks are great with their hands and create needlework, woodwork, jewelry, and so forth. Others are skilled in music, the arts, or poetry, while still others are creative in how they interact with people through conversation, storytelling, or providing hospitality. Anytime you generate something new and different, tangible or intangible, you are being creative.

Often as people retire and find more time on their hands, they explore new venues for creativity, and that exploration is generative in itself. Some people might say, "Oh, I'm not creative at all," but they don't realize that their garden brings joy and color to others or that they have the capacity to draw a shy person into a conversation. Open yourself to the variety of ways you can be creative. Generative activities of any kind can not only enhance your well-being, but also bridge generations and support your connections with other people.

1. Which, if any, of the creative outlets that the ladies used appeal to you?

2. What are your current creative outlets? Are you satisfied with these, or do you feel the need for a greater creative component in your life?

3. What creative outlet(s) have you always wanted to try? What opportunities to engage in it are available to you? What would be your next step to explore the possibilities?

4. What kinds of obstacles (including negative self-talk and old scripts) tend to keep you from creative activities that

interest you? What are some ways you can overcome those obstacles?

Commitment to "Use It or Lose It"

Lifelong learning keeps our minds engaged and allows for the expansion of our capacities through the new things we learn. As our lives change in our later years, learning new things can support our vitality and sense of usefulness and value.

1. Create a list of the frontiers of learning you might want to explore. The following questions may help you do so:
   - What are you curious about?
   - What skills would you like to acquire?
   - What subjects have always intrigued you that you now want to explore?
   - What classes, certifications, or other training might you want to pursue to build on your earlier experience and interests?
   - What physical activities would you like to pursue? What games, sports, or body-maintenance disciplines (yoga, Tai Chi) appeal to you?

2. What current activities do you want to continue or expand to keep your body strong and your mind sharp as you age? How might you adapt these activities to fit your changing circumstances?

3. What resources for ongoing learning do you know about? (See Appendix B for some ideas. Your local library, community college, or university can also be a great place to start.)

4. How do you plan to use your new learning? Sharing with others? Personal fitness? Writing a book? Getting a job? Something else?

Sense of Purpose

When men and women move into retirement, one of the biggest issues they confront—aside from finances and health maintenance—is redefining themselves and identifying their purpose, their reason to be. Changing circumstances require us to come with up with different answers to some big questions: *Why am I here? What matters to me? What is worth the investment of my time and energy? What do I hope to accomplish in the future?* Increasingly, in later years, the big question becomes *What legacy do I want to leave for later generations?*

These are not onetime decisions, of course. Because of the various changes in later life, remaining flexible can be important in exploring what the next life-stage purpose will be. As you saw also with the ladies, some redefining and "evolving," as Claire put it, is needed along the route. You might want to take some time now to explore your own sense of purpose and consider how it might evolve.

1. How have you defined your purpose through the various decades of your life so far? List the decades and then describe your sense of purpose in each.

2. Revisit the list of values you wrote down at the beginning of this chapter (question 1 under the heading "Self-Knowledge"). What do your most important values tell you about what your current purpose is or should be?

3. Define your current life purpose, taking into consideration your resources, location, health status, and values. If you have difficulty doing this, the questions listed at the beginning of this section ("Why am I here?" and so on) might help you focus.

4. What steps do you need to take to implement your life purpose?

5. How do you visualize your legacy to future generations? What steps do you need to take now to make sure that legacy comes to fruition?

Spiritual Connection

Many people, including the majority of my ladies, consider religious belief and practice a vital part of life. Developed over time through formal or informal experience and instruction, it serves as a clear and solid beacon for them. Others stay away from organized religion but find meaningful spiritual connection in nature, a philosophy, or the simple belief in something larger than themselves. Each of us chooses and comes to terms with our beliefs with respect to spirituality, and many find the forms of spiritual connection changing in the later years of life. Some find themselves longing for something deeper, especially as they face mortality issues. Some move into a less restrictive, more open faith than they previously practiced, while others long for a return to the "old ways." Wherever you find yourself on these issues, examining your spiritual desires and assumptions can help you move toward deeper spiritual connection and satisfaction.

1. What, if any, is the role of faith, spirituality, and or religion in your life?

2. What do you want that role to look like as you journey further into aging? What do you want to be sure to include in your spiritual life, and what would you be content to leave behind?

3. What steps can you take now to enhance or explore the role you want faith to play in your future? What practices can you undertake to enhance your personal experience of spirituality?

4. How is your spirituality tied in with your need for community—church attendance, Bible studies, meditation groups,

and the like? If these are important to you, what are some ways you can remain involved?

5. If you do not hold to any particular faith tradition, what provides you with a sense of connection to that which is meaningful in life? How can you tap into that to enhance your well-being?

Use of Inspiring Models

In this book I have focused on five stellar models for aging positively that I encountered during my summers in Nantucket—plus my mother and my wonderful French neighbor. As I worked on the book, many others on the island and at home in Virginia came to mind as well. All of us are surrounded by strong potential role models for growing older with grace. If we look for them, we can tap into their wisdom and follow their examples.

1. Looking at them as role models, what specific benefit did you receive from reading about my golden ladies?

2. What women and men have inspired you at various stages of your life? Which, if any, of these exhibited the kind of balance and vitality that made them good models for positive aging? Consider making a list of your important role models, what they have done to help you, and what lessons you want to remember from their example and/or teaching.

3. Where else might you look to locate good role models for positive aging?

4. What is the most significant contribution a model might make for you as you age? What qualities are you seeking in your model that could enhance your journey?

5. Keep your eyes open for anyone who might meet the requirements you defined for a model. Knowing what you are looking for can help you find it, and being open to the idea seems to facilitate the search. After my experience with the golden ladies, I now see many more models and more silver linings. And, for me, their power is in their existence as real people, living their daily lives for me to witness.

6. Have you considered being a role model or a mentor for someone else? What treasures do you have to share and what silver linings can you provide for those who come after you?

APPENDIX A

A Word About Nantucket Women

BECAUSE NANTUCKET IS WHERE I met my golden ladies, I thought it might be of value to share something about the special nature of Nantucket women. As I have explained, all my golden ladies were washashores, the term used to describe those who are not native to the island. Yet I see in them the same strength and character that island women have shown throughout Nantucket's history.

I have always had an interest in early American history and have been fascinated with the life stories of women who lived in that period. I can still see the shelf in my hometown library that held the wonderful biographical series available to girls during the 1950s and 1960s. I devoured the tales of Martha Washington, Betsy Ross, Abigail Adams (my personal favorite), and Dolly Madison, as well as those of women who came later. I always believed that reading those books gave me a better sense of daily life in early times than any formal history textbook ever did. So during my summers in Nantucket, I was naturally eager to gain a historical perspective on women of the island.

After visits to Nantucket's Peter Foulger Museum in the 1990s and to the Whaling Museum, which absorbed the majority of the Foulger collections in 2005, I developed a deeper appreciation of the quality of these women—their intelligence and commitment to education, their forbearance and faith, their industrious attitude and egalitarian spirit. Some actually went along on whaling trips, helping with the work and even bearing children while on the extended voyages. More often, however, the women ended up taking care of home life on their own while the men were at sea for extended periods. I really came to identify with them because overseas deployment, extended business travel, and out-of-state commutes often left me to tend to our family affairs independently as well.

Although not my personal refrain, I laughed with a degree of understanding when I first read the "Nantucket Girl's Song," recorded in the journal of a woman named Eliza Brock. The journal is dated May 1853–June 1856. Here's an excerpt of the poem:

> Then I'll haste to wed a sailor, and send him off to sea,
> For a life of independence, is the pleasant life for me.
> But every now and then I shall like to see his face,

For it always seems to me to beam with manly grace,
With his brow so noble open, and his dark and kindly eye,
Oh my heart beats fondly towards him whenever he is
    nigh.
But when he says "Goodbye my love, I'm off across the
    sea,"
First I cry for his departure, then laugh because I'm free.[1]

I was intrigued to learn about the many businesses that
were managed by women and their degree of participation
in commerce throughout Nantucket's history. So many
women-owned businesses were located on Center Street
that it was dubbed "Petticoat Row." A number of years
ago, while taking one of my regular walks down Center
Street, an art print in a shop window beckoned to me—and
I couldn't resist. The scene depicted what I saw as the quint-
essential Nantucket woman, spyglass in hand, gazing out
to sea from a captain's walk atop her house. Her straight
back and her determined stance told me that she would
survive and thrive. The picture now hangs in my home in
Virginia and reminds me of the thread of strong women that
is woven through Nantucket's history and, I like to think,
runs through me as well.

During another summer, a friend and I attended the "Gutsy
Girls of Nantucket" exhibit at the Coffin School, which
added to my broadening picture of the Nantucket woman

---

1   There is some discussion as to the authorship of this poem and, although it is
in Eliza Brock's journal, it might be attributed to Martha Ford. Nevertheless,
the meaning remains clear.

through time. We learned about such women of renown as Maria Mitchell, the first female astronomer in America, who discovered a comet which was subsequently named for her— "Miss Mitchell's Comet." Lucretia Mott, the famous 1800s Quaker abolitionist and proponent of women's equal rights and social reform, was an island resident. So was Madaket Millie, a consummate Coast Guard volunteer who kept watch for shipwrecks at the west end of the island while also lending her hand to neighbors in need. And there were so many other women—women of courage, intelligence, and independence whose names were less well known but who shaped their families and the culture of the island in significant ways. Learning about them was an inspiring way to spend an afternoon with a good friend.

Then, during the summer of 2010, I had the privilege of viewing an extraordinary Nantucket Historical Association exhibit titled "Sometimes Think of Me: Notable Nantucket Women Through the Centuries." This remarkable display featured many of the women from the Gutsy Girl's exhibit but included others too—a Wampanoag woman named Wanona, who legend tells was gifted in the healing medicinal arts and also known for helping heal the rift between warring tribes, plus the most recent preservationists, artists, and sustainers of culture on the island. Beautiful embroidered narratives crafted by fiber artist Susan Boardman complemented the women's stories. Although this exhibit is not a permanent one at the museum, I have been pleased to be able to revisit its richness through a companion book that features photos of

Susan Boardman's embroidery, the artifacts that were in the exhibit, and wonderful, well-researched biographies written by Betsy Tyler, who holds the Obed Macy Research Chair at the NHA. I believe anyone appreciative of needlework and women's history would enjoy it.[2]

Nantucket's long heritage of strong women continues today. During each summer visit, and as I have worked on this book, I have met extraordinary women, many of whom, like my golden ladies, are powerful models for positive aging. As I continue on my own journey of aging, I am eager to meet more of these remarkable women—to hear their stories, find inspiration in their wisdom, and use them, too, as models for well-being in my later years.

---

2 Susan Boardman and Betsy Tyler, *Sometimes Think of Me: Notable Nantucket Women Through the Centuries* (Nantucket, MA: Nantucket Historical Association, 2010). You can also view some of Susan Boardman's remarkable embroidered narratives at http://www.susanboardman.com.

❧

Resources for Positive Aging

THE FOLLOWING IS NOT intended to be a comprehensive list, but simply an array of resources that might help you build on the attitudes and actions my golden ladies have modeled. I hope these resources help you in your own search for silver linings.

Awakening Possibilities Regarding Aging

- *Composing a Further Life: The Age of Active Wisdom,* by Mary Catherine Bateson, PhD (New York: Knopf, 2010). Following up on ideas expressed in her classic *Composing a Life,* Bateson identifies a new stage in the life cycle—Adulthood II—and draws upon extensive interviews to explore creative possibilities for making the most of this time of life. A cultural anthropologist, the author has taught at Harvard, Amherst, and George

Mason University and served as the keynote speaker at the International Conference on Positive Aging in 2011.

- *The Creative Age: Awakening Human Potential in the Second Half of Life,* by Gene D. Cohen, PhD (New York: HarperCollins Quill, 2000). The late Dr. Cohen was the first chief of the Center on Aging at the National Institute of Mental Health and was the director of the Center on Aging as well as a professor of both health-care sciences and psychiatry at George Washington University. This book cites research that counters harmful myths about aging, then goes on to explore creativity in later years and how it contributes to well-being.

- *The Mature Mind: The Positive Power of the Aging Brain,* by Gene D. Cohen, PhD (New York: Basic Books, 2006). This book draws on twenty-first-century brain studies to show why—and how—creativity, intellectual growth, and relationships can thrive at any age.

Supporting Resilience

- *The Survivor Personality: Why Some People Are Stronger, Smarter, and More Skillful at Handling Life's Difficulties . . . and How You Can Be, Too,* by Al Siebert, PhD, rev. ed. (New York: Perigee, 2010). The late Al Siebert was a recognized researcher in the nature of survival resilience and the founder of the Resiliency Center in Portland, Oregon. This book explores the traits and skills that help some people survive and thrive when others crumble—and shows how these qualities can be learned. The result is better coping, increased success, and a brighter outlook.

- *The Resiliency Advantage: Master Change, Thrive Under Pressure, and Bounce Back from Setbacks,* by Al Siebert, PhD (San Francisco: Berrett-Koehler, 2005). This award-winning book draws on a wealth of research to show readers how to respond well to disruptive change, sustain health and energy under pressure, rebound from setbacks, and find new ways of living and working when the old ways no longer work. Though focused specifically on the work environment, Siebert's suggestions apply beautifully to issues of growing older.

- *The Power of Resilience: Achieving Balance, Confidence, and Personal Strength in Your Life,* by Robert Brooks, PhD, and Sam Goldstein, PhD (Chicago: McGraw-Hill, 2004). Dr. Brooks is a psychologist on the faculty of Harvard Medical School and has lectured internationally on the theme of resilience. Dr. Goldstein is a psychologist on the faculty of the University of Utah with areas of speciality in school psychology, child development, and neuropsychology. In this book they combine their research and clinical experience to show readers how they can develop a resilient mind-set and the skills to cope well with both everyday stress and unforeseen crisis.

Some Positive Foundations for Well-Being

- *Learned Optimism: How to Change Your Mind and Your Life,* by Martin E. P. Seligman, PhD (New York: Vintage, 2006, original ed. 1990). This modern classic, continually in print since 1990, explores the ways that an optimistic outlook can enhance life and—more important—how anyone can develop it. Considered the seminal work in positive psychology, it has been endorsed by the National Institute on Mental Health (NIMH), the National Science Foundation, and other prestigious organizations. A professor of psychology at the University of Pennsylvania, he directs the university's Positive Psychology Center and has served as president of the American Psychological Association.

- *Flourish: A Visionary New Understanding of Happiness and Well-Being,* by Martin E. P. Seligman, PhD, reprint ed. (New York: Free Press, 2011). This landmark work from the "father of positive psychology" moves beyond the idea of crisis management or even happiness to explore the dynamics of profound fulfillment. Seligman suggests the acronym PERMA to denote the five "pillars" of a flourishing life: Positive Emotion, Engagement, Relationships, Meaning, and Accomplishment.

Supporting Spirituality, Peace, and Well-Being

- *Mindfulness for Beginners: Reclaiming the Present Moment—and Your Life,* by Jon Kabat-Zinn, PhD

(Boulder, CO: Sounds True, 2012). Available in a variety of formats—including a book/CD combination, an audio version, and an e-book without audible components—this offering by the founder of the University of Massachusetts Medical School's renowned Stress Reduction Clinic offers a series of mindfulness meditations to help you with stress reduction, the alleviation of depression, chronic pain relief, and more.

- *The 12 Keys to Spiritual Vitality: Powerful Lessons on Living Agelessly,* by Richard P. Johnson, PhD (Liguori, MO: Liguori Publications, 1998). A practicing Roman Catholic and a trained gerontologist, Dr. Johnson is founder of the Johnson Institute for Spiritual Gerontology and Maturing Adult Faith Formation. In this book he presents age itself as a "master teacher" that can school us in the art of "living agelessly"— maturing with wisdom and grace.

- *Healthy Aging: A Lifelong Guide to Your Well-Being* by Andrew Weil, MD, reprint ed. (New York: Anchor, 2011). Weil is the internationally recognized medical and naturopathic doctor who founded the Arizona Center for Integrative Medicine at the University of Arizona. In this book he draws on the relatively new science of biogerontology (the biology of aging) to explore ways we can keep our bodies and minds in good working order as we age.

Resources for Ongoing Learning

- *Osher Lifelong Learning Institute (OLLI)*. This network of institutes, associated with colleges and universities throughout the country, provides a variety of courses that adults of all ages can take for personal fulfillment and the sheer joy of learning. They also sponsor lectures, concerts, and other cultural activities. By visiting their National Resource Center at www. osher.net, you can find an OLLI location near you and explore its learning possibilities.

- *Road Scholar* (previously called Elderhostel). This nonprofit organization provides opportunities for adults to learn, travel, and discover in all fifty states and more than a hundred countries worldwide. Their website is www.roadscholar.org.

- *Senior Net*. This nonprofit organization specializes in computer and Internet education for older adults. It's a great resource for help in learning new technological skills or enhancing existing ones. Their website is www.SeniorNet.org.

- *The Great Courses* (The Teaching Company). These audio and video courses from top university professors are geared to the lifelong learner. The classes—ranging from the arts, business, religion, and history to math, science, and health—are wonderful to do at home alone or with a group of friends. Courses are available in a variety of formats, including CD, DVD, downloading, and streaming. Companion books are often available for purchase as well. The website is www.thegreatcourses.com.

Resources for Finding Meaningful Paid and Volunteer Work

- *Encore.* This organization's website, www.encore.org, explains that its goal is to build "a movement to make it easier for millions of people to pursue second acts for the greater good. We call them 'encore careers'—jobs that combine personal meaning, continued income, and social impact—in the second half of life. While Encore is not a job placement service, it provides free, comprehensive information that helps people transition to jobs in the nonprofit world and the public sector."

- *Volunteer Match.* This nonprofit group connects potential volunteers with local nonprofit organizations in need of help, matching interests, needs, and localities. As they put it, "we bring good people and good causes together." Their website is www.volunteermatch.org.

- *AARP Experience Corps.* The purpose of this volunteer group is to improve literacy in disadvantaged schools by engaging senior adults as tutors for children in grades K–3. The goal is not merely to teach reading, but also "to ensure that every child has a chance to succeed in school and in life." For more information, see their page on the AARP website: www.aarp.org/experience-corps/.

- *Senior Corps (Corporation for National & Community Service).* This federal agency helps senior volunteers "become mentors, coaches or companions to people in need, or contribute their job skills and expertise to community projects and organizations." Guidance and training are available to volunteers. For more information, see www.nationalservicc.gov/programs/senior-corps.

Resources for Finding a Trained and Certified Coach for Transition and Retirement

- *Retirement Options.* Go to www.retirementoptions.com and click on "Find a Coach" to locate individuals who are certified as retirement and retirement transition coaches. Coaches work both in person and by telephone, and some use video chat applications such as Skype or FaceTime.

- *Retirement and Life Renewal* (www.retirement-renewal.com). This is my own website. It provides information about my workshops and group coaching offerings that focus on life renewal and the transition to retirement. Some sessions are based on this book.

- *International Coach Federation.* This organization's website (www.coachfederation.org) provides a listing of certified coaches who have met the ICF professional criteria of education, training, and experience. Each coach has specific coaching specialties and may have additional certifications in the area of their specialty.

Additional Resources for Older Adults

- *Area Agencies on Aging.* Under the auspices of the Administration on Aging (part of the Department of Health and Human Services), the Area Agencies on Aging are located throughout the country. They offer referrals, classes, and a range of other resources and services for older adults. To find one in your area, go to www.aoa.gov and click on "Find Local Programs."

ACKNOWLEDGMENTS

DURING THE MORE THAN four years this book took to complete, many people have helped, supported, and encouraged me in some way or other. For that I am profoundly grateful.

My deepest appreciation, of course, goes to my golden ladies, the subjects of this book, who not only served as my role models and friends, but also willingly shared their stories and wisdom with us all.

For his long and abiding love and confidence, I give my thanks and love to my husband, John. He gave me his unflagging trust throughout the process merely because the book was important to me.

For her ongoing support both technical and moral—talking me off the ledge when technology betrayed or baffled me and providing administrative assistance when my bout with Bell's palsy impeded my work flow—I give thanks and love to my daughter, Kristin.

I appreciate the help I received from Chuck and Elna Soule in obtaining photos of Estelle as well as clarifying some dates and details after her death. I also want to thank Chris Meredith for providing me with and permitting me to use photos of his mother, Maggie, and granting me permission to quote her poetry, which so eloquently expresses who she was and enhanced the telling of her story.

To my early readers—Rita Usher, Patsy Murphy, Annetta Haddox, Geraldine O'Neill, and Mary Jo Jackson—thanks for jumping in even though the polish had yet to be applied to the manuscript and for encouraging me to proceed. I also greatly appreciate Debra Klingsporn's enthusiasm for the project and her introduction to my editor, Anne. And to my later excerpt readers and listeners, who offered an eye and an ear for particular sections and approaches—Barb Schulz, Sandy McGushin, and Karen Decker—thanks so much for the encouraging and helpful feedback. To Sandi Atkins, Elaine Evans, Jean Rich, and Ann Rice, who kept the flame of hope burning, and to Ann for the "silver linings," I say thank you all. And to my friends Jane Evins Leonard and Netta Noorigian, who lent encouragement and support toward the end of the project, helping me through the sticky spots with their "intelligent women's" feedback, I am most grateful for their wisdom and common sense.

As to the professionals who worked for and with me on this project, I was indeed blessed. I thank Deb Tremper at Six Penny Graphics, who was a joy to work with. She listened, and with her great sense of style, designed the cover and interior of this book to be consistent with the essence and intent of the book. I so appreciate my copy editor, Lisa Guest, for taking on this project and adding valuable insights and suggestions that helped make the book better. And of course to Anne Christian Buchanan, who was my developmental editor, my consultant, my teacher, my book midwife, and now, I hope, my friend, go my deepest thanks and gratitude. It has been quite a journey, and Anne's flexibility, patience, keen insights, perseverance, and skilled professionalism served me so well in achieving the completion of this book.

I am indeed a grateful woman, as well as, in my husband's words, an "aspiring ninety-year-old."

ABOUT THE AUTHOR

 PEGGY BROWN BONSEE, a Professional Certified Coach, specializes in life coaching for retirement transitions. Her practice, begun in 1999, draws on her long experience in the fields of health, science, education, and libraries as well as her specialized coach training. She holds certification from the International Coach Federation and specific certification in retirement transition coaching from Retirement Options. Peggy lives with her husband in the foothills of the beautiful Blue Ridge in Northern Virginia and considers herself blessed to be able to spend summers on the island of Nantucket.

CPSIA information can be obtained
at www.ICGtesting.com
Printed in the USA
FSOW04n1252070116
15538FS